The kingdom of the world has become
the kingdom of our Lord and of his Christ,
and he will reign for ever and ever.

REVELATION 11:15

Revelation Down to Earth

· · · · · · · ·

MAKING SENSE
of the
APOCALYPSE OF JOHN

Edwin Walhout

WILLIAM B. EERDMANS PUBLISHING COMPANY
GRAND RAPIDS, MICHIGAN / CAMBRIDGE, U.K.

© 2000 Wm. B. Eerdmans Publishing Co.
All rights reserved

Wm. B. Eerdmans Publishing Co.
255 Jefferson Ave. S.E., Grand Rapids, Michigan 49503 /
P.O. Box 163, Cambridge CB3 9PU U.K.

Printed in the United States of America

05 04 03 02 01 00   7 6 5 4 3 2 1

ISBN 0-8028-4889-3

www.eerdmans.com

I take vast pride in dedicating this book to
ALMA,
cherished Christian wife,
in appreciation for
53 years of patience, love, and resourceful support.

Contents

CONTENTS

CHAPTER 1

Overview

Why Study the Book of Revelation?

Anyone who reads the book of Revelation for the first time and then asks seriously what it is all about must find the answer most elusive. Why is it even in the Bible, and what does it have to do with the gospel of Jesus Christ? What are Christians supposed to get out of it? Is it even worth trying to understand, especially since there are so many different explanations of it?

Revelation Down to Earth explains this difficult book of the Bible from a pastoral point of view. It focuses on seeing what John saw and trying to understand what he meant. The visions have a connection with Jesus and the gospel and the church. John was writing to actual churches composed of actual people. He expected them to gain by reading his book. Now, by reading *Revelation Down to Earth,* you also will come to understand and make sense of John's visions. And you will see what significance Revelation still has for us today.

Where Does This Book Come From?

It is no secret that the Revelation of John has been a very controversial book. Not only does it elicit wildly divergent interpretations still today, but it also has detractors aplenty who either reject it entirely, thinking it has no place in the Bible at all, or simply ignore it.

For the first few centuries, most Christian leaders accepted the book as having been written by the apostle John, the disciple whom Jesus loved and who wrote the Gospel of John. They would, of course, give it high standing and do their best to make sense of it.

Then a few people began to doubt that this same John, the disciple, actually wrote both books. As a result, they stopped taking it seriously. They thought someone known as John the Elder (who wrote the three epistles of John but was not the original disciple) wrote Revelation. In our day there is even one major scholar who thinks it was written by disciples of John the Baptist.[1]

The main argument against authorship by the apostle John is that the style of writing is considerably different from that of the Gospel of John, in such matters as vocabulary and grammar. It is impossible to ascertain for certain who the author is, so we will assume it is the apostle John. There actually are a few similarities in style between the book of Revelation and the Gospel of John, such as the use of the terms *Lamb* and *Logos* (Word) to describe Jesus. Perhaps the style is not so divergent after all.

John lived in Jerusalem (or the surrounding area) until the Jewish rebellion in A.D. 66. This rebellion, of course, is the one the Jews expected Jesus to begin thirty-five years earlier. The Roman armies came and in time subdued the rebels, destroying Jerusalem and the temple by the year 70.

Sometime prior to that year John escaped to Ephesus. The church in this city, dating back to the time of Paul, had become one of the major centers of Christianity. John's status as one of the original disciples of Jesus doubtless garnered him immense respect and authority, so much so that he soon became the de facto bishop of the entire Roman province of Asia.

Persecution of Christians broke out in that area about the year 95, during the reign of Emperor Domitian (for what precise reason is uncertain), and John, as the leader of the Christians, was exiled to a Roman prison colony on the island of Patmos in the Aegean Sea, about thirty miles southwest of Miletus. While on this island John continued to think

---

1. J. Massyngberde Ford, *Revelation*, Anchor Bible 38 (New York: Doubleday, 1975).

about and pray for his churches on the mainland, wondering how he could continue to help them.

John was able to recall personally all the events of Jesus' life on earth. He had been with Jesus during his ministry and knew him well. He had recently written down all his memories in his Gospel. He would clearly remember the great climactic events of the last week of Jesus' life on earth — the triumphant entrance into Jerusalem; the growing disillusionment of the disciples as Jesus refused to start a revolution; the trial, crucifixion, and burial of Jesus; and finally his resurrection and ascension into the sky. He would also vividly remember when God sent the Holy Spirit at Pentecost.

John would have reflected long and hard about the meaning of all those events. He would have tried to understand why they happened, and what effect Jesus wanted them to have on his disciples. The questions John wrestled with are the same questions Christians have today: Is Jesus still active in our world and in our lives? Is he somehow still with us and still powerful among us here on earth?

The book of Revelation is John's answer to these questions. It is his way of continuing to be of pastoral assistance to the churches of Asia, but also to anyone else who reads his book.

Revelation is a continuation of John's earlier writing. In his Gospel John wrote about Jesus as he lived and worked on earth. Now John continues to write about Jesus, but as he lives and works from heaven. The book of Revelation is a sequel to the Gospel of John. One deals with Jesus before the resurrection and ascension, the other deals with Jesus afterward.

In this respect these two documents are comparable to the two documents that Luke wrote, the Gospel of Luke and the book of Acts. The two Gospels, Luke and John, are somewhat parallel in that they both tell about Jesus' life on earth, prior to death and resurrection. In the same way, Acts and Revelation are somewhat parallel in that they tell about Christianity after the resurrection. Acts picks up the story of Christianity where the Gospel of Luke ends. It tells what happens on earth to the disciples and the early church up until Paul's imprisonment in Rome about the year 63. Revelation symbolically tells the story of Christianity from the viewpoint of what happens in heaven and how it affects those on the earth. Acts, therefore, is the sequel to the Gospel of Luke just as Revelation is the sequel to the Gospel of John.

There are obviously significant differences. Acts focuses on the disciples and what they did under the guidance of the Christian spirit. Revelation focuses on Jesus and what he is doing by means of his continuing Spirit. The Acts of the Apostles describes the growth of Christianity in descriptive historical language. The Revelation of John describes the progress of Christianity in symbolic visionary language.

Acts and Revelation are really describing the same things. Acts describes events from the point of view of real historical people living on the earth in faith and obedience. Revelation describes the same events, but from the point of view of what Jesus himself is doing on earth from heaven. That accounts for the great difference between the two books. John uses the language of visions to describe what Jesus is doing in heaven after he ascended.

The book of Revelation is the result of the angel showing John that whatever happens on earth is really the work of Jesus from heaven. John must learn to see that even his own banishment to Patmos is part of the overall scheme of things whereby Jesus is bringing all nations under his control. The angel wants John to see, and then to write down, how Jesus supervises and directs the course of events on earth.

We must see these puzzling visions as insights into how Jesus is bringing all people under his control, how he is healing the nations and drawing all men unto himself. Jesus is progressively sending the gospel to do its work within the civilizations of the world, so that the kingdom of this world is becoming the kingdom of our Lord and of his Christ (Rev. 11:15). We must see Jesus at work not only in the ancient world described in the Bible but also throughout history ever since, and specifically in our world today. John's message is that Jesus is Lord. He is Lord of all, "King of kings and Lord of lords" (Rev. 19:16).[2] The powers he injected into life and history are the most powerful, controlling, dominant, and authoritative forces ever to influence the world, and they have continued to shape history ever since. The visions of Revelation are given to us to help us understand this.

---

2. All biblical quotations in this book, unless otherwise indicated, are from the New International Version (NIV).

How This Book Is Put Together

There is no unanimity among scholars concerning the major divisions of the Apocalypse of John. For example, the New International Version lists sixteen major divisions. Author Harry Boer finds thirteen.[3] William Hendriksen[4] and R. C. H. Lenski,[5] both well-respected authors and scholars, divide the book into seven major divisions, but Lenski confesses to bafflement. Another excellent biblical scholar, Robert Mounce,[6] has eleven divisions, including a prologue and an epilogue.

Another interpretation divides the book into three major sections, supposedly written at three different times by unknown persons. The "John" mentioned in the book is affirmed to be John the Baptist, but the actual authors are believed to be John the Baptist's disciples. According to this interpretation, chapters 4 through 11 were written first, during the time before John knew about Jesus. Chapters 12 through 22, since the name of Jesus is mentioned in this section, were supposedly written by John's disciples during or after the ministry of Jesus. The beginning chapters, 1 through 3, the letters to the churches, are said to have been written last, by followers of John the Baptist who had been converted to followers of Jesus.[7]

There is another, more logical explanation for the organization of this book. Revelation is composed of a sequence of four major divisions, as follows:

1. Seven Churches (1:9–3:22)
2. Seven Seals (4:1–7:17)
3. Seven Trumpets (8:1–14:20)
4. Seven Bowls (15:1–22:5)

In addition to these major parts are a prologue and an epilogue. This division of the book is easy enough to see, and more important, it is not superimposed. This outline comes right out of the book itself.

There is a connection between these four parts. They are not four

3. *The Book of Revelation* (Grand Rapids: Eerdmans, 1979).
4. *More Than Conquerors* (Grand Rapids: Baker, 1939).
5. *The Interpretation of St. John's Revelation* (Minneapolis: Augsburg, 1943).
6. *The Book of Revelation*, NICNT (Grand Rapids: Eerdmans, 1997).
7. Ford, *Revelation*.

separate manuscripts merely juxtaposed to make one volume; there is continuity from one section to the next.

The Divisions of This Book
Connect with Each Other

These four major divisions — churches, seals, trumpets, and bowls — are not only sequential but also cumulative. They not only describe things that happen one after another *sequentially*, but more importantly they describe things that build upon one another *cumulatively*. This concept is crucial to understanding the book of Revelation.

What happens in the second set of visions depends on what has already happened in the first set; what happens in the third set depends on what happens in the second; and what happens in the fourth set depends on what happens in the third. They are cumulative.

The sequence of churches, seals, trumpets, and bowls describes four stages in a process, and this process is meant to show how Jesus works on earth from heaven by means of the gospel. The visions of Revelation show how the gospel is working in the world and how we can actually trace its effects. The gospel is the most overwhelming and powerful force in the world: the force that controls the direction history is taking. Jesus is Lord of the nations even in our modern twenty-first-century world. The book of Revelation is given to us by God precisely to show us how Jesus is Lord and how he is exercising his control over the nations of the world.

There is, accordingly, embedded within this enigmatic book of Revelation a most profound and important philosophy of history, of real and actual historic events — or rather a theology of history, since it involves the control of God through Jesus over our human history.

The Main Point of the First Segment:
Seven Letters

This first set of visions represents the first stage in the process by which Jesus accomplishes his purpose. It is simple enough to understand. Jesus begins his conquest of the nations by establishing churches within the existing cultures of the human race. These churches are composed of people who have heard about Jesus, who recognize that in Jesus the purpose of God is definitively revealed, and who therefore follow Jesus as Lord and Master. They hear the gospel (the story of Jesus from birth to ascension), they believe the gospel, and they demonstrate their faith by finding the purpose of their lives in simple obedience to God. That is what a church is — a group of believers who congregate around the Lord Jesus.

Churches are established through the efforts of people who spread the gospel by telling others about Jesus. They may be sent out formally, like Barnabas and Paul, or they may be ordinary people who simply tell neighbors and friends the story of salvation. It does not matter who tells the story; it matters only that it is told, and that those who believe truly surrender themselves to Christ.

God provided the Bible for us so that we can know Jesus as the fulfillment of the old covenant as well as the initiator of the new covenant. Word-of-mouth transmission of the gospel was sufficient in the early generations before the New Testament was written, but often stories that are passed on only by word of mouth can become garbled and embellished, sometimes so drastically that one can hardly find an element of truth in them anymore. Many such legends about Jesus did as a matter of fact come into being in what we call New Testament apocryphal literature. That is why we have the Bible as the definitive collection of scrolls about Jesus and the early churches. The Bible, including this book of visions, provides authentic accounts of the gospel.

The purpose of the first three chapters of Revelation, the letters to the churches, is to inform us that we must look at the churches, which are established (with all their weaknesses!) as the place where the healing of the nations begins. They comprise not just individuals coming to believe, but individuals joined together in the bonds of the Spirit of Jesus. That is the beginning stage of Christ's strategy as revealed to John.

The Main Point of the Second Segment:
Seven Seals

The second stage is the opening of the divine scroll by the breaking of its seals. God the Father is holding a sealed scroll in his right hand, and no one can be found to open it until at last "a Lamb, looking as if it had been slain" (5:6), breaks the seals and opens it. When he opens the seals one by one, great tragedies occur on earth.

This second set of visions, the seals, builds on the first set concerning the churches. First, Jesus sees to it that churches are established; second, he opens the heavily sealed scroll.

The scroll symbolizes God's purpose, especially as it relates to the human race. It speaks to the questions of why God created a human race in the beginning and what he expects the human race to accomplish. Sin complicated these expectations. Yet God's expectations must and will be fulfilled even in a world that constantly chooses to ignore and violate his wishes. God will reverse the decision of mankind as described in the story of Adam and Eve and persuade this voluntarily wicked race of humans to change its mind and choose righteousness.

The sealed scroll in this second set of visions represents God's plan to overcome and negate the Adamic decision of sin and to establish instead the true rule of God among the nations of the earth. This scroll contains God's eternal purpose for us, sealed so as to be unknown until Jesus comes to open it up for all to see. This second division builds on the previous visions of the churches; it shows what happens in the world when churches are established.

When the Lamb that had been slain opens the seals, horror and tragedy come pouring forth out of the scroll. There are four horses and their riders representing a sequence of disaster in which Christians are persecuted and the rich and mighty of this world are overthrown. The presence of churches in any given culture highlights two vastly different lifestyles at work, and therefore precipitates conflict and persecution.

When Christians live according to the law of God, they expose the wickedness of those who do not. The presence of churches in any community exposes the ungodly lifestyle of wickedness. More than that, they expose the track of sin downward into greater and greater ruin. And still more, wicked people turn against godly people and persecute them. Just as the Jews in Jesus' time mistreated Jesus, so too unbelievers have mistreated Christians ever since. The gospel shows this, indeed precipitates it. But the gospel also assures us that in the end the mighty and powerful forces of evil will cringe in fear, crying out for the mountains to fall on them so as to escape the wrath of the Lamb (6:16).

This second set of visions, the seals, is showing the second stage in the process by which God achieves his goal of healing the nations. First, churches are introduced into the communities of the world; second, the differences between two incompatible lifestyles are exposed, thus precipitating violent conflict between them, conflict which produces martyrs in the churches and will eventuate in the absolute vanquishing of wickedness. Jesus did say, after all, "Do not suppose that I have come to bring peace to the earth. I did not come to bring peace, but a sword" (Matt. 10:34).

The Main Point of the Third Segment: Seven Trumpets

The third set of visions entails the blowing of trumpets by seven angels. Actually this set of visions is the content of the opening of the seventh seal in the second set, so the continuity is obvious (Rev. 8:1-2). In the ancient world trumpets were blown to announce major events, such as the arrival of some great personage, or were used to call people to the temple or, in warfare, to summon soldiers to battle.

In Revelation the angels blow their trumpets and natural disasters develop on one-third of the earth, the sea, and the heavens: momentous conflicts between mythical creatures, a woman clothed with the sun taking refuge in the desert, great dragons arising out of the sea and out of the earth, and the harvesting of the earth by God's angels.

When churches in various parts of the world expose incompatible lifestyles (merely by showing their existence), they precipitate opposition. Open conflict occurs between the forces of evil and the forces of good. Enormous powers of wickedness appear in the civilizations being challenged by the gospel. Great suffering ensues, but God somehow manages to safeguard his churches so long as they flee to him, and in the end righteousness prevails. In this setting the trumpet call of God summons Christians (churches) to persevere, to fight the good fight of faith, and to live faithfully in spite of extreme opposition.

These visions do not merely describe one specific epoch of human history; they represent what happens always wherever the gospel goes. First, churches are established; second, churches expose two incompatible lifestyles and precipitate conflict; third, Christians are summoned to fight, to follow the Lord Jesus into the great battle against Satan and his followers.

From heaven Jesus is constantly starting new churches throughout the world. The effect of this is to continually expose the inadequacies and evils of the surrounding cultures that have been built on godlessness. This exposure of the nature and consequences of sin always results in determined opposition, spiritual and moral warfare within actual historical communities. Jesus calls us to persevere, to follow steadfastly, and to wear the white linen garments that symbolize the righteous deeds of the saints. These are the first three stages of God's plan as revealed to John through the visions of Revelation: the churches, the seals, and the trumpets.

The apostle John expected his readers in the seven churches of Asia Minor to be able to understand the significance of these visions in terms of their own relationship to God, to Jesus, to their cities, and to the Roman Empire. They would see themselves as the churches among which Jesus himself is walking, and by means of which Jesus is challenging the evils evident in the Greco-Roman way of life. They would understand that opposition and conflict are unavoidable at their stage of Christian witness, and they would be fortified to endure martyrdom in the assurance that the spirit of Christ will someday prevail in all peoples on the earth. They would hear the trumpets of God calling them to get involved in the great spiritual battle being waged throughout the earth.

The Main Point of the Fourth Segment: Seven Bowls

The fourth and final series of visions is that of seven angels pouring out the contents of the bowls they carry. The bowls contain plagues and are called the "bowls of God's wrath on the earth" (16:1). All the events in the entire book of Revelation originate in heaven. Jesus dictates the letters to the churches from heaven, the seals are broken on the scroll of God in heaven, angels in heaven sound the trumpets, and now more angels administer the wrath of God from heaven.

But the effect of all these events is felt on earth. Horrible disasters and catastrophes fall upon the wicked. All the terrible powers of evil gather for a mighty onslaught against the Lamb of God, and they are thoroughly and utterly defeated. The power of the devil and his hosts is completely annihilated while the city of God is constructed in eternal peace, eternal shalom.

There is a very important principle involved here. The action of God is seen specifically in the affairs of this earth. The entire sequence of events is the activity of God in the actual progress of human history. The events of history, including the things that are happening today in the modern world, fit into this four-step pattern that the book of Revelation is showing us.

Discerning This Divine Pattern

There are two distinct levels on which to see this fourfold process. The first pertains to any given national culture, to that of, say, the original Roman world or of the invading barbaric tribes of the Dark Ages, or even to that of modern Europe and America, or of Nigeria, South Africa, Australia, India, China, or Japan. If you trace the history of one distinct community or nation, and if the gospel has taken hold at all in that history, then you should be able to trace at least the beginning stage in that history.

The second level applies to the human race as a whole, to human history in its totality. Remember the great universalistic passages of the New Testament: disciple the nations (Matt. 28:19), every knee will bow (Rom. 14:11), he is Lord of all (Acts 10:36), and the kingdom of the world has become the kingdom of our Lord and of his Christ (Rev. 11:15). What Genesis 1 tells us about man created in God's image and about the human responsibility to multiply and subdue the earth is as much a definition of the destiny of man as it is of the origin of man. God wants the entire human race, in its totality, to function as his image in the work of developing the potentials of nature. That is the goal not only of creation but also of redemption.

The book of Revelation describes the process by which God accomplishes the purpose he defined originally in the creation of the human race. The ongoing process of time and life and history is the process described so vividly and enigmatically in the Apocalypse of John.

The human race, at the beginning of the twenty-first century, is surely far from the ultimate goal of freely choosing obedience to God in perfect shalom and righteousness. The ugly heads of grotesque beasts of evil are still emerging all over our culture. They deceive many, but they do not destroy the work of God. Even this is part of God's plan. It is, in fact,

11

the gospel that triggers such blatant hatred of all that is good and noble and right and true.

We cry out, "How long, how long, how much longer does this intolerable situation have to last?" And we need to hear again the instruction to wait a little longer, as well as the command to prophesy again even though our stomachs turn sour. Above all, we need to see again, with John, that white stallion whose majestic rider bears the name "Faithful and True" and the "Word of God" (19:11-13), who is even now treading out the winepress of the wrath of God against sin and evil.

Principles of Interpretation
That Apply to This Book

The following is a list of some of the basic hermeneutical principles that have been consciously employed in writing this explanation of the Apocalypse of John.

1. The book of Revelation as a whole is *pastoral* in nature. Everything in it possesses concrete, practical, immediate, personal, moral, and social value for the people who read it. It is not arcane religious speculation about the end of the world, nor is it abstract systematic theology. John wants all his readers to be strengthened to endure patiently the various afflictions that attend their service of the Lord. They must learn to align themselves with the strategy of God in the perennial conflict of good versus evil.

2. The entire document (other than the prologue and the epilogue) is visionary and therefore *symbolic* in nature. Even the seemingly more prosaic letters of chapters 2 and 3 are parts of visions and need to be treated as symbolic. The same applies to chapter 20, the much-discussed chapter on the millennium. All of these are strictly symbolic.

3. The visions of Revelation are intended to be *existential* throughout — not the philosophy of existentialism, but rather existential in that they provide insight into the present existence of readers at any given time in history. If an interpretation of a given vision does not help to clarify something in our present world, then we are missing the point. The visions are designed, like parables, to show us things about life and history that we might otherwise never see.

4. The perspective of Revelation is consistently *theistic*. The visions

12

show what God is doing in life and history by means of the gospel of Jesus Christ, the Spirit of Christ, and the Christian church. This is extremely important, especially in our age, which has largely lost the theocentric perspective. Even some Christians scoff at the claim to be able to trace what God is doing in our world. But God gives these revelations to Jesus, who passes them on to John, to the churches of Asia Minor, and to us. They show God at work through the ascended Lamb of God, at work from heaven but on earth.

5. The visions of this book need to be understood as descriptive of real events and happenings. They are *historical* in perspective. Some interpreters, building on this insight, have treated the sequence of visions as prophecies of successive epochs of history. For example, they believe certain visions predict the fall of the Roman Empire, and some visions describe the Middle Ages, the Reformation, and the modern world.

That is not what is meant here by historical. The visions are historical in the sense that they describe processes that are really and truly happening within the countries of the world, wherever the gospel takes root. They are historical in the sense that the actual progress of human civilization is determined by the gospel and that the power of Jesus' Spirit is the decisive force in leading the human race slowly to its goal of imaging God in the way it conducts itself. History is going somewhere, and it is being directed by the King of kings and the Lord of lords (19:16)!

CHAPTER 2

The Prologue

Revelation 1:1-8

John's first vision, that of Jesus shepherding his churches, begins in 1:9. The first eight verses of this chapter are introductory to the manuscript as a whole, a preface or prologue to the main body of visions.

In ancient times, when a person first took a papyrus scroll in his hand, he did not know what was inside; there was normally no title or name of the author on the outside. Custom was that as soon as the scroll was unrolled, the first things to be read were the names of the author and of the person to whom the scroll was being sent. In this scroll, however, this identification is not the very first thing to be read; instead, that information is in verse 4: "John, to the seven churches in the province of Asia."

The first three verses provide what we today might call the provenance of the book as a whole, that is, some explanation of how it came to be written. There is also a blessing upon people who read it or listen to it being read (literacy was still a relatively rare achievement in those days).

After the author and the destination come a formal benediction in verses 4 and 5 and a formal doxology in verses 5 and 6. Verses 7 and 8 contain a succinct summary of the purpose of the book and an assurance of the reliability of the things written in it.

This is how the preface is put together:

1. Why and how this book was written (1:1-3)

15

2. Identification of author and recipients (1:4)
3. The benediction and doxology (1:4-6)
4. Assurance of reliability (1:7-8)

Why and How This Book Was Written

The revelation of Jesus Christ, which God gave him to show his servants what must soon take place. He made it known by sending his angel to his servant John, who testifies to everything he saw — that is, the word of God and the testimony of Jesus Christ. Blessed is the one who reads the words of this prophecy, and blessed are those who hear it and take to heart what is written in it, because the time is near. (1:1-3)

■　　■　　■　　■　　■　　■　　■

The revelation of Jesus Christ . . .

The very first phrase of the book uses the Greek word *apokalupsis,* meaning "unveiling." By using this specific word, John tells us that in the past something has been hidden, covered up, but now it has been unveiled, opened up, revealed for all to see.

In the light of the next clause, "which God gave him," it appears that Jesus is the subject, the one doing the revealing, not the one being revealed. This perspective is confirmed by a passage in the last chapter: "I, Jesus, have sent my angel to give you this testimony for the churches" (22:16). Jesus sends his angel to show John, the seven churches, and us things that otherwise might remain hidden from our sight.

. . . which God gave him to show his servants what must soon take place.

The word *him* in this sentence means Jesus, since he is the only person yet mentioned. God gave Jesus an *apocalypse,* the purpose of which is to show Christians "what must soon take place."

Soon could mean almost anything: next year, next decade, next century, or next millennium. The specific Greek word used here means "with speed, quickly, speedily, soon," or "shortly"; it is sometimes translated

16

"hastily" or "immediately." The *soon* Jesus is talking about is the *soon* of now, of currently, of the present.

To anticipate the rest of the book, Jesus shows us forces that the gospel introduces into human life and history, forces that are therefore always operative in present time.

These many forces, both good and evil, may have confused the actual people to whom John sent this manuscript. Jesus wants his servants to be able to differentiate among the great variety of forces functioning in the world. In particular he wants them to see how the ultimate force of the gospel is functioning as it comes into conflict with the powers of evil in this world. So *soon* in this case means immediately, right now, and continuing perpetually. The visions John writes about in Revelation describe what is going on and has gone on in life and history at every moment since the ascension of Jesus into heaven.

> *He made it known by sending his angel to his servant John, who testifies to everything he saw — that is, the word of God and the testimony of Jesus Christ.*

Jesus from heaven communicates these things to John on earth by means of "an angel." The word *angel* means messenger. Dozens of angels are described in the successive visions, all of them messengers, all of them bearing a message from heaven, but this angel is the one assigned specifically to guide John in these visions and explain the meaning to him (compare 22:16).

John describes everything he saw as "the word of God." That is interesting phraseology. Normally the term *hear* is used in connection with the word of God, not *see*. But John says he sees "the word." He is referring to the visions he sees and records in this scroll. The visions themselves are communications from God and are therefore "the word of God."

John also describes what he sees as "the testimony of Jesus Christ." The visions are not only a word direct from God, but also, simultaneously, a message from Jesus Christ. *Word* and *testimony* are rough synonyms; what comes from God and what comes from Jesus are not two different things but are the same thing.

Identification of Author and Recipients

John, To the seven churches in the province of Asia . . .

It is widely believed that the apostle John, in his older years, became the pastor or spiritual advisor of the churches in the Roman province of Asia. These churches owed their existence mainly to the apostle Paul, who worked for three years in the city of Ephesus. Using Ephesus as his headquarters, Paul sent out assistants to explain Jesus to the communities of other nearby cities. As Acts informs us, this work was exceptionally successful, so much so that the residents of Ephesus forced Paul to leave town. In his later years Paul continued his interest in these churches by writing letters (Philemon, Colossians, Ephesians) and by sending Timothy as his representative, writing two letters to him there (1 and 2 Timothy).

What we now know as Paul's letter to the Ephesians was, in all likelihood, originally a circular letter intended to be read by all the churches in the area of Ephesus. Similarly, John's book of Revelation is also designed to be a circular letter, sent to make the rounds of all the churches in Asia.

Many scholars estimate that Paul died about A.D. 67, so it is likely that John became the chief pastor (or bishop) of Ephesus and these churches sometime after that date. Scholars also estimate the date in which Revelation was written to be about 96, when John would surely have been a very old man.

Benediction and Doxology

Grace and peace to you from him who is, and who was, and who is to come, and from the seven spirits before his throne, and from Jesus Christ, who is the faithful witness, the firstborn from the dead, and the ruler of the kings of the earth.

To him who loves us and has freed us from our sins by his blood, and has made us to be a kingdom and priests to serve his God and Father — to him be glory and power for ever and ever! Amen. (1:4-6)

The Benediction

A benediction is a blessing from God upon his people. A doxology is a word of praise from people to someone else, often to God but in this case to Jesus.

Grace and peace to you . . .

The word *grace* connotes the favor of God which results in our conformity with God's will. It is the power of God that gradually works within people so as to enable them to image their creator more faithfully. The word *peace* translates the Hebrew idea of shalom, a community living together in harmony, joy, love, and peace. This too is evidence of the Spirit of God at work among people.

. . . from him who is, and who was, and who is to come . . .

This is a title describing God the Father. Clearly it does not refer to Jesus, who is mentioned separately later. John wants his readers to understand that past history, current events, and future contingencies all reside within the omnipotent and omniscient hands of God; not merely does God himself exist eternally, but our existence — past, present, and future — lies entirely within God's control.

Never think about God in the abstract. Always think about him in the concrete, in the actions he performs within the world we live in. John reminds us that He Who Is (Hebrew Yahweh) is the one in full control of whatever is happening in the present time in our world. Furthermore, God determines what is "to come" just as surely as he has determined what happened in the past.

. . . and from the seven spirits before his throne . . .

It is hard to know with certainty what this refers to. The scene is analogous to the court of a king, where several people wait to go on errands for the king. However, in keeping with the principle that the presence and activity of God is not to be understood abstractly, we should understand the "seven spirits" as connected to the seven churches. These seven spirits represent the power of God functioning within the seven churches to which John is sending this scroll.

. . . and from Jesus Christ, who is the faithful witness, the firstborn from the dead, and the ruler of the kings of the earth.

Three enormously important phrases describe Jesus here.

1. Jesus is the *faithful witness*. We may receive all the information Jesus presents in the gospel, including his virgin birth, his childhood and youth, his public ministry, his teachings and miracles, his death, his resurrection, and his ascension, as an authentic message from God himself. Have no doubts about what comes from Jesus: it comes ultimately from God.

2. Jesus is also the *firstborn from the dead*. Disregard the other people who were raised from the dead by Old Testament prophets and by Jesus himself. They all died again. When Jesus arose from the dead, he did so in such a way that he cannot die again. He is the first and only human being to escape from death entirely. Furthermore, the notion of firstborn suggests also that there will be others in the family. This in turn assures us that the exact same thing that happened to Jesus in his resurrection will also happen to those believers who are found in him.

3. Jesus is *the ruler of the kings of the earth*. This affirmation has been largely lost in the contemporary Christianity of the twenty-first century. Almost unanimously this is regarded as a prediction for the future, not as a description of the present. Many think Jesus' kingship is hidden now in heaven, and that it will only be made manifest when he comes again to set up a millennial kingdom on earth.

But if we think this way, we overlook that Jesus is now, and has been ever since his resurrection and ascension, the controlling power over affairs on earth. Jesus' power is not hidden at all. It is functional and visible precisely everywhere the gospel prevails, everywhere the Spirit of Christ dominates, everywhere the church grows. The power of Christ from heaven is the most decisive influence within the ongoing civilization of earth. Jesus *is* the ruler of the kings of the earth.

The Doxology

To him who loves us and has freed us from our sins by his blood . . .

John directs this word of praise to Jesus. Long ago, in his own mind, John worked out the paradox of Jesus' death. Jesus chose voluntarily to let himself be crucified, knowing full well he could avoid it if he chose to. John came to realize that neither he nor others would honestly confront their own utter sinfulness unless forced to do so by what Jesus did. Afterward John himself, along with Peter and the rest of the disciples, saw what an enormous mistake they had made in their expectations of what Jesus should do, and in their complicity in the crucifixion of Jesus.

In the light of Jesus' death and resurrection John learned to know himself, to repent of his false ways, and to accept the yoke of discipleship more exactly. John now phrases it in such a way that Jesus' love, as shown on the cross, has resulted in believers being released from their sinful ways of life.

> *. . . and has made us to be a kingdom and priests to serve his God and Father . . .*

This is visible wherever there are people who serve him. These subjects of King Jesus constitute his "kingdom." That is where the tangible evidence of Jesus' kingdom can be seen — in those who love and follow him.

Jesus is also ruler of the kings of the earth, even over people who do not explicitly believe in him and obey him, those who may in fact consciously reject him. The evidence here is that the power of the gospel and of the Spirit of Christ is more decisive in the movement of the nations than is the power of the devil. Recognize that this is so, and trace it out as history moves along.

Jesus has also made us to be "priests." Jesus' kingdom is composed of priests. Christians are not only subjects, they are also functionaries, allowing themselves to be ruled and controlled by Christ. They respond by becoming people whose very being is a song of praise, a doxology. They become living sacrifices to God.

> *. . . to him be glory and power for ever and ever! Amen.*

Jesus does not draw the praise and doxology merely to himself — that is, as a man — but redirects it to God his Father in heaven. That is the way it must be. A Christian's life and obedience must be directed to God the Father, the creator, and must be subject to Jesus as king. This is the precise purpose of God when he created Adam (mankind) on the earth.

Assurance of Reliability

Look, he is coming with the clouds, and every eye will see him,
even those who pierced him; and all the peoples of the earth will
mourn because of him. So shall it be! Amen. "I am the Alpha and
the Omega," says the Lord God, "who is, and who was, and who
is to come, the Almighty." (1:7-8)

. . . .

. . . he is coming with the clouds . . .

It is customary to understand this sentence as describing Jesus' second
coming. However, the Christians to whom John was writing would not
have understood it that way. They would, on the contrary, have understood the reference as a fulfillment of a prophecy made centuries earlier
by Daniel: "In my vision at night I looked, and there before me was one
like a son of man, coming with the clouds of heaven. He approached the
Ancient of Days and was led into his presence. He was given authority,
glory and sovereign power; all peoples, nations and men of every language worshiped him. His dominion is an everlasting dominion that will
not pass away, and his kingdom is one that will never be destroyed" (Dan.
7:13-14).

Daniel is describing the coming of the Messiah, the person whom
God will send in the future to establish God's rule among men. John
knows that this person has already come. It is Jesus.

John's intent here in Revelation is to assure his people that the "one
like a son of man" (Dan. 7:13) has already come. The coming of the son
of man has already occurred, and even more to the point, his coming is
continuing every day. Long ago Jesus had promised his disciples to be
with them always, to the very end of the age (Matt. 28:20). This is what
John is reaffirming for his churches.

In his ascension Jesus disappeared into the clouds. But just as surely
as there are still clouds in the sky, so too Jesus is still coming right along
with them. Those clouds that hid Jesus from John's view decades earlier
are still the symbols that Jesus is permanently active from heaven on our
behalf.

The overall thrust of this sentence, "he is coming with the clouds," is

22

the assurance that God is at work through Jesus Christ, by means of the gospel and the Holy Spirit, in the salvation of the human race. John's later visions will show how God is actually doing this, but for now John wants to assure his people that God is working through the ascended Lord Jesus to accomplish his purposes. They may rest assured that whatever setbacks befall their lives, nothing will countermand the power and purpose of God in the gospel of Jesus Christ.

Jesus is Lord. Already. Now. Just as the clouds received the ascending Jesus years ago, so too ever since has Jesus been *coming* by his Holy Spirit. Open your eyes. See what is happening. Recognize the intense power of King Jesus. In time every eye will see him, even those who are still his enemies. A great deal of trouble and misery is yet in store for this world. That does not diminish his control. Our Lord Jesus himself endured his share of misery while on earth. He is in control and *coming* every moment. Do not ever doubt God's grace and power.

"I am the Alpha and the Omega," says the Lord God . . .

What greater assurance can there be than this? God *was* in the beginning and he *will be* in the ending. He began time and history and the universe when he spoke his mighty word of creation. He is actively involved in controlling and directing the course in which our world proceeds, and he will see to it that everything will ultimately, infallibly, and inevitably arrive at the conclusion he has in mind. What John is about to communicate to us comes with the divine assurance that this word from God is infallible, that it will indeed accomplish that for which it has been sent. God will infallibly achieve his purpose, which he set out originally in the creation of the world, namely, the production of a human race whose function is to subdue the earth, imaging God in the process.

FIRST SEPTET

The Seven Churches

This is the first of the four major divisions of the book of Revelation. This septet describes the seven churches to which John is writing. The first stage in God's strategy with the gospel is to establish churches within existing cultures. That is the foundation upon which everything else in this book will be built; it is step one of four. The vision of Jesus among his churches is presupposed as the background in all the succeeding visions described in Revelation.

This first section can, in turn, be subdivided into two parts:

1. A vision of the ascended Lord *Jesus* resplendent in glory, and
2. The specific shepherding letters sent to the seven *churches*.

John sees the ascended Lord in a glorious vision, and this Lord then instructs John what to say to the churches.

CHAPTER 3

Jesus Resplendent

Revelation 1:9-20

The Occasion

I, John, your brother and companion in the suffering and kingdom and patient endurance that are ours in Jesus, was on the island of Patmos because of the word of God and the testimony of Jesus. On the Lord's Day I was in the Spirit . . . (1:9-10)

* * * * * *

. . . the suffering and kingdom and patient endurance . . .

As their pastor, John identifies with his seven congregations in three ways: suffering, kingdom, and patient endurance. It is useful to consider these three items together. Christians at the time were suffering; they were undergoing persecution and discrimination of various kinds in the Roman Empire — and it would only get worse.

But more importantly, John's parishioners also share in kingdom, in Christ's lordship, and in his victory over death and sin, his victory over Satan. Jesus' enemies were able to persecute Jesus. They were even able to put him to death, but that was all they could do. Jesus would not remain in the grave. He rose from the tomb alive, demonstrating that whatever powers his enemies may have are vastly inferior to his own.

John now tells us that we also share that ultimate power. The enemies of Christ can do terrible things to his people; they exiled John to the island of Patmos, for example. But they could not destroy his spirit. Just as John was strong in exile, we also have the strength through Christ to endure. The enemies of Christ cannot control the life and soul of those who believe. Christ is Lord, and all who believe in him share in his victory over the powers of evil. Remain faithful to the Lord and share, by faith, in the kingdom of Jesus. The enemies of the Lord will not overcome those who are faithful.

Therefore, John concludes, let us resolve to continue in quiet and patient endurance of all these present troubles. We share in the suffering of Jesus, but more importantly we share in the kingdom!

On the Lord's Day I was in the Spirit . . .

The Jewish Sabbath is on the seventh day of the week. It is a holy day, from sundown Friday till sundown Saturday. Jesus rose from the dead on the first day of the week, and since this resurrection was the single most compelling reason that his followers continued to worship Jesus Christ as Lord, Christians began to value Sunday as a holy day more than Saturday.

On one such holy day John was relaxing and thinking about his churches on the mainland, and thinking also about the Lord Jesus in heaven. Perhaps he was wondering how he could help his churches to appreciate more intensely the wonderful person he himself knew Jesus to be.

Suddenly, he experienced an incredible event that showed him the answer to his question. He saw Jesus, not now disappearing up into the clouds over the Mount of Olives, but standing right there among the churches, resplendent and triumphant. John knew that he must now show his people how to recognize Jesus living among them; that they should not think of him as faraway, distant, or remote, but as one who is nearby, one who is indeed standing right there next to them.

The Command

. . . and I heard behind me a loud voice like a trumpet, which said: "Write on a scroll what you see and send it to the seven churches:

to Ephesus, Smyrna, Pergamum, Thyatira, Sardis, Philadelphia and Laodicea." (1:10-11)

. . . .

We are not told how soon after he saw this vision that John actually wrote about it. There are dozens of visions in this book of Revelation. We do not know how much time elapsed between the experience and the writing for any of them. Whether he saw all these things in one day or received these visions over a span of weeks or months we are not told. Did he write down each of them right after he saw it, or did he wait until they had all been given? (Did he perhaps forget exactly what one series of visions had been about? See what he says about the seven thunders in 10:4.) It does not matter when John wrote about his visions. It only matters that God commanded him and he obeyed.

On his own island of Alcatraz, John had no access to writing materials, to pen and ink, or (even more scarce) to papyrus to write on. His exile was probably not so severe as prison. Perhaps his exile meant simply that he had to get out of the province of Asia and never come back. On the island of Patmos, where he was sent, it is possible that his upkeep and care were still his own responsibility. If this were the case, he would have asked his friends to supply his needs, including writing materials.

The Vision

I turned around to see the voice that was speaking to me. And when I turned I saw seven golden lampstands, and among the lampstands was someone "like a son of man," dressed in a robe reaching down to his feet and with a golden sash around his chest. His head and hair were white like wool, as white as snow, and his eyes were like blazing fire. His feet were like bronze glowing in a furnace, and his voice was like the sound of rushing waters. In his right hand he held seven stars, and out of his mouth came a sharp double-edged sword. His face was like the sun shining in all its brilliance. (1:12-16)

. . . .

. . . seven golden lampstands . . .

John explains the symbolism of the lampstands in verse 20: "the seven lampstands are the seven churches." This is an interesting metaphor for John to use, comparing a church to a lampstand, a menorah. This comparison suggests the function of a church, namely, to be a light in the world (Matt. 5:14). In his Gospel John used the phrase to describe Jesus himself: "I am the light of the world" (John 8:12). Jesus, from heaven, sends his light, his truth, and his power into the world by means of churches. The function of a church is to reflect and transmit the light that flows from the resurrected and ascended Lord Jesus.

John sees Jesus relating not to individual persons but to churches. Christians therefore should join together as believers, establishing God's churches on the earth.

. . . someone "like a son of man" . . .

Many years earlier in his Gospel John had used the phrase "Son of Man" to describe Jesus (John 3:13-14). The term has a long history among the Jewish people, going back at least to Daniel 7:13, where it surely means the Messiah, the prophecy having been fulfilled with the coming of Jesus. John wants no doubt to describe the same Jesus who years ago lived on earth, who died, rose again, and ascended into the clouds, fulfilling in this unexpected way the purpose of a messiah, a christ.

But why does he describe him as *like* a son of man? Why not a son of man identically? This term accentuates the change that occurred in Jesus' existence when he rose from the dead and ascended into heaven. Passing through the rigors of death and resurrection transformed Jesus in ways that, while not negating his true humanity, brought him into a new dimension of human existence.

We cannot, from our *this side* perspective, know precisely what the *other side* looks like. Just what changes took place in Jesus' humanity when he rose from the dead we don't know for sure. The best we can do is to look at Jesus between the resurrection and the ascension and note the differences the Bible suggests between what Jesus was before and after his resurrection.

The apostle Paul suggests that we may expect what happened to Jesus to happen also to us in exactly the same way, for as he says, "We [shall] bear the likeness of the man from heaven" (1 Cor. 15:49). John, in his vision, sees Jesus as he exists after ascension, but significantly he sees him on earth standing invisibly among his churches, shepherding them through the trials of life in the Roman Empire. John wishes to emphasize that the true shepherd and pastor of the churches is not John himself, or any other undershepherd, but Jesus from heaven. All churches must look directly to Jesus for their wisdom, their strength, and their comfort.

There is symbolism in each of the items by which John describes Jesus:

> *. . . a robe reaching down to his feet and . . . a golden sash . . .*

These suggest the official apparel of either a priest or a king, or in this vision perhaps both. The culminated Jesus is seen as the epitome of all the official functions of Old Testament Israel: the priest who is also a king, and the king who is also a priest.

> *. . . hair . . . white like wool . . .*

Here John's depiction of Jesus again picks up the imagery of Daniel (Dan. 7:9). The woolly whiteness may suggest, as in Isaiah 1:18, holiness, or righteousness. The symbolism picks up Old Testament themes, and thus conveys the impression that Jesus is the fulfillment of Jewish tradition.

> *. . . eyes . . . like . . . fire . . .*

Again, an echo of Daniel (Dan. 10:6). The figure possesses eyes that penetrate deep into the realities of people, of life, and of time, not only observing but also exerting power in the purging influence of fire. Jesus is not only looking at what is going on in the churches, he is cleansing out the impurities with holy fire.

> *. . . feet [of] bronze . . .*

Perhaps John sees these feet in contrast to the feet of clay in Daniel 2:33. The reign of Christ from heaven does not rest upon feet of clay but upon the stable foundation of precious metal purified by fire.

> *. . . voice . . . like the sound of rushing waters.*

Like the sound of constantly breaking waves on the shore, so the voice of the Lord dominates the environment. His voice is inescapable, forceful, controlling. In the next section John will give specificity to this voice as Jesus directs his message to each of the seven churches in turn. What he is about to say cannot be ignored or evaded.

In his right hand he held seven stars . . .

The "seven stars are the angels of the seven churches" (Rev. 1:20), Jesus himself explains to John. The word *angel* means messenger, and here Jesus says that anyone who functions as a messenger of the gospel, who undertakes the responsibility of disseminating the gospel, is being held as a star in his right hand. He would mean people like Timothy and Titus; Epaphras, Luke, and John himself; Peter, Barnabas, Paul, Epaphroditus, and John Mark; and doubtless many others who are unnamed in the Scriptures. The term may be understood collectively; all active messengers in any true church are included in the term *angel*.

. . . a sharp double-edged sword.

A sword is hardly part of a priest's equipment, but it would be included in the wardrobe of a king. The controlling concept of John's vision here is that of kingship rather than of priestliness. The sword, significantly, is not in Jesus' hand or buckled to his waist; it is protruding from his mouth. The imagery suggests that the manner in which Jesus exerts his power is not by human strength, ingenuity, or intimidation but by the power of his word, the energy of truth, the irresistible force of the gospel.

Think of Isaiah's dictum, "My word . . . will not return to me empty, but will accomplish what I desire and achieve the purpose for which I sent it" (Isa. 55:11). And also of John's own insight, "The Word became flesh" (John 1:14). Jesus, while on earth, incarnated God's eternal word, his purpose for the human race as a whole. And he achieved the purpose for which God sent him; he did not return to God empty. Even now Jesus is sending that same word into the world so that the eternal purpose of God's word will ultimately be accomplished. That word begins its relentless onslaught on the reign of evil and terror by establishing churches as beachheads in the domain of the enemy.

His . . . brilliance.

"His face was like the sun shining in all its brilliance." In Greek the word translated "face" means not merely the face as such, but the entire appearance, the total effect of the visionary being. You don't look directly at the sun because it blinds you. Similarly, though John sees the ascended Lord in the detail he has described, now, because of the brilliance of his appearance, he can only close his eyes and fall at his feet as though dead.

The resplendent Lord must dominate not only John but also every one of us as we seek to find our way through life as disciples of Christ. Religion is not about asserting our own willpower, our own insight, or our own ingenuity; it is about learning to see Jesus in all his glory and submitting all that we have and are to his dominant control. We die with him only to be raised again to live with him, already now in this life. We lose our life in him only to find it again. Jesus Christ our Lord is here, and he is standing among his churches!

John wants his people to see Jesus in the capacity of both priest and king, a royal priest and a priestly king. Earlier in Revelation John wrote that Christians become "a kingdom and priests" (1:6). John is urging his readers to develop a vision of Jesus that sees him as the example par excellence of what we all become when we follow him as Lord. Combine the religious element and the secular element, the priest and the king, and understand that Jesus leads us in living our lives on earth but in a deeply religious orientation.

Do not think *only* of the past or *only* of the future in this regard. Think existentially. Think in the present. This Jesus, whom John is describing so extravagantly, is coming now. He is present constantly among his churches — among all his churches everywhere. He is the sovereign Lord who in his own humanity has defeated all the inhuman powers allied against him, and who is sharing his own priesthood and kingdom with all who follow him.

He is not only standing among the churches in the ancient Roman province of Asia, but he is standing here also today in the beleaguered churches of the world, in the Orient, in Africa, in Europe, and in the Americas. Jesus is just as surely here today as he was in the days of John. Time and distance do not diminish the glory and the power of Jesus. He remains as resplendent today among modern churches as he was then among the ancient churches.

The Consolation

When I saw him, I fell at his feet as though dead. Then he placed his right hand on me and said: "Do not be afraid. I am the First and the Last. I am the Living One; I was dead, and behold I am alive for ever and ever! And I hold the keys of death and Hades.

"Write, therefore, what you have seen, what is now and what will take place later. The mystery of the seven stars that you saw in my right hand and of the seven golden lampstands is this: The seven stars are the angels of the seven churches, and the seven lampstands are the seven churches." (1:17-20)

. . . .

. . . I fell at his feet as though dead.

Whether John literally fell prone on the ground when he received this vision or actually sees himself in the vision, falling down as if dead, John means to suggest that he surrendered himself entirely to the one "like a son of man" in his vision. All of his own independent personal resources became as if dead before the imposing magnificence of the ascended Lord Jesus. This reaction is surprising. We might rather expect to see John energized to ever greater and more diligent efforts to proclaim the gospel. Rather than revitalizing him, however, the vision paralyzes him. John is "as though dead."

While on earth, before his death and ascension, Jesus had told people who wanted to be his disciples that they must learn to deny themselves. "If anyone would come after me, he must deny himself and take up his cross and follow me" (Matt. 16:24). This is what John is actually demonstrating as he falls to the ground before Jesus. He is surrendering his entire being to Jesus. This is the response we all as Christians must learn to make if we would follow him.

"Do not be afraid."

Jesus understands that we are overwhelmed by this vision of his appearance. We are reduced to immobility, paralysis, stupefaction, deadness. We are in awe of the utter power and majesty of the risen Lord. In counseling John not to be afraid, Jesus means more than a psychological feeling of being afraid or scared. He means to tell John to not be afraid that at this exact moment he is "as . . . dead." He is useless and unimportant. Jesus doesn't want this vision to reduce John to a withdrawn nonentity. It is well, Jesus is saying, that you fall on your face before me, but now that you have done so, let me pick you up and make you truly my disciple, going where I send you, saying what I tell you, doing what I command you.

Next, Jesus describes himself in a series of portraits, all designed to amplify John's vision of him even further. The following phrases describe the same thing, that is, Jesus.

"I am the First and the Last."

The Greek words are *protos* and *eschatos,* first and last. Jesus is encouraging us to understand that everything we hold to be important in life must begin and end with him.

"I am the Living One . . ."

Not merely is he alive again, but he is life itself, that is, human life. Jesus is the epitome, the paradigm, and the essence of humanity. He is what human life is all about, the incarnation of God's eternal plan for the human race, a second and perfected Adam.

". . . I was dead, and behold I am alive for ever and ever!"

In our vision of Jesus we must not overlook the process by which he became what he now is. He was born of the virgin Mary, he grew up and learned obedience as a child, he worked with his hands as a carpenter, he proclaimed the kingdom of God, he healed the sick and raised the dead, he himself died and rose from the dead — and now as the climax of this historical process Jesus is alive in such a way that he cannot die again, for ever and ever.

When we see Jesus in our own private vision, we must see not only that our own personal individual lives are entwined in his, but also that the welfare of the entire human race is involved in Jesus. The historical process by which Jesus became what he now is must be duplicated by the human race in its unity, together as one. That is what Jesus is actually accomplishing now in his work on earth from heaven.

"And I hold the keys of death and Hades."

Jesus is affirming that, because he has passed through the historical process of death and resurrection, he has not only overcome death in his own personal life, but he also holds the power which enables the entire human race to do the same. The human race can assure itself of not being destroyed, of not succumbing to the debilitating effects of sin, of having a future for ever and ever. Do it Jesus' way. He has the keys to the future, to life, to success, to perpetual progress for the entire human community.

Jesus told John to write it all down (1:11). He didn't want him to miss a thing. John is about to see precisely how Jesus will bring down the forces of Satan and bring healing to all nations. He needs to pay close attention. Jesus is showing him the process by which he will make all things new, totally eradicating all that is ugly or evil or wrong or sinful. He is creating a new world where righteousness will dwell. Jesus is talking about our world, the very real churches and people who are valiantly struggling against the powers of evil. Jesus commands John to write to them and show them what is really happening behind the scenes of the life and history they see in front of them. He must show them how the tribulations they are undergoing in their lives are part of the great process by which Jesus is bringing all knees to bow before him and all tongues to confess that he is Lord. He will give them courage and faith and obedience through the visions he writes down.

CHAPTER 4

Jesus Shepherding

Revelation 2–3

The Pattern of the Seven Letters

Jesus, whom John is now seeing in a vision of magnificent glory and authority, dictates to John what he must write to each church. Besides receiving the book as a whole, each church receives a special letter directed specifically to it.

The seven letters are stylized, following a common pattern. At the beginning of each letter Jesus refers to one of his own characteristics, usually one already mentioned in John's vision of Jesus. This characteristic is then utilized in the letter as a standard against which to measure the spiritual health of the church.

Jesus analyzes both the good things and the bad things in each church, warning against the evil and encouraging the good. He evaluates how well each church reflects his own character. That is the standard by which Jesus evaluates these churches in these letters. A church's success is measured by the extent to which it images Christ Jesus, that is, the extent to which the nature of Jesus is incorporated into its life and witness. The same is true still today. Churches should reflect one or more of the attributes of Jesus.

The Letter to Ephesus

"To the angel of the church in Ephesus write: These are the words of him who holds the seven stars in his right hand and walks among the seven golden lampstands: I know your deeds, your hard work and your perseverance. I know that you cannot tolerate wicked men, that you have tested those who claim to be apostles but are not, and have found them false. You have persevered and have endured hardships for my name, and have not grown weary.

"Yet I hold this against you: You have forsaken your first love. Remember the height from which you have fallen! Repent and do the things you did at first. If you do not repent, I will come to you and remove your lampstand from its place. But you have this in your favor: You hate the practices of the Nicolaitans, which I also hate.

"He who has an ear, let him hear what the Spirit says to the churches. To him who overcomes, I will give the right to eat from the tree of life, which is in the paradise of God." (2:1-7)

. . . .

". . . him who holds the seven stars in his right hand and walks among the seven golden lampstands . . ."

The metaphor is comparable to a shepherd holding his staff and walking among his sheep, and with a similar meaning — Jesus is shepherding his churches through the uncertainties of life, particularly the persecutions that erupt from time to time. This is the part of John's vision directed especially to Ephesus, and by which Jesus judges the condition of the church.

". . . I know your deeds, your hard work and your perseverance."

These good Christian people in Ephesus have worked hard, they have persevered, and they have indeed endured hardships. More specifically they have tested false apostles and rejected their teachings. And commendably, they have not grown weary. They have been Christians for twenty or more years, perhaps as many as forty years, but they are not "burned out," as our modern saying goes.

". . . You have forsaken your first love."

The original joy, enthusiasm, conviction, and devotion that the church of Ephesus once had are now missing from their service. They need to get it back. If they don't, and the trend continues, their lampstand, their church itself, will be removed; it will burn itself out.

The warning is not only for Ephesus but also for any and all churches. Churches that no longer sense the loving presence of Jesus among them will slowly lose their love for him, and the reason for having a church at all will vanish. If there is no sense of need for Jesus, there is, in the end, no sense of service to him either. No need, no service, no church. That is the direction the church is heading in, and it should be avoided by all means.

". . . You hate the practices of the Nicolaitans . . ."

Historians have not been able to identify this group with certainty. There may have been in the vicinity of Ephesus some prominent person named Nicolaus who advocated certain beliefs and practices that were opposed to the spirit of Christ. In the letter to Pergamum (2:14-15), the term *Nicolaitan* is used in connection with Balaam, with the practice of eating food sacrificed to idols, and also with sexual immorality. Perhaps this Nicolaus was a contemporary Balaam, teaching those same things. Jesus, therefore, is commending the Christian people in Ephesus for resisting and overcoming this threat.

"To him who overcomes . . ."

Overcoming means sensing deeply the presence of the Lord Jesus and living accordingly, overcoming the pressures to conform to the spirit of the world rather than to the spirit of Christ, precisely as this church has demonstrated in its rejection of Nicolaitanism.

". . . the tree of life, which is in the paradise of God."

Everyone who perseveres, who accepts the shepherding guidance of Christ Jesus and serves him with genuine love and faith and hope, will, by

39

that very token, be with Jesus in the paradise of God, eating from the tree of life.

This promise does not refer to life after death. Jesus means to encourage us today by saying that already in this life a living faith and trust in Jesus is the same as eating of the tree of life, being in the paradise of God.

The Letter to Smyrna

"To the angel of the church in Smyrna write: These are the words of him who is the First and the Last, who died and came to life again. I know your afflictions and your poverty — yet you are rich! I know the slander of those who say they are Jews and are not, but are a synagogue of Satan. Do not be afraid of what you are about to suffer. I tell you, the devil will put some of you in prison to test you, and you will suffer persecution for ten days. Be faithful, even to the point of death, and I will give you the crown of life.

"He who has an ear, let him hear what the Spirit says to the churches. He who overcomes will not be hurt at all by the second death." (2:8-11)

.　.　.　.　.　.　.

". . . him who is the First and the Last, who died and came to life again."

Here is a church whose model is the one "who died and came to life again." In his earlier life on earth Jesus endured the humiliation of being rejected by his own people. The Christians in Smyrna must contrast that humiliation of Jesus with his present exaltation at the right hand of the Father in heaven, and they must learn to take that contrast as the pattern by which they themselves must live. With him they must die to sin and come to life in righteousness.

"I know your afflictions and your poverty — yet you are rich!"

John draws the comparison: you are living in poverty, but in fact you are very rich! In this sense they have died and come to life again with Jesus, here and now. Though they endure poverty on earth, they already enjoy the glory of heaven in a new life of the spirit.

> ". . . *those who say they are Jews and are not, but are a synagogue of Satan.*"

Rough language! Smyrnan Christians were enduring hostility and persecution from the Jewish synagogue. Unconverted Jews never liked to see their synagogue community invaded by the gospel, their brothers and sisters agitating to update their lives around Jesus rather than the Law. In fact, they expelled these Christian brethren, who then formed a new community centered on Christ.

But Jesus says the truth is with the church, not with the synagogue. In fact, he calls the synagogue "a synagogue of Satan" because of the way they react to the Christians they have expelled. In spite of their profession, they have played into the hands of Satan, just as the Jews in Jerusalem had done earlier when they rejected Jesus.

Jesus asserts that these unconverted Jews are not really Jews. "They say they are Jews but they aren't." Jesus wants his followers to understand that the true meaning of Judaism is not found in maintaining the ancient traditions, but in following Jesus. Jesus is the true Jewish Messiah. True Judaism therefore means believing this and following Jesus. Rejecting and not following Jesus is equivalent to rejecting true Judaism. Jesus is the fulfillment of the entire course of Old Testament religion.

> ". . . *you will suffer persecution for ten days.*"

Smyrnan Christians, however, are not to worry. They may be persecuted for a while, but it will pass ("ten days" is a figure of speech, it is symbolic). What is important is that they be faithful to their Lord so long as they live, even to the death if need be. If they do that, they will demonstrate that they are indeed wearing "the crown of life." That is what true life is: to be faithful to the Lord in all circumstances.

> "*He who overcomes will not be hurt at all by the second death.*"

In 21:8 certain people are consigned to a second death: "the fiery lake of burning sulfur." Faithful Christians do not have to worry about being drowned in this dreadful lake of fire.

41

In 20:6 John writes, "Blessed and holy are those who have part in the first resurrection. The second death has no power over them." Second death cannot happen to people who have part in the first resurrection. But what then is this first resurrection?

"The first resurrection" refers to the resurrection of which Jesus is the first. Jesus is the First and the Last. His is the first resurrection; if you believe in Jesus you share in his resurrection. But to share in this first resurrection is the same thing as to escape the lake of fire, which is the second death.

The first death would be the death of Adam and Eve, described in Genesis 3, namely, the death that is identical with choosing to eat from the wrong tree. To choose the way of sin is itself to choose death. Sin is the death of the spirit, of that which is best and holiest in man. All of us are in Adam. All of us participate in this first death.

We must be resurrected from that moral and spiritual death. This happens in Christ, who is the first man to rise from Adam's death. As the apostle Paul puts it again and again in his letters, to be in Christ means to be in his death and resurrection. Die to sin and rise to righteousness. Dying to sin is dying to the first death — in other words, participating in the first resurrection.

Those who are genuinely in Christ, in his resurrection, need not fear the second death. This second death is the finalizing of the first death. When we die physically, our ultimate destiny becomes irreversible. Those who refuse the first resurrection in Christ, who persist in the first death, will finalize their ultimate destiny when they die physically. The lake of fire symbolizes this finalization of the first death. Christians do not have to worry about that fate.

The Letter to Pergamum

"To the angel of the church in Pergamum write: These are the words of him who has the sharp, double-edged sword. I know where you live — where Satan has his throne. Yet you remain true to my name. You did not renounce your faith in me, even in the days of Antipas, my faithful witness, who was put to death in your city — where Satan lives.

"Nevertheless, I have a few things against you: You have people there who hold to the teaching of Balaam, who taught Balak to entice the Israelites to sin by eating food sacrificed to idols and by committing sexual immorality. Likewise you also have those who hold to the teaching of the Nicolaitans. Repent therefore! Otherwise, I will soon come to you and will fight against them with the sword of my mouth.

"He who has an ear, let him hear what the Spirit says to the churches. To him who overcomes, I will give some of the hidden manna. I will also give him a white stone with a new name written on it, known only to him who receives it." (2:12-17)

.   .   .   .

". . . him who has the sharp, double-edged sword."

In John's original vision, the sword is in Jesus' mouth (1:16). It therefore represents what Jesus says, his word, the gospel. This sword cuts against sin, opposing and destroying sin wherever it is found. The symbolism goes back to the Garden of Eden, where the cherubim wave flashing swords back and forth to guard the way to the Tree of Life (Gen. 3:24). The church in Pergamum must measure itself against this sword in Jesus' mouth. Are they withstanding temptation and sin? Having regained Paradise through faith in Jesus, are they guarding their lives well?

". . . where Satan has his throne."

Pergamum was an ancient capital of Asia, and still remained a center of administration where the Roman emperor was worshiped as a god. Hence Jesus uses the symbol of power, a throne, to signify this unique danger to the faith of the young church in Pergamum.

A recent wave of persecution — perhaps the same one in which John was banished — had resulted in the capture and death of one of their church leaders, Antipas. Through it all the Pergamum church maintained its faith and obedience to the Lord. They overcame Satan in that crisis.

". . . You have people there who hold to the teaching of Balaam . . ."

But there is another temptation they are facing, the outcome of which is still in doubt. Some members of the church in Pergamum hold to teachings similar to those of Balaam in the Old Testament, errors now being resurrected by someone called Nicolaus, whose followers are known as Nicolaitans. These errors involve "eating food sacrificed to idols and . . . committing sexual immorality."

The apostle Paul had earlier dealt with both of these problems in long letters to the Corinthians (1 Cor. 7–10) and to the Romans (Rom. 14).

The problem regarding idol food was twofold. First, it was common practice to purchase meat from butchers who secured their supplies from the surplus of pagan temples; and second, people would often attend civic events in these temples, including festivals in which foods blessed by pagan priests were served. The Jewish heritage was to avoid not only this food but also all nonkosher foods. By participating in such events Christians may seem to be engaging in acts of worship to some particular heathen god.

The problem regarding sexual immorality was also connected with the pagan temples. Young women functioned as priestesses in these temples, serving the male clientele who were symbolically worshiping the goddess of the temple by engaging in sexual adventures with them.

Jesus, through John, is warning them now to guard themselves against such compromises, which may well have the long-range effect of diminishing their loyalty to him. Wield the sword of the Spirit against those foes.

> *"To him who overcomes, I will give some of the hidden manna. I will also give him a white stone with a new name written on it . . ."*

The hidden manna, the white stone, and the new name are very likely references to customs connected with public festivals held in the pagan temple. The white stone with a name on it probably is equivalent to our modern ticket with the seat number on it. Present the stone with your name on it to the doorkeeper of the temple, and you will be admitted. Christ gives each believer a new character and a new lifestyle, represented by the new name. Symbolically, this new name provides admission to the temple of God.

Still symbolically, at the festival in the temple of God these persons with new names may partake of the hidden manna, that is, the sustenance of life eternal. If you are in the Lord Jesus by faith, then you receive his Spirit who will sustain you through good times and bad.

The Letter to Thyatira

"To the angel of the church in Thyatira write: These are the words of the Son of God, whose eyes are like blazing fire and whose feet are like burnished bronze. I know your deeds, your love and faith, your service and perseverance, and that you are now doing more than you did at first.

"Nevertheless, I have this against you: You tolerate that woman Jezebel, who calls herself a prophetess. By her teaching she misleads my servants into sexual immorality and the eating of food sacrificed to idols. I have given her time to repent of her immorality, but she is unwilling. So I will cast her on a bed of suffering, and I will make those who commit adultery with her suffer intensely, unless they repent of her ways. I will strike her children dead. Then all the churches will know that I am he who searches hearts and minds, and I will repay each of you according to your deeds. Now I say to the rest of you in Thyatira, to you who do not hold to her teaching and have not learned Satan's so-called deep secrets (I will not impose any other burden on you): Only hold on to what you have until I come.

"To him who overcomes and does my will to the end, I will give authority over the nations — 'He will rule them with an iron scepter; he will dash them to pieces like pottery' — just as I have received authority from my Father. I will also give him the morning star. He who has an ear, let him hear what the Spirit says to the churches." (2:18-29)

. . . .

"*. . . the Son of God, whose eyes are like blazing fire and whose feet are like burnished bronze.*"

Jesus sees with blazing eyes what goes on in the churches, and with his bronzed boots he tramples out whatever he sees that is impure. This picture of what Jesus sees and does in the churches is now directed specifically to the church in Thyatira.

> *"I know your deeds, your love and faith, your service and perseverance, and that you are now doing more than you did at first."*

Jesus, the one "who searches minds and hearts" (Ps. 7:9), sees growth and improvement in the church of Thyatira. Their later love and works of faith exceed the first. They are not, like Ephesus, moving downward toward perfunctory obedience, but upward, serving more faithfully as time goes on.

> *". . . You tolerate that woman Jezebel . . ."*

Jesus sees Jezebel, a local prophetess who is leading some of them into the same sins as Pergamum, immorality and idol food. The original Jezebel was, of course, the Phoenician wife of Old Testament king Ahab. She introduced the idol religion of her home country into Israel, and the prophet Elijah opposed her strenuously (1 Kings 18).

> *"So I will cast her on a bed of suffering . . ."*

Jesus, with his bronzed feet, comes to her and gives her the suffering she deserves. He promises to bring great tribulation upon her and her followers. He will not allow such immorality and idolatry to survive in the church. Jesus is thus promising to "trample out the vintage of the grapes of wrath," as the song puts it, separating the good wine from the discarded pulp (Rev. 14:18-20). What his eyes see, his feet deal with.

> *". . . I will repay each of you according to your deeds."*

These good Christians in Thyatira must not think their faith in Jesus is separate from the way they live. In those days there was a prevalent notion that what one does in one's mind is the only thing that is really important, not what one does with one's body. Jesus was telling them, and us, that Christians must not use that justification for accepting Jezebel's teachings. If they do they will get what they have chosen, namely, being "dashed to pieces" by the wrath of the Lord.

On the contrary, those who follow Jesus humbly and sincerely, in their physical life as well as in their intellectual life, will also get what they have chosen, namely, "authority over the nations."

Matthew writes, "he will reward each person according to what he has done" (Matt. 16:27; see also Rev. 22:12; Rom. 2:6-11; 2 Thess. 1:6), and also "by their fruit you will recognize them" (Matt. 7:16). Jesus promises the Christians in Thyatira that they will get what their lives deserve. Live a life of faith and obedience and the Lord will bless you. Live a life of sin and self-indulgence and the Lord will punish you. It's that simple.

"To him who overcomes and does my will to the end, I will give authority over the nations . . . just as I have received authority from my Father."

John is reflecting the last words of Jesus recorded by Matthew: "All authority in heaven and on earth has been given to me" (Matt. 28:18).

"Authority in heaven," of course, means the authority of God. In this passage from Matthew Jesus is affirming that God will be working out his purposes precisely through the continued ministry of Jesus from heaven. But Jesus also claimed "all authority . . . on earth." He means that whatever awesomely evil powers may be evident in human civilization, Jesus is in the process of overcoming them just as surely as he overcame them in his own personal life. His resurrection and ascension is the pledge that he can and will have authority over all.

The astounding thing in this letter to Thyatira, however, is that Jesus promises to give this same authority to those who overcome by doing his will to the end. These people, in this church, will exercise "authority over the nations." Incredible!

Jesus does not mean in the first instance political authority, or economic authority, or judicial authority. He means specifically spiritual authority, the authority that controls the spirit, the same authority that motivates people to do what they do, the inner drive that determines the way they live. Some people may be motivated by self-aggrandizement, or a lust for money or power or knowledge. They may be craving for revenge, or maybe something nobler, like a desire to help the unfortunate. There are hundreds of drives and motivations that shape the pattern of our behavior as human beings.

Ultimately, however, such drives can be reduced to two categories: those that are beneficial and those that are not. Some drives contribute to the overall welfare of people and some do not. Selfishness does not contribute to goodness, selflessness does. Revenge does not produce harmony and peace, forgiveness does. Wars of aggression do not encourage shalom, international cooperation does. Spiritual authority is exercised in two basic forms, that of God and that of the devil. One is for good and the other is for evil; one is creative, the other is destructive.

Jesus is instructing the church in Thyatira — and of course all churches — that he is constantly exercising supreme authority from heaven on earth. He has already demonstrated that his authority on earth is greater than that of Satan — by patiently enduring all the powers that Satan could throw at him, and then calmly overcoming them in his resurrection and ascension.

Jesus wants his churches to understand this clearly; what is happening in the churches and in the nations where those churches work is exactly the process by which Jesus is exercising his authority on earth.

Christians, because of their commitment to Jesus as Lord, put their allegiance to God higher than any other loyalty they may exercise — whether to family or friends, nation or government, religious institution, university, or corporation. Christians have numerous loyalties, but supreme over all is loyalty to God as he exercises his power through Christ and the gospel and the Spirit.

As the number of Christians increases in any given social unit, there will be growing pressure to do things right, with justice and compassion, in truth and in love. Any entrenched powers of evil will feel this pressure and resist mightily. Hostility and conflict will inevitably ensue. But Christ's promise is that in the end truth, justice, and love will increase and eventually overcome. Jesus wants his church in Thyatira to see what is happening in their city in this perspective.

If you look at history, you can see that it has actually worked out that way. Fewer than three hundred years after this was written the Roman Empire, once implacably hostile to Christ, succumbed to the gospel so that Christian faith became the dominant attitude in the empire. The same process is at work wherever there are Christians and churches. This is an example of how Jesus gives authority over the nations to his followers.

The Letter to Sardis

"To the angel of the church in Sardis write: These are the words of him who holds the seven spirits of God and the seven stars. I know your deeds; you have a reputation of being alive, but you are dead. Wake up! Strengthen what remains and is about to die, for I have not found your deeds complete in the sight of my God. Remember, therefore, what you have received and heard; obey it, and repent. But if you do not wake up, I will come like a thief, and you will not know at what time I will come to you.

"Yet you have a few people in Sardis who have not soiled their clothes. They will walk with me, dressed in white, for they are worthy. He who overcomes will, like them, be dressed in white. I will never blot out his name from the book of life, but will acknowledge his name before my Father and his angels. He who has an ear, let him hear what the Spirit says to the churches." (3:1-6)

. . . .

". . . him who holds the seven spirits of God and the seven stars."

This figure of speech seems to be derived somehow from a royal court in which numerous officials stand around waiting for instructions from the king. Jesus himself would be like an executive officer through whom all commands are processed. He has the powers of God, "the seven spirits," in his control, and also the churches, "the seven stars." He sends these spirits into the churches, and they respond by obeying God's commands. The church in Sardis must evaluate itself by asking whether it understands itself clearly to be held in the hand of Christ, that the Lord controls its life from heaven.

". . . you have a reputation of being alive, but you are dead."

Sadly, Jesus' evaluation is negative. The church has an excellent reputation for being vigorous and energetic, but appearances here are deceiving. The church in Sardis is busy, but the motivation for its activity is not what it should be: the members are not motivated sufficiently by the Spirit of God.

49

The specifics of this anomaly are not provided. We do not know precisely why Jesus reviews the church in Sardis so negatively. We don't know what gives the impression of great spirituality to those observing on the outside, while within there is nothing but dead men's bones. Jesus spoke of it earlier in Matthew 23, where he describes scribes and Pharisees as hypocrites. The term *hypocrisy* means exactly what the church in Sardis is accused of — vigorous religious activity without a genuinely spiritual drive behind it.

> *"He who overcomes will, like them, be dressed in white. I will never blot out his name from the book of life . . ."*

Dressed in white means walking with Christ in righteousness and holiness. Jesus promises that those Christians who can sort out the implications of living according to the Spirit of the Lord will receive the white garments which symbolize purity and righteousness and all that is good and beneficial.

Jesus will not remove their names from "the book of life." The symbolism of this term is comparable to the term "tree of life" (Gen 2:9). Eating of the tree of life is one way of saying that one's name is engraved in the book of life. If you live in such a way as to demonstrate the effects of the Spirit of Christ, and if you conform your life to the commands of God, then you are truly alive. You have life, life as God intended it to be from the beginning and as Jesus desires you to have it. You have life, not death. You are eating from the tree of life. Your name is in the book of life.

The Letter to Philadelphia

"To the angel of the church in Philadelphia write: These are the words of him who is holy and true, who holds the key of David. What he opens no one can shut, and what he shuts no one can open. I know your deeds. See, I have placed before you an open door that no one can shut. I know that you have little strength, yet you have kept my word and have not denied my name. I will make those who are of the synagogue of Satan, who claim to be Jews though they are not, but are liars — I will make them come and fall down at your feet and acknowledge that I have loved you. Since you have kept my command to endure patiently, I will also keep you from the hour of trial that is going to come upon the whole world to test those who live on the earth.

"I am coming soon. Hold on to what you have, so that no one will take your crown. Him who overcomes I will make a pillar in the temple of my God. Never again will he leave it. I will write on him the name of my God and the name of the city of my God, the new Jerusalem, which is coming down out of heaven from my God; and I will also write on him my new name. He who has an ear, let him hear what the Spirit says to the churches." (3:7-13)

. . . .

". . . him who is holy and true, who holds the key of David."

This metaphor, "the key of David," goes back at least to Isaiah, in a passage which appears to be a messianic prophecy as well as a local one: "I will place on his shoulder the key to the house of David; what he opens no one can shut, and what he shuts no one can open" (Isa. 22:22). Whatever the immediate reference of Isaiah may have been, Jesus is appropriating the phraseology here to suggest that the church in Philadelphia needs to examine itself in the light of this figure of speech.

The house of David may be equated therefore with the kingdom of Christ, Jesus being a descendant of David and the inheritor of the promises made to David. The kingdom of Christ is in turn the kingdom of God, since God exercises his sovereignty over the human race now through his Son Jesus. So the intent of the metaphor is to confirm that it is Jesus who controls entrance into the kingdom of God. Jesus not only holds the key, but he himself is the key.

The record of Jesus' life, the gospel, is our key. Jesus instructed his original disciples, "I will give you the keys of the kingdom of heaven; whatever you bind on earth will be bound in heaven, and whatever you loose on earth will be loosed in heaven" (Matt. 16:19). Wherever the gospel of Jesus Christ is believed, there the kingdom of Christ is to be found. The key to entrance into the kingdom, therefore, is in believing the gospel. Jesus wants the church in Philadelphia to examine whether or not

51

they are in the kingdom of Christ, and to determine that by whether they truly believe the gospel.

"See, I have placed before you an open door . . ."

Continuing the metaphor of keys and doors, Jesus reminds the church that there is "an open door" for them, presumably one through which Jesus expects someone or something to move.

The passage is often interpreted to mean the opportunity to do mission work, to evangelize. Yet, in the immediate context of Philadelphia it could also mean an open door for others to come in, into the church.

Philadelphia is the original Church of the Open Door, welcoming all who believe. Jesus says, "I will make those who are of the synagogue of Satan, who claim to be Jews though they are not, but are liars — I will make them come and fall down at your feet and acknowledge that I have loved you." People of the Jewish faith continue to confront claims that Jesus is their Messiah. Yet some eventually come to believe, thus becoming members of the church and passing through the open door.

". . . I will also keep you from the hour of trial that is going to come upon the whole world to test those who live on the earth."

Very likely the reference is to some egregious governmental hardship placed upon Christians, the harbinger of which was John's own banishment to Patmos. In that case the term "the whole world" would mean the whole Roman Empire. Perhaps John could sense that an empire-wide persecution was about to break out.

Understand this promise in the broader biblical context. Adam and Eve faced their trial, and failed. Old covenant Israel faced the trial, and failed (crucifying their Messiah). Jesus faced his trial, and did not fail. Christian people constantly face their trials; those who overcome do not fail.

Accordingly, the "trial that is going to come" is in reality a trial that is coming constantly. God's people always face the *test* of whether or not they will be faithful during opposition, discrimination, scorn, and outright persecution. When Jesus says he will keep them from that "hour of trial," he does not mean that they will escape it altogether but that they will remain faithful through it.

The point is that "the hour of trial" is always upon us, testing whether we live faithfully as Christians or not. Either we obey God or we do not. Either we live in the spirit of Christ or we do not.

"I am coming soon."

If we take this statement out of context, we will be thoroughly puzzled. John wrote these words in the latter part of the first century. But Jesus has not returned yet, so what can be meant by *soon*?

The Greek word used here is *tachu*. "I am coming *tachu*." The term can bear a variety of meanings in Greek — quickly, speedily, hastily, soon, shortly, immediately, suddenly, easily, or readily. Its primary meaning is not necessarily chronological or sequential, as in the sense of this year or next year. Jesus is saying that when the hour of trial comes upon this church in Philadelphia, Jesus himself will be there immediately to shepherd them safely through it. When you need his help he will be there.

The words "I am coming" are translated from the Greek word *erchomai*. This word is in the present tense, so that the adverb *tachu*, "soon," does not negate that sense of something occurring in the present. Jesus is always coming, always present. His coming is immediate, at hand, now as well as soon.

This fits in with the previous context, the hour of trial. It also suggests to us that Jesus is not here talking about his second coming, as we ordinarily understand it. We do not have to wait until the end of the world to experience Jesus' presence. He is always with us, especially in the times that severely try our faith.

The Letter to Laodicea

"To the angel of the church in Laodicea write: These are the words of the Amen, the faithful and true witness, the ruler of God's creation. I know your deeds, that you are neither cold nor hot. I wish you were either one or the other! So, because you are lukewarm — neither hot nor cold — I am about to spit you out of my mouth. You say, 'I am rich; I have acquired wealth and do not need a thing.' But you do not realize that you are wretched, pitiful, poor, blind and naked. I counsel you to buy from me gold refined in the fire, so you can become rich; and white clothes to wear, so you can cover your shameful nakedness; and salve to put on your eyes, so you can see.

"Those whom I love I rebuke and discipline. So be earnest, and repent. Here I am! I stand at the door and knock. If anyone hears my voice and opens the door, I will come in and eat with him, and he with me.

"To him who overcomes, I will give the right to sit with me on my throne, just as I overcame and sat down with my Father on his throne. He who has an ear, let him hear what the Spirit says to the churches." (3:14-22)

. . . .

". . . the Amen, the faithful and true witness, the ruler of God's creation."

Jesus identifies himself to the Laodicean church in these three ways:

1. the *Amen* (Amen, firm, faithful, true)
2. the *martus* (martyr, witness)
3. the *arche* (beginning, authority)

Try to combine these three items into one composite picture of Jesus. It is a description that emphasizes reliability, authority, and trustworthiness. Notice how the terms *faithful and true* explain the meaning of *Amen.* Jesus is the standard by which to evaluate all things, the entire creation of God. That is how the church in Laodicea must see Jesus, and from that perception they must evaluate their own lives. They need to see Jesus as the *arche* of the entire universe, its beginning, its ruler, and they must accept this reality as faithful and true and then live accordingly.

". . . you are neither cold nor hot."

This is not so different from the church in Ephesus, which has lost its first love, or the church in Sardis, which has a better reputation than its actual character. Perhaps this condition is to be expected more or less in the second generation. The first people to come to believe in Jesus do so in great joy and commitment, but their children perhaps merely accept their new religion without getting excited by it; they are "neither cold nor hot."

> *"But you do not realize that you are wretched, pitiful, poor, blind and na-ked. I counsel you to buy from me gold refined in the fire, so you can be-come rich; and white clothes to wear, so you can cover your shameful na-kedness; and salve to put on your eyes, so you can see."*

Notice the parallels: poor — gold, blind — salve, naked — white clothes.

The Christians in the Laodicean church are evaluating themselves in non-Christian ways. They must, however, learn to do that in a Chris-tian way. They think they are wealthy, but Jesus sees that they are poor — they possess external wealth but internal poverty. They think they are wise, but Jesus thinks they are blind — social and financial proficiency does not necessarily demonstrate spiritual and moral integrity. They display themselves in up-to-date fashions, but Jesus sees their naked-ness — stylish designer clothing does not compensate for lack of righ-teousness.

> *"Those whom I love I rebuke and discipline."*

Jesus loved this church in Laodicea. We should too. Jesus *loves* all seven of these churches in the book of Revelation. We should too. It may be that Jesus is "about to spit you out of my mouth," but he has not yet done it. Laodicea is still a church of the Lord Jesus Christ. Jesus loves them and will continue to do so until it may become necessary to remove their lampstand, as he expresses it in the letter to Ephesus. If that happens, of course, then they are no longer a church.

As long as they remain a church, Jesus loves them. It is precisely be-cause they are a genuine church, in spite of their serious flaws, that Jesus rebukes them as strongly as he does. Severe discipline from the Lord is precisely the evidence that he loves us.

> *"I stand at the door and knock."*

One of the most quoted expressions from the entire book of Revelation, this sentence has puzzled some of us, namely, those who want to empha-size the sovereignty of God in salvation, insisting that grace is a gift of

God, not an achievement of man, "not [of] works, so that no one can boast" (Eph. 2:9). They see God answering their knock at the door.

This interpretation, however, makes little sense except in an abstract way. It is not we knocking at the door, but Jesus. Jesus *knocks* at the door and we answer; we choose to open the door to salvation and invite him into our lives.

It was Adam and Eve's choice to disobey God. It was Jesus' voluntary choice to reverse the decision of Adam and Eve. And it must be a genuine human choice to believe in Jesus and open the door of one's life to him. If you do not do this, then you are not saved.

The sovereignty of God should not be understood as canceling out the necessity of human decision. The two aspects — the divine and the human — are not mutually exclusive. They are not *either/or* but are *both/ and*. Salvation is completely a gift of God, and at the same time is completely a decision of man. The two are congruent, simultaneous. We experience the sovereign grace of God precisely in our decision to repent and believe, thus opening the door to Jesus.

Jesus wants this church in Laodicea to examine itself to see whether it has indeed opened the door for Jesus, or whether it has drifted into the attitude that it can do things pretty much as it pleases, deceiving itself again.

"To him who overcomes, I will give the right to sit with me on my throne, just as I overcame and sat down with my Father on his throne."

This is an extremely insightful comparison. If you know algebra, you will see the form of an algebraic equation here: a Christian is to Jesus as Jesus is to the Father. Jesus overcame the powers of temptation, of sin, and of death, and his reward is to sit with God on his throne. If we overcome as Jesus did, then our reward will also be to sit with Jesus on his throne.

The church in Laodicea must learn to see its challenge as the test of whether or not it will overcome. Will it confront the challenge, learn how to repent, "open the door" to Jesus, and thus sit with Jesus on his throne, or will it turn away, close the door, and be "spit out"?

*   *   *

These seven letters seem so out of character with the rest of the book of Revelation that it is difficult to discern what purpose they serve. Would the sequence of visions be impaired if they were left out altogether, if the book moved directly from the original vision of Jesus resplendent to the opening of the seven seals?

But this is the way the book of Revelation has come down to us, so it is to be presumed that the Lord intended it to include these letters. The purpose of these letters can be found in the following reasons:

1. The entire manuscript, the whole book of Revelation, including all the subsequent visions, is a *letter* to the churches.

2. Further, the whole book of Revelation is designed to be of some *pastoral value* to the churches: informative, cautionary, encouraging — whatever — but of real practical value to the people to whom the book is sent.

3. Still further, this practical value for the churches is not merely a prediction of some distant events to happen in the far-off future, but of immediate, local, *existential, contemporary* processes.

4. The seven letters are included not only for the benefit of those seven churches themselves but, in the Lord's broader design, for *all churches* everywhere, showing them the method of Christian self-evaluation. The variety of churches and their specific testing ought to be a model for us in our great proliferation of churches today.

5. These letters provide the assurance that a church does not have to be flawless to be a *genuine church*. Jesus is pictured as shepherding all of these seven churches, the ones with severe shortcomings as well as those who are chastised little. We must be very careful in denouncing other churches for what we may perceive as unacceptable shortcomings.

6. The letters are a reminder that we should *build upon the virtues* of a church, not upon its weaknesses and sins. Build upon the work of Christ in the church, not the work of the devil.

7. Lastly and perhaps most importantly, we should see these individual churches to which the letters are sent, frail and weak as they are, as nonetheless being the *locus of the omnipotent power of God* as exercised by the gospel of the Lord Jesus Christ. It is through them, and other congregations like them, that God is healing the nations — first the Roman Empire, then the barbarians of Europe, and eventually the entire human race. Churches, flawed though they all are, are nonetheless the first stage of the process whereby the Lord is redeeming the human race.

SECOND SEPTET

The Seven Seals

Revelation 4:1–8:5

Linking the First and Second Septets

In the first septet, the seven churches, John sees Jesus standing among his churches, shepherding them through the spiritual pressures of life on earth.

In this second septet, the seven seals, John sees Jesus in the guise of a Lamb, standing in the throne room of God in heaven. Resurrected and ascended, Jesus proceeds to do what no one else there can do, namely, open the seven seals which fastened the scroll in God's hand. As each seal is opened, vast, turbulent forces are unleashed out of the scroll to wreak their damage on the world.

There is a significant connection between this second septet vision and the first septet. The connection is not only *sequential,* that one comes after the other, but also *cumulative.* What happens in the second septet builds on what is shown in the first septet. This chapter will define the main point of the second septet and then connect it with the first septet by, first, discovering the essential purpose of the opening of the seven-sealed scroll in God's hand, and second, seeing how this relates to the vision of Jesus shepherding his churches.

The Scroll

Scrolls, in general, contain information of one kind or another. Letter scrolls, such as we have here, remain sealed in transport from one place to another, and no one really knows what they contain. No one but the person to whom the scroll is sent has authority to open it, just as today it is illegal to open another person's mail.

The scroll is in God's right hand; it is a letter he wishes to send to his churches. But no one in the courtroom has authority to open it and disclose its contents. No one knows what information it contains. Such a scroll could contain all kinds of different information. This particular scroll contains the plan of God for the world and for the churches.

Accordingly, this part of the vision is about God's plan for the world he created. It explains why God created the world and produced human beings within it. God is going about the process of leading the human race to the destiny he wants for it. He is supervising the process of history, and he will reverse the wrong decision of Adam so that the human race will choose obedience rather than disobedience.

The Lamb

The Lamb who has been slain is the only one able to unseal the scroll. Only Jesus can open it. Jesus, as John has written elsewhere, is the incarnation of God's plan; he is the Logos (Word) of God (John 1:1-14). Jesus can open the scroll because he has already done so. He opened the seals by what he did in his life on earth.

Jesus incarnates God's plan. When God created Adam and Eve by his word (logos), he instructed them to produce a civilization that imaged his own character, replenishing the earth and subduing it as images of God. Adam and Eve failed this assignment. Now Jesus comes to earth as the last Adam and does precisely what God wanted Adam to do: he lived perfectly within the process of social and cultural development. Jesus imaged God perfectly, thus fulfilling the logos of God. That is why Jesus is able to open the seven-sealed scroll in God's hand. Jesus incarnates, epitomizes, summarizes, actualizes, demonstrates, and reveals the plan of God for the human race.

In the life, death, resurrection, ascension, and session of Jesus, God is demonstrating in miniature his requirement for the human race. By incarnating this eternal logos of God, Jesus encapsulates in one individual the purpose of God for the total communal life of the human race. Take the process of Jesus' life as one human person and expand it to embrace the entirety of humanity, and you see the reason why Jesus is capable of unsealing the scroll of God. He has, as a matter of fact, already done so by means of his crucifixion, resurrection, and ascension.

In this second septet we see the result of the earthly ministry of Jesus within the ongoing life of the nations of the world. The effect of Jesus' own life on earth, culminating in his life in heaven, is what John now sees in the opening of the seals. The impact of Jesus' life on the process of history is seen in the symbolism of what happens when the Lamb opens the seals one by one. Jesus' incarnation has unleashed divine powers into the fallen and corrupted culture of mankind.

What God wrote in this scroll (his word, his logos, his plan), Jesus reveals as he opens the seals one by one. Jesus' life on earth *is* the actual opening of the seals. The effect of Jesus' life on earth is, among other things, to show us how God is working in human history. The idea of *opening* is the idea of revealing, of exposing, of demonstrating, of communicating.

There is a causal and cumulative connection between this second septet and the first septet. The connection is not difficult. Christ establishes churches within fallen civilization, and these churches embody a godly lifestyle that clearly conflicts with the ungodly lifestyle that dominates the culture in which they are found. The difference between good and corrupt lifestyles would not be seen if there were no churches.

This is the significance of the opening of the seals. They show what effect the coming of Jesus has in the world that has built its civilization on the principles of Adam. Jesus introduces a new orientation, the orientation of faith, obedience, and love. As people receive this new orientation in faith, they form churches, which embody the new lifestyle of truth, honesty, and godliness. And this presence within an ungodly community challenges others to either repent and enter the new community or to harden themselves and stir up trouble. This is what is represented by the disasters that emerge when Jesus opens the seals.

When the seals are opened, we see the vast differences that the coming of Christ brings about in God's plan for the redemption of the world. Disasters, troubles, and anxieties are revealed, showing us how the com-

61

ing of Christ into this world provokes and initiates conflict between godliness and ungodliness.

Church History

This second septet describes what has been happening on earth ever since Jesus completed his work on earth.

The divine powers that Jesus injects into human history are exactly the powers which have created the churches of the first septet, and which are in turn channeled into human culture through those churches, producing the effects we see in the second septet. Those powers first create churches, and then pass via the churches into the surrounding social structures, where they create havoc in the godless contemporary world.

This second septet must be seen as not only *subsequent* to the first septet but also *cumulative* upon it. The powers of the Spirit of Christ are being channeled into human civilization through actual churches. Real people in real churches affect the real civilization, calling other real people to repent and believe and thus to confront the usurping powers of evil in human society. When people do not repent they initiate persecution, hatred, and violence — shown symbolically in the things that happen when Jesus opens the seals.

The contents of the second septet may be subdivided into two sections, as follows:

1. The Throne Room (4-5)
2. Opening the Seals (6:1-8:5)

CHAPTER 5

The Throne Room

Revelation 4–5

The Thrones

After this I looked, and there before me was a door standing open in heaven. And the voice I had first heard speaking to me like a trumpet said, "Come up here, and I will show you what must take place after this." At once I was in the Spirit, and there before me was a throne in heaven with someone sitting on it. And the one who sat there had the appearance of jasper and carnelian. A rainbow, resembling an emerald, encircled the throne. Surrounding the throne were twenty-four other thrones, and seated on them were twenty-four elders. They were dressed in white and had crowns of gold on their heads. From the throne came flashes of lightning, rumblings and peals of thunder. Before the throne, seven lamps were blazing. These are the seven spirits of God. Also before the throne there was what looked like a sea of glass, clear as crystal.

In the center, around the throne, were four living creatures, and they were covered with eyes, in front and in back. The first living creature was like a lion, the second was like an ox, the third had a face like a man, the fourth was like a flying eagle. Each of the four living creatures had six wings and was covered with eyes all around, even under his wings. Day and night they never stop saying: "Holy, holy, holy is the Lord God Almighty, who was, and is, and is to come." Whenever the living creatures give glory, honor and thanks to him who sits on the throne and who lives for ever and ever, the twenty-four elders fall down before him who sits on the throne, and worship him who lives for ever and ever. They lay their crowns before the throne and say: "You are worthy, our Lord and God, to receive glory and honor and power, for you created all things, and by your will they were created and have their being." (Rev. 4)

. . . .

. . . and there before me was a throne in heaven with someone sitting on it.

One day John was daydreaming about Jesus and the churches when suddenly he envisioned a door opening into heaven. A voice invited him to enter. Upon entering he saw a huge room with someone sitting on a throne, and many courtiers filling up the room.

John does not say it in so many words, but it can be none other than God himself who is sitting on the throne. He is represented as sitting on the throne of the universe that he created, and as supervising its operation, functioning as absolute monarch over the entire world.

Surrounding the throne were twenty-four other thrones, and seated on them were twenty-four elders.

The number twenty-four is not common in Hebrew literature. It is, however, two times twelve, and the number twelve is prominent. Twelve is the number of sons of Jacob. Likewise in the beginnings of Christianity, twelve is the number of disciples Jesus chose to accompany him. The symbolism of twenty-four is a combination of the Old Testament and New Testament, twelve tribes plus twelve disciples, Israel in the past plus the church in the future (compare 21:12-14).

The significance of this, in turn, is that God is in charge of events both in the Jewish past and in the Christian future. God is sovereign over all of life and history, over all creation, but his deputies are the tribes of

Israel and the Christian church. It is precisely in them and through them that God is directing the affairs on earth so that his ultimate purpose will be achieved. The twenty-four thrones surrounding the throne of God depict the agencies by which God is achieving his goals in history.

> *Before the throne, seven lamps were blazing. These are the seven spirits of God.*

Seven is indicative of the seven churches. These churches blaze like lamps before the throne of God. The seven lamps (really "torches" in the Greek meaning) represent the way the Spirit of God functions in congregations of Christian people, not only these seven but also all churches everywhere.

"I am the light of the world" (John 8:12), said Jesus, and then added, "You [too] are the light of the world" (Matt. 5:14). The light that the churches shine into the world is the continuation of the selfsame light which Jesus brought into the world, the light of God's plan being worked out in human life and society.

> *Also before the throne there was what looked like a sea of glass, clear as crystal.*

It is hard to visualize an entire sea within the throne room, huge though the room may have been. The sea here is symbolic; it symbolizes the opposite of the wild, tempestuous sea of human culture. Jesus stilled the storm on the Sea of Galilee (Mark 4:39), and something of that symbolism contributes to this visionary sea before the throne of God. God, through the gospel and by the Spirit, is in the process of bringing shalom into the violent tempests of human civilization.

> *In the center, around the throne, were four living creatures, and they were covered with eyes, in front and in back. The first living creature was like a lion, the second was like an ox, the third had a face like a man, the fourth was like a flying eagle.*

The Greek word *zoa* is used here; it means living things. John sees four weird creatures in God's presence. Jewish readers would have been prepared for such anomalies, even four of them, from Ezekiel 1:5. In Ezekiel

65

these four things represent the motivating powers that cause the wheels of life to move, just as a stream causes the machinery of the mill to function and an engine causes an automobile to move. The symbolism in Revelation is parallel. The four living creatures represent life in all its many forms throughout the earth. God's concern is to redeem the entire creation, including all forms of life, as Paul suggests also in Romans 8:20-21.

> *They lay their crowns before the throne and say: "You are worthy, our Lord and God, to receive glory and honor and power, for you created all things, and by your will they were created and have their being."*

The twenty-four elders are the spokesmen for the four living things. Similarly human beings, because they are at the top of the natural order of life on earth, are the representatives and spokesmen for all of life. When humans go wrong, as Paul suggests, the entire creation goes wrong (Rom. 8:20), but when humans come around to the right all the world comes right as well. When the four living things want to praise God, the twenty-four elders vocalize that praise, for God created all things.

The Scroll

> Then I saw in the right hand of him who sat on the throne a scroll with writing on both sides and sealed with seven seals. And I saw a mighty angel proclaiming in a loud voice, "Who is worthy to break the seals and open the scroll?" But no one in heaven or on earth or under the earth could open the scroll or even look inside it. I wept and wept because no one was found who was worthy to open the scroll or look inside. (5:1-4)

. . . .

. . . a scroll with writing on both sides and sealed with seven seals.

This scroll represents God's plans, his blueprints, for the human race. Inside the scroll are not just writings, but the pent-up powers and forces and energies that will shape the course of human civilization throughout the earth till the end of time.

66

It was highly unusual in those days for a scroll to have "writing on both sides." This feature has special symbolism in it; it suggests the dual aspect of events in life and history, divine and human. Historians see and record events as they happen from an earthly, human perspective. But God wants us to know that behind all these events is the hand of a master planner. We may read one side of the scroll, the human side, but there is another side, the divine side. We must try to read both sides. These visions in Revelation will help us do just that.

In ancient times scrolls would normally be kept from unrolling by means of a few dabs of wax, or seals. Making an impression in the wax before it hardened with a ring or other instrument would then authenticate official documents.

> *. . . no one in heaven or on earth or under the earth could open the scroll or even look inside it.*

There was "no one in heaven or on earth or under the earth" with the personal qualifications and credentials needed, not merely to understand God's purposes, but to implement them, to unleash them. There was no one with the authority and power to unleash these forces of God into the ongoing turmoil of human history, surely not the emperors Tiberius or Caligula or Nero or Domitian, and not even saints like Peter or Paul or even John himself. John is distressed and deeply saddened that no one can be found to put God's strategies and purposes into effect. There was no one to do God's will, to achieve his purpose. John "wept and wept."

The Lamb

Then one of the elders said to me, "Do not weep! See, the Lion of the tribe of Judah, the Root of David, has triumphed. He is able to open the scroll and its seven seals."

Then I saw a Lamb, looking as if it had been slain, standing in the center of the throne, encircled by the four living creatures and the elders. He had seven horns and seven eyes, which are the seven spirits of God sent out into all the earth. He came and took the scroll from the right hand of him who sat on the throne. And when he had taken it, the four living creatures and

67

the twenty-four elders fell down before the Lamb. Each one had a harp and they were holding golden bowls full of incense, which are the prayers of the saints. And they sang a new song: "You are worthy to take the scroll and to open its seals, because you were slain, and with your blood you purchased men for God from every tribe and language and people and nation. You have made them to be a kingdom and priests to serve our God, and they will reign on the earth."

Then I looked and heard the voice of many angels, numbering thousands upon thousands, and ten thousand times ten thousand. They encircled the throne and the living creatures and the elders. In a loud voice they sang: "Worthy is the Lamb, who was slain, to receive power and wealth and wisdom and strength and honor and glory and praise!"

Then I heard every creature in heaven and on earth and under the earth and on the sea, and all that is in them, singing: "To him who sits on the throne and to the Lamb be praise and honor and glory and power, for ever and ever!" The four living creatures said, "Amen," and the elders fell down and worshiped. (5:5-14)

. . . .

". . . the Lion of the tribe of Judah, the Root of David, has triumphed. He is able to open the scroll and its seven seals."

The image of Lion comes from Genesis 49:9-10, the image of Root from Isaiah 11:1, 10. Clearly John means to say that Jesus continues Jewish tradition by fulfilling messianic prophecies. Jesus' ancestry is that of Judah and David. But what is operatively significant is not his genealogy but that he "has triumphed." The Jew, the Davidian has triumphed, he is victorious over sin.

The choice, which Adam and Eve made wrongly, Jesus made correctly. The temptation to which Adam succumbed, Jesus resisted. The battle of the human race, which both Adam and Jesus incarnated, and which Adam lost, Jesus won. The proof is the resurrection. Satan has hurled all his forces at Jesus, crushing him in the utmost power of evil, into death itself, but Jesus calmly endures it all and rises from the dead. There is no power exercised by Satan that is able to destroy or corrupt or entangle Jesus. He has conquered the power of Satan, overcoming it in a life of faithful obedience to the Father in heaven, and demonstrating his success finally and irreversibly in his resurrection, ascension, and session at the Father's right hand.

> *Then I saw a Lamb, looking as if it had been slain. . . . He came and took the scroll . . .*

John had been told about a Lion, but what he sees is a Lamb. Not a proud, majestic lion but an innocuous, weak, dead-looking lamb. Both images describe Jesus. Jesus the Lion overcame the devil, but he did so as Jesus the Lamb — dying as a lamb, rising as a lion.

But John mentions these details of the vision for a purpose. It is precisely because of what Jesus did as a lamb that has given him the authority and power of a lion, namely, the privilege of taking the scroll from the hand of God and of cracking open the seals.

Jesus' death and resurrection is the qualification for unleashing the powers of God's Spirit into the seemingly helter-skelter process of human life and history. The redemptive powers of God that have previously been localized in the nation of Israel are now pervading the universal family of the human race. The powers of righteousness, justice, peace, truth, goodness, joy, love, faith, hope, and all the other divine attributes that hitherto have been directed only to the Jews have now through the Lamb-Lion exploded into all nations on earth. This is what John wants us to see.

> *"You have made them to be a kingdom and priests to serve our God, and they will reign on the earth."*

The four living things as well as the twenty-four elders sing when they see the Lamb come forward to take the scroll. They know what the action means. It means Jesus has made people "from every tribe and language and people and nation . . . to be a kingdom" for God. No longer just the Jews, but now all peoples. They sing vigorously, for they know that in Jesus God has made a gigantic step forward to achieve his purposes on earth.

John tells us "they will reign on the earth." Do not imagine some far-off millennial kingdom in the distant future. John is describing the present. The result of Jesus' death and resurrection is to create a kingdom for God on earth. Not merely a kingdom over which God rules, but a kingdom in which everyone rules. Every person who enters the kingdom becomes a ruler, a king or a queen. They "reign on the earth." That includes every follower of Christ who has ever lived, while he or she lives.

Christians reign over temptation, sin, and the devil. Indeed, they reign even over the devil himself in the sense that they obey God, not the devil. They are not controlled by sin but by Christ. Therefore they reign with Christ, in the same sense that Christ reigned over the devil while on this earth. They become kings and priests. God's kingdom is a body of people each of whom images God's freedom and power in reigning with Christ over sin and evil.

> *"Worthy is the Lamb, who was slain, to receive power and wealth and wisdom and strength and honor and glory and praise!"*

Myriads of angels sing adulation to the Lamb, affirming with transcendent wisdom that Christ has received imposing credentials from God by means of his death and resurrection.

The resurrection itself is the means whereby Jesus achieved the status that the angels describe in these seven attributes. When Jesus rose from the dead, he emerged out of one state and into another. The new state is that of "power and wealth and wisdom and strength and honor and glory and praise." Jesus did not merely resume his prior state of existence after the resurrection; he entered a new, glorified, perfected state of being. That is what the angels chant and what the entire universe echoes.

We now see why the Lamb is capable of unsealing the scroll in the right hand of God. He has already done so in real life. It is a done deal, as they say. Jesus has already unsealed the scroll by showing what it means to be human, and thus confirmed his authority by means of his resurrection from the dead. Jesus has already demonstrated God's plan, he has already received the authority of God, and he has already unleashed his redemptive spirit into the chaos of human life — all because he conquered death.

John wants the churches, both then and now, to understand that this vision of the scroll and the Lamb concerns an event already past in real human history. He wants us to understand, from the viewpoint of heaven, what the death, resurrection, ascension, and session of Jesus really means for the ongoing process of human history. God is achieving his ultimate purpose for the world by means of the gospel, the churches, and the spirit of Jesus. The power of Jesus is dominant over all other powers functioning within human civilization.

> *Then I heard every creature in heaven and on earth and under the earth and on the sea, and all that is in them, singing: "To him who sits on the throne and to the Lamb be praise and honor and glory and power, for ever and ever!"*

"Every creature" responds to the song of the four living things and the twenty-four elders. The entire universe responds with an echoing song of praise to the Lamb. What Jesus has accomplished via the cross and resurrection and ascension is of benefit to the entire universe. The entire universe will ultimately be the recipient of the redemptive power of the Lamb who is a Lion.

CHAPTER 6

Opening the Seals

Revelation 6:1–8:5

The First Four Seals

I watched as the Lamb opened the first of the seven seals. Then I heard one of the four living creatures say in a voice like thunder, "Come!" I looked, and there before me was a white horse! Its rider held a bow, and he was given a crown, and he rode out as a conqueror bent on conquest.

When the Lamb opened the second seal, I heard the second living creature say, "Come!" Then another horse came out, a fiery red one. Its rider was given power to take peace from the earth and to make men slay each other. To him was given a large sword.

When the Lamb opened the third seal, I heard the third living creature say, "Come!" I looked, and there before me was a black horse! Its rider was holding a pair of scales in his hand. Then I heard what sounded like a voice among the four living creatures, saying, "A quart of wheat for a day's wages, and three quarts of barley for a day's wages, and do not damage the oil and the wine!"

When the Lamb opened the fourth seal, I heard the voice of the fourth living creature say, "Come!" I looked, and there before me was a pale horse! Its rider was named Death, and Hades was following close behind him. They were given power over a fourth of the earth to kill by sword, famine and plague, and by the wild beasts of the earth. (6:1-8)

·   ·   ·   ·   ·   ·   ·

The opening of the first four seals should be taken together as a unit. In each case John:

1. Hears one of the four living things saying, "Come" (6:1, 3, 5, 7).
2. Watches a horse emerge from the scroll (6:2, 4, 5, 8).
3. Describes the rider on the horse (6:2, 4, 5, 8).
4. States what the horse and rider do (6:2, 4, 6, 8).

It is evident that this scroll contains not merely information about God's will, but the actual working of it as well. Something happens as each seal is broken. We are not just being lectured, we are being shown. God's purpose is not simply something to understand, it is something to see at work — God's word at work, God's word that does not return to him useless but in fact accomplishes everything he desires (Isa. 55:11). We must learn to hear God's word by seeing it in action.

All four of these horsemen bring evil: conquest, war, famine, and death. As a unit, therefore, these four horsemen of the Apocalypse should be seen as representing the total forces of evil in human life and culture.

Furthermore, these four horsemen show a sequence of evil. What the first rider does prepares the way for what the second rider does, and what the second rider does ensures that the third rider will come, and the third rider in turn guarantees the coming of the fourth rider. Wherever the first rider conquers, there will follow, in order, war, famine, and death. This is what this first series of four seals represents.

> . . . a white horse! Its rider held a bow, and he was given a crown, and he rode out as a conqueror bent on conquest.

Elsewhere in Revelation Jesus is depicted riding a white horse (19:11). Many people think this reference in chapter 6 must be to Jesus also, since the idea of conquest better fits Jesus than it does some evil power.

The reference is not to Jesus but to Satan, since it is an integral part of this series of four. All the other riders are symbols of evil powers; this rider is also. Jesus is opening the seals, which makes it unlikely that he is also one of the riders coming out of the scroll.

The whiteness of the horse, sometimes a symbol of purity and goodness, here would have to be understood as a counterfeit whiteness — deceptive, illusory, delusive, seductive. Follow me, says the devil, and I will bring you a good life. Adam and Eve heard this voice, followed its instructions, and suffered its consequences. Jesus also heard this voice, refused its blandishments, and now leads the way into true whiteness.

Yet this rider is given a crown. Satan is wearing a crown, the laurel wreath symbolizing victory. This is a usurped crown, not his by right. He rides "out as a conqueror bent on conquest." Satan wants to gain control over something that is not his by right. He sees God's creation and looks to sabotage it. He sees Adam and Eve and looks to ruin them. He rides out into God's good creation, trying his best to conquer and spoil it.

This is what John sees in the opening of this first seal. From the very beginning of time Satan has been pretending to be the lord and ruler of creation, bent on the conquest and ruination of the world over which God said, Behold, it is very good (Gen. 1:31). Wherever you see evidence of sin, evil, corruption, ruination, spoilage, crime, injustice, hatred, violence, and the like, there you see the rider on this pseudowhite horse bent on claiming God's good creation as his own, bent on its conquest and its ruin.

> *. . . a fiery red one. Its rider was given power to take peace from the earth and to make men slay each other. To him was given a large sword.*

The redness of this horse represents the blood shed in war. Its rider takes shalom away from the earth. *Shalom,* "peace," is the word that describes the totality of what God wants for his creation: not merely absence of war and violence, but the positive presence of love, cooperation, faithfulness, justice, trustworthiness, harmony, goodness, and all other virtues which spring from the creative hand of God. Shalom is the condition in which God created Adam and Eve, and it is the destiny, the telos, of the entire human race. What Satan wants is to take this away from the earth, so wherever he succeeds in seducing people, instead of affairs becoming better, they become worse. People no longer live in shalom with each other. They hate, they covet, they steal, they murder, they fight, they wage war, they ruin, and they destroy.

The sword brandished by the devil in this way is large. Its power is awesome. In the Second World War, how large and irresistible the sword wielded by Adolf Hitler in Germany and by Josef Stalin in the USSR seemed to be! How impossible it seemed to escape from under it for those caught in that devilish conquest. Jesus wants us to see, not only on the individual level but also on the national level, what happens when Satan comes into power. Violence ensues. A huge sword takes peace from the earth.

> . . . *a black horse! Its rider was holding a pair of scales in his hand. . . . "A quart of wheat for a day's wages, and three quarts of barley for a day's wages, and do not damage the oil and the wine!"*

In our world scales usually represent the scales of justice, the weighing of evidence on both sides in a judicial dispute. In the context here, however, the scales refer to the domain of economics. They weigh out the amount of food a man gets for a day's wages.

Work for one day and you can buy a quart of wheat, enough to sustain you for one day. Or you can get three quarts of barley, less nourishing but more in quantity. But you don't get any oil or wine for that same day's wage. The point is that prices are high, and you can barely eke out a daily existence. It is an environment of starvation wages, or a potential famine driving prices up for scarce food supplies.

The picture is of economic austerity, if not outright famine. Jesus wants us to see that once we commit ourselves to follow Satan, we plunge ourselves into a community of violence and war, which in turn results in scarcity, economic distress, even famine. Once a nation (or an individual) opts to define its own future rather than follow God's way, a process of deterioration ensues which can hardly be halted.

The resources of the nation are expended in building up military might to enforce its will upon others, and that in turn creates an economic situation in which the regular needs of daily living become secondary to building up the war machine. The squandering of national resources need not be exclusively in military might; it could also be in sequestering national resources and wealth for private purposes — catering to the personal lusts and prestige of those in control of government.

A wrong spiritual commitment leads directly to a wrong political expression, and this in turn leads to wrong economic priorities.

. . . a pale horse! Its rider was named Death, and Hades was following close behind him. They were given power over a fourth of the earth to kill by sword, famine and plague, and by the wild beasts of the earth.

The pale horse is sickly, symbolizing disease and death. That is the end result of the process these four seals represent. It is the same vision Adam and Eve heard from God in Genesis 3: eat of the Tree of the Knowledge of Good and Evil at your own peril, for it will lead you to death. These four seals show us in a bit more detail how that process works: wrong commitment, wrong priorities, wrong living conditions, death. One leads to the next.

. . . power over a fourth of the earth . . .

God allows Satan to act, to tempt us, to succeed in gaining our allegiance. But he does not allow Satan to gain complete control — only one-fourth, 25 percent. This figure, as all of John's vision, is symbolic of course. Satan's authority and control over the world is but partial, never coming near to overwhelming the authority of God.

Jesus does not want us to become negative, paranoid, or downbeat, responding only to the evils around us. He wants us to know that, as powerful as evil may be in the world, it is still severely limited and controlled by God. Time and destiny are in the hands of God, not the devil. The churches in ancient Asia could use such encouragement, especially in the first three centuries when the full power of the Roman emperor was, at times, mobilized to exterminate the Christian faith.

The Fifth Seal

When he opened the fifth seal, I saw under the altar the souls of those who had been slain because of the word of God and the testimony they had maintained. They called out in a loud voice, "How long, Sovereign Lord, holy and true, until you judge the inhabitants of the earth and avenge our blood?" Then each of them was given a white robe, and they were told to wait a little longer, until the number of their fellow servants and brothers who were to be killed as they had been was completed. (6:9-11)

. . . .

. . . the souls of those who had been slain because of the word of God . . .

Clearly this fifth seal represents a change from the first four seals. John sees no fearsome horsemen emerging to work havoc, but instead he sees the people who had been slain during their evil surges. John sees the results of the four horsemen, the murder of people obstinately refusing to accept their godless efforts. This phraseology includes all Christians who die, whether or not they are martyrs in the narrow sense of that word. All who die while remaining faithful to the Lord are witnesses to the redeeming grace of God.

"How long, Sovereign Lord, holy and true, until you judge the inhabitants of the earth and avenge our blood?"

John hears the Christian people who have passed into death. He hears them asking when the promises of God, and their Christian hope, will be fulfilled. How long will it be before God makes all things right on the earth, judging the godless and establishing true shalom?

The question is not unlike the one the apostle Paul addressed in his first letter to the Thessalonians. There, Christians were wondering what good it was to be a Christian if one died before Christ returned to set up his kingdom. Paul replied that living people would have no advantage over those who died because all would be raised from the dead. In a second letter to them, Paul explained that several things must happen before Christ's kingdom would be complete. Don't expect it to happen immediately, he tells them. Look first for the signs, which he then describes: the renunciation of faith and the man of sin.

John, in the fifth seal, sees the same question being raised: "God, when will your promises be fulfilled?"

. . . wait a little longer . . .

They were told to "wait a little longer." They must learn to be patient, understanding that the working out of God's purpose takes time. Much time. It has been two millennia already, and the kingdom of Christ has not been perfected yet.

John's purpose in writing these visions was to encourage and strengthen the believers in the seven churches of Asia. Jesus and John are addressing the question of the living: How long, in view of the fact that so many of us are dying, before Christ succeeds in perfecting his reign on earth? It is not that the souls of the dead are being restless and impatient in their graves. They know Jesus reigns from heaven, and that he is already establishing his reign on earth. They just want to know how long it will take. "How long" must we wait?

> *. . . until the number of their fellow servants and brothers who were to be killed as they had been was completed.*

God answers them. Keep waiting until the full number of Christians who are ordained to die have actually done so. God wants us to understand that time is in his hands. He knows what he is doing. A great many more people will have to be born and die before the final completion of God's plan. Leave the matter of timing and duration to God. Just be obedient, faithful — and patient.

The Sixth Seal

I watched as he opened the sixth seal. There was a great earthquake. The sun turned black like sackcloth made of goat hair, the whole moon turned blood red, and the stars in the sky fell to earth, as late figs drop from a fig tree when shaken by a strong wind. The sky receded like a scroll, rolling up, and every mountain and island was removed from its place.

Then the kings of the earth, the princes, the generals, the rich, the mighty, and every slave and every free man hid in caves and among the rocks of the mountains. They called to the mountains and the rocks, "Fall on us and hide us from the face of him who sits on the throne and from the wrath of the Lamb! For the great day of their wrath has come, and who can stand?"

After this I saw four angels standing at the four corners of the earth, holding back the four winds of the earth to prevent any wind from blowing on the land or on the sea or on any tree. Then I saw another angel coming up from the east, having the seal of the living God. He called out in a loud voice to the four angels who had been given power to harm the land and the sea: "Do not harm the land or the sea or the trees until we put a seal on the foreheads of the servants of our God." Then I heard the number of those who were sealed: 144,000 from all the tribes of Israel. From the tribe of Judah 12,000 were sealed, from the tribe of Reuben 12,000, from the tribe of Gad 12,000, from the tribe of Asher 12,000, from the tribe of Naphtali 12,000, from the tribe of Manasseh 12,000, from the tribe of Simeon 12,000, from the tribe of Levi 12,000, from the tribe of Issachar 12,000, from the tribe of Zebulun 12,000, from the tribe of Joseph 12,000, from the tribe of Benjamin 12,000.

After this I looked and there before me was a great multitude that no one could count, from every nation, tribe, people and language, standing before the throne and in front of the Lamb. They were wearing white robes and were holding palm branches in their hands. And they cried out in a loud voice: "Salvation belongs to our God, who sits on the throne, and to the Lamb." All the angels were standing around the throne and around the elders and the four living creatures. They fell down on their faces before the throne and worshiped God, saying: "Amen! Praise and glory and wisdom and thanks and honor and power and strength be to our God for ever and ever. Amen!"

Then one of the elders asked me, "These in white robes — who are they, and where did they come from?"

I answered, "Sir, you know."

And he said, "These are they who have come out of the great tribulation; they have washed their robes and made them white in the blood of the Lamb. Therefore, they are before the throne of God and serve him day and night in his temple; and he who sits on the throne will spread his tent over them. Never again will they hunger; never again will they thirst. The sun will not beat upon them, nor any scorching heat. For the Lamb at the center of the throne will be their shepherd; he will lead them to springs of living water. And God will wipe away every tear from their eyes." (6:12–7:17)

. . . .

There was not much action in the fifth seal, only a picture of dead saints voicing their impatience. The sixth seal, on the other hand, brings vivid and impelling drama: terrifying events in the world of nature — earth, moon, stars, sky, mountains, islands. People are frightened into senseless and frantic reactions. Four angels are controlling the otherwise devastating winds. Another angel is planting the seal of God on the forehead of God's servants. There is a census of Old Testament saints and a vision of New Testament saints, countless in number. Majestic voices are raised in praise of God. And finally, these people dressed in white robes are identified.

Catastrophe in Nature

There was a great earthquake. The sun turned black . . . the whole moon turned blood red, and the stars in the sky fell to earth. . . . The sky receded like a scroll, rolling up, and every mountain and island was removed from its place.

This portentous language focuses on the omnipotent power of God the creator. This is in sharp contrast to the fourth seal, which attributes power over a mere fourth of the earth to the figures of Death and Hades. While the devil's four horsemen are given authority to ruin a quarter of the world, the authority of the Creator includes the entirety of the solar system. It is as if Jesus is saying to John: "You think Satan is awesome? Take a look at what God can do!" The devil can create nothing; he can only spoil what he finds. God not only creates everything, he also protects it from disintegration.

Once again, do not take this vision literally (take none of Revelation's visions literally). It is symbolic. The significance of the natural catastrophes is to be seen in the effect they have on people. What we see in this first part of the vision is the shaking up of the spiritual kingdom of darkness functioning in the world.

Since the fall of Adam the human race has been enthralled by the spiritual power of sin and evil, by the devil. John now sees these entrenched powers of evil being challenged, shaken, and overcome. Jesus has already accomplished this in his own life by means of his resurrection from the dead. And he is continuing the process in the human race as a whole by means of the gospel, the church, and the Holy Spirit.

John wanted those early Christians in Asia to see that the gospel was shaking up the powers of the Roman Empire, threatening the religious, philosophical, and spiritual foundations upon which the empire was built. And he wants Christians today to see that the same process has been continuing ever since: the gospel is shaking up the spiritual powers of evil that are still working to try and conquer the soul of the human race. The visions of Revelation are given to help us see and understand.

The Wrath of the Lamb

Then the kings of the earth, the princes, the generals, the rich, the mighty, and every slave and every free man hid in caves and among the rocks of the mountains. They called to the mountains and the rocks, "Fall on us and hide us from the face of him who sits on the throne and from the wrath of the Lamb! For the great day of their wrath has come, and who can stand?"

The result of the great upheavals in nature is that everyone on earth trembles in abject fear. The upheavals represent the spiritual powers of darkness, while the people, the powerful kings and princes as well as the lowly slaves, represent all the people under the domination of Satan.

What power is able to make the minions of Satan cower in fear? Not military might like cruise missiles or nerve gas. Or political power wielded by presidents and parliaments. These could either be instruments of evil or of good, but they are not nearly powerful enough to overcome Satan and his followers.

It is the power of "the wrath of the Lamb." The thought of a lamb does not usually invoke fear. But this Lamb has been slain. And he has come back to life. Jesus rose from the dead and is sitting in a place of power at God's right hand in heaven. It is that feat which constitutes the heart of the threat to Satan's domain.

What a contrast between Christ and Satan. All of Satan's powers are pictured in the first four seals — he can destroy and ruin and make trouble, but only to a limited extent. Jesus can take death and make life come from it. Jesus reverses Satan's work. What Satan ruins, Jesus redeems. What Satan spoils, Jesus perfects. What Satan kills, Jesus resurrects. The work of Satan in sin and evil is destructive by nature. The work of Jesus in righteousness and goodness is constructive by nature. The great portents in nature, which begin this vision, are not to destroy God's creation but to destroy the stronghold of Satan. Their purpose is to destroy Satan's kingdom in order to reestablish God's kingdom.

The wrath of God and of the Lamb are identical. It is one wrath exercised in conjunction by both God and the ascended Jesus. It is wrath directed against the devil and his dominion, affecting everyone on earth and redeeming many — as the later part of this vision shows.

The Four Winds

> . . . *four angels standing at the four corners of the earth, holding back the four winds of the earth to prevent any wind from blowing on the land or on the sea or on any tree.*

Think of the four corners of the earth as the four directions: north, south, east, and west. God has four angels stationed, one in each direction, to prevent these powerful winds from completing the ruin of earth suggested in the earlier part of the vision.

God's purpose is not negative, not ruinous. God does not wish to destroy any part of his creation, including man, even those in rebellion against him. His purpose is to destroy that which destroys, to remove the negative powers from his good creation. The angels restraining the winds show this to us. The powers that rage back and forth in our human societies — war, disease, poverty, conflict, competition, hatred — must be eliminated, destroyed. That is what the symbolic shaking up of the solar system suggests.

Now this shake-up is held in check. God's angels restrain the winds that would complete and finalize the destruction. Satan is in the process of being destroyed, but his destruction does not carry with it the destruction of humanity. This is what we are to see in this vision.

The Seal of God

> . . . *another angel coming up from the east, having the seal of the living God.*

Here we see the positive value of the four angels of the winds. They provide the opportunity for this fifth angel to do his work. The wrath of God and of the Lamb is working toward the annihilation of the powers of ruin, but at the same time an angel is impressing the seal of God on the forehead of people who are being drawn out of Satan's realm into that of Jesus.

The Christians in the churches of Ephesus, Smyrna, Pergamum, and the other cities should see this in terms of their own lives. There are vicious powers of evil at work in human life and society within the world as they know it. But the wrath of the Lamb has been let loose within that same society. The gospel is being proclaimed. People are being taken out from under Satan's control, and they are being baptized into the name of the Lord Jesus Christ.

The gospel is doing two things simultaneously. By taking people away from the control of Satan, it weakens the power of the devil, but by the same token it strengthens the kingdom of Christ. It destroys the destroyer and seals the foreheads of the saints. This is what John is describing here.

The Old Testament Saints

. . . the number of those who were sealed: 144,000 from all the tribes of Israel. From the tribe of Judah 12,000 were sealed, from the tribe of Reuben 12,000, from the tribe of Gad 12,000, from the tribe of Asher 12,000, from the tribe of Naphtali 12,000, from the tribe of Manasseh 12,000, from the tribe of Simeon 12,000, from the tribe of Levi 12,000, from the tribe of Issachar 12,000, from the tribe of Zebulun 12,000, from the tribe of Joseph 12,000, from the tribe of Benjamin 12,000.

Some interesting things to note about this section: the tribe of Dan is not listed, and Joseph is; his son Manasseh is listed, yet Ephraim, his other son, is not.

We must again remember that this is a vision. Everything is symbolic. Even the particular numbers — 12,000 from each tribe and the total of 144,000 — are nothing more than symbolism. The Jewish people were accustomed to thinking in terms of twelve tribes, so the number twelve would indicate completeness, all the tribes, and the number

12,000 would merely extend the idea of twelve, and then twelve twelves would give the total of 144,000.

By no means let yourself think that only 144,000 actual people will be saved from Old Testament times. And certainly do not make that number mean a select few Christians who will be privileged to attain special honor in the life to come. Take it simply to mean that every one whom God has ordained to be sealed in the past has been sealed, with the promise also that the same will be true in the future.

The Great Multitude

. . . a great multitude that no one could count, from every nation, tribe, people and language, standing before the throne and in front of the Lamb.

In this vision John sees the effect of the spread of the gospel throughout the earth. God's great goal is the redemption of the entire human race, the reversal of the decision of Adam and Eve in the beginning, and John now sees a multitude of people that no one can count.

This vision shows the contrast between Old Testament and New Testament. Old Testament Israel, the twelve tribes, has done its work; its mission is accomplished. Now New Testament Israel, the Christian church, continues the work of God, bringing the Spirit of Christ to all nations, discipling them and baptizing them in the name of the Lord. This part of the vision is a picture of the expansion of the kingdom of Christ among all human beings in the world, continuing until the very climax of God's purpose. Much the same is suggested by the imagery of 21:12-14.

The Great Tribulation

"These are they who have come out of the great tribulation; they have washed their robes and made them white in the blood of the Lamb."

The multitudes that John saw were all dressed in "white robes." The question comes up in his vision: Who are these people, and where did they come from?

The answer is that these are the people "who have come out of the great tribulation." These are the people who have laundered their dirty clothing in the blood of Christ, thus making them white and pure.

Many Christians regard this great tribulation as a unique special event to occur at some *future* date just prior to the return of Jesus Christ from heaven. Extreme pressure of one kind or another will be put on Christians during that period of time, and those who survive until Christ's return are those who "come out of the great tribulation." In other words, these are only those Christians who survive that future crisis.

This is not what John is saying. Look to the second half of the sentence, namely, they who "have washed their robes and made them white in the blood of the Lamb." John is talking about all Christians. The "great tribulation" does not mean some future crisis confronting the church, but the constant pressure every Christian is under always, every day, to persevere in faith and obedience. People who persevere throughout their lives, daily washing their robes in the blood of Christ; constantly living in the Spirit of the Lord; finding the righteousness, which is the product of faith; maintaining that commitment to the end of their lives — these are the people John wants us to see.

More concretely, John would want the Christian people in Sardis, Laodicea, Philadelphia, Smyrna, Pergamum, and elsewhere to see themselves involved in this "great tribulation" which has come upon the earth. He would want them to see the tribulation of the troubled times brought about by the gospel throughout the Roman Empire.

John would want Christians today to understand that the same disturbed condition of human society is continuing wherever the gospel takes root. Christ challenges the powers of evil wherever the gospel goes, creating tension, trouble, and tribulation. Every Christian is in it and is called upon to persevere to the end, to survive the tribulation, overcoming it and living in the presence of the ascended Lord.

*   *   *

There is much action in this sixth seal. See it in its wholeness, in relation to the preceding seals. The first four seals portray the sequence of evil in its destructive course among the nations of the world. The fifth seal shows godly people seemingly overwhelmed by the enormous power of evil entrenched in civilization, wondering when God is going to change all that. Then this sixth seal shows what God is, as a matter of fact, doing. This sixth seal is an answer to the fifth seal. Christ wants us to see that the gospel is an irresistible force in the world, far more powerful than the forces of evil, and that before it people cringe desperately in fear. He wants us to see that God is holding in check all the winds of fortune, while the gospel is spread and people are brought to faith and to the righteousness that comes from faith. He wants us to know that we are called upon to persevere even though the world around us is in turmoil, surviving that tribulation by faith in the Lamb.

The Seventh Seal

When he opened the seventh seal, there was silence in heaven for about half an hour.

And I saw the seven angels who stand before God, and to them were given seven trumpets.

Another angel, who had a golden censer, came and stood at the altar. He was given much incense to offer, with the prayers of all the saints, on the golden altar before the throne. The smoke of the incense, together with the prayers of the saints, went up before God from the angel's hand. Then the angel took the censer, filled it with fire from the altar, and hurled it on the earth; and there came peals of thunder, rumblings, flashes of lightning and an earthquake. (8:1-5)

. . . .

This seventh seal does double duty. It completes the septet of the seven seals, and it also introduces the next septet of the seven trumpets. When the seventh seal is opened, John sees seven angels who are then each given a trumpet. But before they blow the trumpets another angel enters the vision. He functions as a priest, holding "a golden censer," making an offering to God. That offering is the main significance of this seventh seal.

He was given much incense to offer, with the prayers of all the saints . . .

87

In the fifth seal the saints were wondering how long before their hopes were fulfilled. In the sixth seal they were encouraged to persevere in the great tribulation. Here in the opening of the seventh seal is a vision of how the prayers of the saints are handled, what use they are, and how prayer works.

The angel mixes the incense in his censer with the prayers of the saints. God's people do not always know precisely what to pray for; our prayers are, at best, tainted with both the finite and the sinful limitations of our lives. Our prayers need to be cleansed and purified. That is what John sees in this part of the vision: prayers purified by angelic incense. This is what John sees as "the smoke of the incense, together with the prayers of the saints, [going] up before God from the angel's hand." Who knows how much of our prayers remain after the impurities are removed from them?

Then the angel took the censer, filled it with fire from the altar, and hurled it on the earth . . .

Our prayers, all by themselves, accomplish nothing. In themselves they are quite powerless. And, for that matter, if everyone's prayers were answered precisely as presented, great confusion would result. People pray for different, sometimes contradictory things. In the Civil War both sides prayed for victory. Just praying for something does not guarantee that it will happen.

Not only must our prayers be purified of improper elements, they must also be energized by a power greater than any human power. This is what John sees when the angel takes burning coals from the altar and ignites the mixture in the censer. The angel adds the power of God to the purified prayers of the saints.

God does hear and answer our prayers, but first he cleanses them and energizes them. Therefore, we must accept that answers to our prayers may come in almost unrecognizable forms. God's answer may even appear at times to be negative, a denial of what we ask for. We should be very humble about our prayers, never pretending to tell God what he must do for us. Rather, we must always and only ask for him to do what he knows is best for us.

. . . and there came peals of thunder, rumblings, flashes of lightning and an earthquake.

Strange answers to our prayers: thunder, lightning, and earthquakes! Again, understand this symbolically.

The prayers of the saints are purified, then they are ignited, and then they are cast back into the earth where they produce turbulence. The turbulence is the same as that depicted elsewhere as caused by the gospel. This is how the gospel brings that turbulence into the sin-dominated world. Because of the message of the gospel, people pray to God their Father in heaven, in the name of the Lamb who is a Lion. These prayers, energized by the Holy Spirit working in those who pray, bring the powers of righteousness, truth, justice, love, honor, and peace into direct conflict with their opposites. The result is turbulent conflict, an *earthquake* of conflict, between the opposing forces of good and evil.

The saints pray and their prayers are returned to them, hurled to the earth energized by the Spirit of God. God is pleased with the prayers of his people, but he also wants action. He wants us to actively work toward accomplishing what we are praying for. God will help you, sustain you, protect you, encourage you, and empower you. You pray indeed, and God is pleased, but now work at it and do what you can with the power of God within you to make it happen. That is what John sees in this seventh seal, and that is what the seven churches need to understand about their prayers.

*　　*　　*

Compare this second septet, the opening of the seven seals, with the first septet, the letters to the seven churches.

In this Apocalypse Jesus is showing John and us how we must understand the events that are happening on earth. Jesus first draws our attention to the actual churches established by the gospel. Some of them may be weak, some may be strong, but they are all churches as long as they remain in the Lord Jesus and are responsive to his care. That is the first septet.

Bring that vision up-to-date. There are in our world not only thousands of actual churches but also dozens of different denominations, all of whom think they are at least in some respects more faithful than others. Christians must learn to recognize, first, that all churches are to be honored as being under the care of the same Lord, and second, that every church is subject to the cautionary warnings of the Lord, comparable to those in this first septet. The Lord shepherds us all, but he also corrects us all.

In the second septet, the opening of the seals, Jesus wants the churches he has just addressed to see how the dominating forces of the gospel actually work in the world. First he shows them how the forces of evil constantly work in human civilization, moving from one evil to another, always in the direction of destruction. Then he shows the powers of God at work, with capacities much greater than those of the devil.

The main point of comparison is that through the churches shown to us in the first septet, the conflict of the second septet is generated. Wherever the church of the Lord Jesus is established, there the contrast between two ways of life will be seen. The presence of people living according to the will of God will show in stark contrast the nature of life lived according to the will of the devil. Conflict must necessarily result wherever the gospel is proclaimed and churches are established. That is important to understand. *Conflict must necessarily result.* But the conflict is predetermined to be won by God, whose authority and power have already been demonstrated in the death and resurrection of Jesus Christ, the slain and resurrected Lamb of God who, when seen directly, turns out to be the Lion of the tribe of Judah.

The Seven Trumpets

Revelation 8:6–14:20

The first step in Christ's gospel strategy for reversing the original decision of Adam and Eve is the establishment of churches, local communities of people who through faith in Jesus Christ encourage one another in godly living. This is the theological significance of the first septet, the letters to the seven churches.

The second step is the exposure of the chasm between two incompatible ways of living: godly and ungodly. Where churches are established, there necessarily follows an increasingly well-defined disjunction between the two lifestyles. This is what the second septet wishes us to visualize.

When God's scroll is finally opened, we receive information, but this information is not abstract, it is concrete. We receive the information in the scroll by seeing how God works in real life and history. It is theology, not written in books but in history. It is action theology, the Word at work. It is said and done, for what God says he does. His word does not return to him useless and empty, accomplishing nothing (Isa. 55:11). The information we receive from the scroll is insight into the gospel at work. So, for example, if the ancient Roman emperors came to fear the presence of Christians in the empire, it was not because of any overt political or military threat but because of this deeply spiritual challenge to the very foundations of imperial power.

Now we have a third septet, seven angels blowing trumpets in turn.

91

The septet of the seven trumpets will add to the picture we already see in Revelation. Trumpets in the ancient world were used to herald the approach of an important personage or the imminence of an important event, together with a summons to do something about it.

These angelic trumpets call our attention to the most decisive and significant dynamics of life and history. We busy ourselves with the many details of life, all important in their way, but the trumpeters call us to focus our attention on the matter of ultimate interest: the progression of the conflict between good and evil. Not only do the trumpeters call our attention to these important events, they summon us to get involved. The opening of the seals shows us what is going on; the trumpets call us to battle.

The angels are proclaiming that God is battling the powers of Satan and redeeming his people from satanic domination. They are calling us to get involved. The angels show us the action from both sides of the conflict between Christ and his opponents.

The several visions in this septet therefore compel us to confront the intense combat going on in human civilization and perceive that it must end finally in the annihilation of one of the combatants. Ultimately, the earth does not have room for both a godly way of life and an ungodly way. The seven trumpets show us the nature of this mortal conflict and the dynamics of the forces on both sides.

Trumpets 1-4

The first four trumpets are a group, as were the first four seals:

1. Hail and fire burn up one-third of the earth (8:7).
2. A burning mountain transforms one-third of the sea into blood (8:8).
3. A burning star befouls one-third of the rivers, turning them bitter (8:10).
4. The sun, moon, and stars are stricken, losing one-third of their light (8:12).

The angels who blow the trumpets, of course, are angels of God, so that whatever tragedy occurs, it must be seen also as being sent by God.

The disasters are envisioned as occurring in nature, the creation of God, but should be understood as symbolic of the inefficiency of human civilization when developed in a godless way. Nothing goes as it should. This very inefficiency should make people realize something is wrong and should therefore goad them to repent.

Trumpet 5

In the fifth trumpet a star falls from heaven, causing a violent explosion, so that the abyss of hell is opened. Out of the abyss pours smoke, which then congeals into locusts. The locusts swarm over the earth but are able to harm only those people who have not been sealed with the seal of God. The locusts are then transformed into fierce warhorses, ready to follow their leader Abbadon into battle.

If the resurrection of Jesus is the key that opens the abyss, then we should see the emergence of Abbadon and the locust-horses as the response of the devil. He wants to smother the new Christian movement, but he can only harm his own.

Trumpet 6

The sixth trumpet is a vision in three parts:

1. Four angels, stationed at the Euphrates River, are released to kill a third of mankind. They employ colorful caricatured horses and riders to do so, but the remaining people do not get the message and therefore do not repent from their evil deeds.
2. An angel holds a little scroll, which John is advised to eat. He does so and finds it sweet in the mouth but sour in the stomach. It is a picture of the gospel, which John must continue to proclaim.
3. Two witnesses proclaim the gospel. What happens to them parallels what happened to Jesus himself while on earth.

This sixth trumpet reminds us that there are two major forces at work in the world. The evil force of Abbadon functions as a warning that the ways of sin just do not work, and thus serves as a call to change our ways.

We can, however, only see the nature of sin as its grossness and deceit are highlighted by the opposing power of Christ. The gospel exposes the horrible shortcomings of sin, but does so at some peril. Bitterness comes with the gospel as well as sweetness, a bitterness demonstrated in the death of Jesus and in the parallel sufferings of people who follow him. We can absorb this suffering, as Jesus did, because of the resurrection to follow, as the vision shows.

Trumpet 7

A woman gives birth to a son. A huge red dragon waits to devour the baby, but the mother and baby are rescued. The dragon then attacks the rest of the woman's descendants. He does so by summoning two great beasts, one out of the sea and the other out of the land. But in the very midst of these massive attacks, people are being redeemed by the thousands as the gospel continues its victorious path through human history. The vision closes with a picture of the two harvests of earth, one of the wicked and one of the righteous.

The seventh trumpet penetrates deeper into the nature of the conflict between Christ and the devil, providing another avenue for us to see, understand, and participate more fruitfully in the work of the gospel.

The more powerful the gospel becomes within any given society, the more clearly its opposite will be displayed. The emergence of gross evils in a civilization where the Christian faith is strong does not mean a weakening of the gospel; it means the opposite. Christians must expect this to happen. The more thoroughly the Spirit of Christ is absorbed into the socioeconomic fabric of life, the more clearly the remaining evils will appear. They are, in fact, shown to be evil by the prevailing climate of Christian opinion. If there were no Christian presence, there would be no contrast against which to measure evil. Evil would be accepted as standard. This insight should be the net result of this trumpet septet.

CHAPTER 7

The First Five Trumpets

Revelation 8:6–9:12

The First Four Trumpets

Then the seven angels who had the seven trumpets prepared to sound them.

The first angel sounded his trumpet, and there came hail and fire mixed with blood, and it was hurled down upon the earth. A third of the earth was burned up, a third of the trees were burned up, and all the green grass was burned up.

The second angel sounded his trumpet, and something like a huge mountain, all ablaze, was thrown into the sea. A third of the sea turned into blood, a third of the living creatures in the sea died, and a third of the ships were destroyed.

The third angel sounded his trumpet, and a great star, blazing like a torch, fell from the sky on a third of the rivers and on the springs of water — the name of the star is Wormwood. A third of the waters turned bitter, and many people died from the waters that had become bitter.

The fourth angel sounded his trumpet, and a third of the sun was struck, a third of the moon, and a third of the stars, so that a third of them turned dark. A third of the day was without light, and also a third of the night.

As I watched, I heard an eagle that was flying in midair call out in a loud voice: "Woe! Woe! Woe to the inhabitants of the earth, because of the trumpet blasts about to be sounded by the other three angels!" (8:6-13)

. . . .

The first angel sounded his trumpet, and there came hail and fire mixed with blood, and it was hurled down upon the earth. A third of the earth was burned up, a third of the trees were burned up, and all the green grass was burned up.

Angels are the messengers of God. Therefore, what they do is from God. The hail and fire that produce a rampant forest fire come from God. He is sending a warning to show the people of the world that something is wrong with the way they live, and to induce them to repent.

Once again, this entire book is a vision, and everything in this vision is symbolic. Do not think of literal forest fires. Remember that we do not find literalism in the next three trumpets either. Visualize rather all the tragedies, disappointments, sorrows, setbacks, failures, and negative events that characterize human life in general. Connect these in turn with the curse of God in Genesis 3 upon the woman, the man, and the serpent. Life as we know it is not all that it should and could be. These first four trumpets picture that condition.

The second angel sounded his trumpet, and something like a huge mountain, all ablaze, was thrown into the sea. A third of the sea turned into blood, a third of the living creatures in the sea died, and a third of the ships were destroyed.

It seems as though John sees a meteorite. But again, understand it symbolically. A literal meteorite would not turn a third of the ocean, salt water, into blood. This trumpet affects the maritime part of our civilization, the fishing and shipping industries.

The third angel sounded his trumpet, and a great star, blazing like a torch, fell from the sky on a third of the rivers and on the springs of water — the name of the star is Wormwood. A third of the waters turned bitter, and many people died from the waters that had become bitter.

John sees another meteorite, this time with a name, Wormwood. Not just the seas are affected this time, but fresh water, upon which people are dependent for their very lives.

The fourth angel sounded his trumpet, and a third of the sun was struck, a third of the moon, and a third of the stars, so that a third of them turned dark. A third of the day was without light, and also a third of the night.

We are dependent on the sun for light and heat. If literally a third of the potency of the sun were removed, we would all perish. But for John the result of the diminution of the sun, moon, and stars is a loss of one-third of daylight and night light. He visualizes tragedy of a high magnitude, even if he is not aware of modern scientific insights.

These four trumpets show that there are forces at work in the ordinary affairs of life that are not immediately obvious to our view. The problems and difficulties of life, associated with God's curse on the sin of Adam and Eve, should remind us that we are not living in the Garden of Eden, in Paradise, in shalom. God sends these setbacks and troubles to remind us that we need constantly to repent of our evil ways and turn to God for guidance and help. We are living in a fallen world that still suffers under God's curse, the curse of sin. To get out from under God's curse we must follow Jesus, the Lamb that was slain, who became the Lion of spiritual power.

. . . I heard an eagle that was flying in midair call out in a loud voice: "Woe! Woe! Woe to the inhabitants of the earth, because of the trumpet blasts about to be sounded by the other three angels!"

The first four trumpets are one unit, representing the condition of the human race ever since the fall of Adam and Eve, that is, from the beginning of human existence. The next three trumpets suggest the effect that the coming of Christ has within this fallen world. The eagle flying high in the sky with its raucous call suggests that something new — and much worse — is about to happen. Not worse for God's purpose, but for the entrenched powers of wickedness.

The Fifth Trumpet (the First Woe)

The fifth angel sounded his trumpet, and I saw a star that had fallen from the sky to the earth. The star was given the key to the shaft of the Abyss. When he opened the Abyss, smoke rose from it like the smoke from a gigantic furnace. The sun and sky were darkened by the smoke from the Abyss. And out of the smoke locusts came down upon the earth and were given power like that of scorpions of the earth. They were told not to harm the grass of the earth or any plant or tree, but only those people who did not have the seal of God on their foreheads. They were not given power to kill them, but only to torture them for five months. And the agony they suffered was like that of the sting of a scorpion when it strikes a man. During those days men will seek death, but will not find it; they will long to die, but death will elude them.

The locusts looked like horses prepared for battle. On their heads they wore something like crowns of gold, and their faces resembled human faces. Their hair was like women's hair, and their teeth were like lions' teeth. They had breastplates like breastplates of iron, and the sound of their wings was like the thundering of many horses and chariots rushing into battle. They had tails and stings like scorpions, and in their tails they had power to torment people for five months. They had as king over them the angel of the Abyss, whose name in Hebrew is Abaddon, and in Greek, Apollyon.

The first woe is past; two other woes are yet to come. (9:1-12)

. . . .

. . . a star that had fallen from the sky to the earth.

This star has a key which opens up the abyss, from which emerges an army of locusts whose king is the angel of the abyss, Abaddon — Apollyon — Satan. Someone or something exerts such influence as to deploy this army of evil into the world. This army that has been shut up, penned in, and unable to escape is now enabled to emerge from its prison. Or perhaps it is compelled to emerge and expose itself to public view.

It could not be Satan himself who releases this army, since he emerges as the king of this underworld army. He himself has been confined. It is not by his own initiative that he breaks out. He is drawn out. He is forced out.

It is Christ who has this power. It is Christ who has the key of Death and of Hades. But why does Christ do this awful thing, releasing hordes of evil powers into the world? Is this consistent with his purpose of healing the nations?

> *They were told not to harm the grass of the earth or any plant or tree, but only those people who did not have the seal of God on their foreheads. They were not given power to kill them, but only to torture them for five months.*

Strange! Locusts who are told not to harm grass, plants, or trees, their natural foods. Instead they may harm people — locusts harming people — but only those who are not sealed with the seal of God. They are told to harm them, torture them, but not to kill them, and only for five months. The time limit represents the normal time of the year for locusts to appear, five months in the growing season, not in the winter. But the vision is symbolic.

The powers of evil in any given civilization are limited in their authority and influence. For a long time they have been imprisoned; now they are released for a short time, but under rigid restraints. Translate this vision into the actualities of time and space, of history and human life. The ministry of Christ is causing the temporary releasing of locusts, of evil that harms only the enemies of God.

Take the actual experience of Jesus as the paradigm. His ministry in Galilee and Judea triggered the emergence of animosity, hatred, criticism, and violence, even death. Without his ministry these evils were hidden within the hearts of the priests and Pharisees. His ministry was the occasion for their breaking out of these hiding places into actual and open opposition.

But who was harmed by this visible emergence of hatred, this coming out into the open of evil? Not Jesus. He was crucified in great pain and sorrow, but he rose again, victorious, from the dead. Even his disciples (excluding Judas) were not harmed because they lived to repent of their lapse of faith. The only ones harmed were those not sealed by the seal of God, all those who refuse to believe in the Lord Jesus.

What John sees is the continuation of this process in the life and experience of all Christians thereafter. Wherever Christ comes with the gospel, wherever churches are established, wherever the Spirit of Jesus controls and empowers people to live for God, there opposition is found. There great swarms of locusts of evil emerge to wreak what havoc they can, attacking Christians and making all kinds of trouble and suffering for them, as they did for Jesus himself. But in the end, they do not harm those who are sealed with the Spirit of God. They harm only themselves, hardening themselves into mindless opposition to God and to his Christ.

> *During those days men will seek death, but will not find it; they will long to die, but death will elude them.*

People will long to die. The forces aligned against truth and godliness produce pressure, both physical and psychological, which makes life extremely miserable.

Take Judas as an example. He chose to oppose the Lord Jesus, and then could not live with his decision. Perhaps, in those ancient times, those who persecuted the Christians found they had unleashed forces within themselves that they had not contemplated, and found themselves tormented by guilt. Perhaps, in modern times, those who supported the Nazis' organized massacre of helpless people came to hate themselves for it.

Sin comes with its own built-in punishment, a certain amount of self-loathing and self-hatred that thoroughly destroys the sense of contentment and joy which forgiveness in Christ brings.

Do not interpret this passage as referring to some remote future time when life will become intolerable. It does not refer to some temporary great tribulation envisioned to happen prior to Christ's return.

Rather, it refers to the very real, constant, and unavoidable effect of conscious opposition to Christ and his Spirit. People simply cannot live comfortably with that. It is unnatural, contrary to the very essence of human nature. Christ's purpose is to restore the original intent of the Creator, bringing human beings into the kind of life defined by the biblical term "image of God" (Gen. 1:27). Those who oppose this, oppose that which makes up the optimal human existence. And that very opposition is what creates the situation described in John's vision: people who are miserable with life, wishing they were dead but not actually being able to commit suicide.

> *They had as king over them the angel of the Abyss, whose name in Hebrew is Abaddon, and in Greek, Apollyon.*

Both names, Abaddon and Apollyon, mean Destroyer. The names remind us that the devil, Satan, is not a creator. Only God is the creator. Satan can only destroy what is already there — not destroy in the sense of uncreate, but in the sense of ruin, spoil, poison, desecrate. Satan and his forces are vandals, spoilers, defilers, powers that take what is there, what God has created, and do their best to violate it. In Adam he succeeded to some extent, but the result is not betterment but sorrow, such intense sorrow that people wish they were dead. Satan is the king of those evil forces that are exposed by the coming of Christ.

> *The first woe is past; two other woes are yet to come.*

The fifth trumpet was the first woe; the sixth and seventh trumpets are the second and third woes. In the first woe we saw the effect of the gospel on those whose wickedness it exposed. In the next woes we shall see what other effects the gospel has on the world.

CHAPTER 8

The Sixth Trumpet

Revelation 9:13–11:14

There are three major visions triggered by this sixth trumpet:

1. Four Euphrates angels (9:13-21)
2. The angel with a little scroll (10:1-11)
3. Two witnesses (11:1-14)

The first five trumpets focused on what happens to evil as a result of Christ's ministry. Trumpet six continues the theme, but also makes a transition to show what happens to Christians at the same time. The gospel affects unbelievers in a negative way, bringing unhappiness and guilt; now John's vision will show how believers fare under the same influence of the gospel and in the same world where the wicked live as well. The four Euphrates angels continue to depict how the various influences of evil function, whereas the angel with the little scroll and the two witnesses show us something of the way Christians function in the same world.

Four Euphrates Angels

The sixth angel sounded his trumpet, and I heard a voice coming from the horns of the golden altar that is before God. It said to the sixth angel who had the trumpet, "Release the four angels who are bound at the great river Euphrates." And the four angels who had been kept ready for this very hour and day and month and year were released to kill a third of mankind. The number of the mounted troops was two hundred million. I heard their number.

The horses and riders I saw in my vision looked like this: Their breastplates were fiery red, dark blue, and yellow as sulfur. The heads of the horses resembled the heads of lions, and out of their mouths came fire, smoke and sulfur. A third of mankind was killed by the three plagues of fire, smoke and sulfur that came out of their mouths. The power of the horses was in their mouths and in their tails; for their tails were like snakes, having heads with which they inflict injury.

The rest of mankind that were not killed by these plagues still did not repent of the work of their hands; they did not stop worshiping demons, and idols of gold, silver, bronze, stone and wood — idols that cannot see or hear or walk. Nor did they repent of their murders, their magic arts, their sexual immorality or their thefts. (9:13-21)

. . . .

. . . "Release the four angels who are bound at the great river Euphrates."

In one of his earliest letters, the apostle Paul told the Christians in Thessalonica that the day of the Lord will not come until the forces that are restraining evil in the world are removed. As strong and powerful as the hold of evil on human life may seem, there is still something holding it back, keeping it from exercising total dominance over human civilization. Life is not as bad as it could get. Paul predicts that when this restraining force is removed, life for everyone will become even more intolerable (2 Thess. 2).

The four angels who are bound at the Euphrates River represent this same insight. The historic nations of the Mesopotamian valley, notably the Assyrians and the Babylonians, served as symbols of evil to the Jewish people. As long as God kept them in check during Old Testament times, Israelite life could continue to flourish, but when God raised them up to invade the southern countries, Israel was in trouble. This cultural background of the time provides perspective on this vision of John.

> *. . . the four angels who had been kept ready for this very hour and day and month and year were released to kill a third of mankind.*

This situation is somewhat comparable to that of Judah during the prophetic years of Jeremiah, who warned insistently that God would send down the Babylonians from the north. The Euphrates angels have been kept in check, but now they are loosed to bring havoc wherever they go. John sees these Babylonian angels released by God to kill off a third of the human race. The angels deploy armies of "two hundred million" to achieve their ends.

God is sending his messengers to destroy one-third of the people on earth. God, not the devil, is sending them. Many, many people will be killed. It is difficult for us to comprehend that a good, loving, and creative God could do such a thing. Yet that is what does happen, and John sees it in his vision.

God wants all people to be honorable and just, to live peaceably, nobly, righteously, and justly. But people do not live this way. They do not live as God desires. God must do something to show people the wrongness of their way of life. Adversity, sorrow, pain, discouragement, failure, deprivation, and even death are avenues by which God demonstrates to us that our way of life is wrong.

What John sees in this vision is a culmination of these warnings, a great gigantic explosion of catastrophe that should persuade everyone to repent and seek a good life under God. Yet, even this final warning is not enough. People still do not repent from evil and turn to God. Look to the experience of Jesus while on earth as the ultimate example.

> *The rest of mankind that were not killed by these plagues still did not repent of the work of their hands; they did not stop worshiping demons, and idols of gold, silver, bronze, stone and wood — idols that cannot see or hear or walk. Nor did they repent of their murders, their magic arts, their sexual immorality or their thefts.*

The people of Jeremiah's day did not repent when he warned them of the terror from the north. John sees the same reaction to the warning brought by the armies of the four Euphrates angels.

People do not repent when life goes awry and brings disaster rather than happiness. Judah did not repent when Jeremiah warned them of impending doom. They were not willing to accept personal responsibility for the way events went. Adam and Eve refused to accept responsibility for their sin. This has been characteristic of individuals everywhere. People don't readily or easily accept fault when things are going wrong.

Something must happen to show us precisely that it is our fault when things go wrong, that we are indeed sinners. Not necessarily that everything bad can be traced to some individual sin, but that in general all sorrows need to be connected with God's curse on Adam and Eve after their sin. Pain and sorrow, disappointment and heartache are God's curse on the human race. When we experience it, as we all do, we need to accept our share of the responsibility.

The ministry of Jesus on earth leads us to this acceptance of responsibility, and to our repentance. Few of the people of Jesus' time would have seen themselves as sinners in need of repentance. Jesus had to show them inescapably that their commitment was not really to God but to their own success.

Jesus showed them by allowing them, no, forcing them, to do to him exactly what they wanted to do. By putting himself in their hands Jesus was forcing them to expose what was deepest in their hearts, disclosing attitudes they may not even have known were there. And they killed him. They killed the Son of God. By rejecting Jesus they confirmed that, deep in their hearts, they rejected God.

Then Jesus showed these same people how godless and profane their deed was by rising from the dead. Peter and the other disciples, as well as thousands of countrymen, saw themselves for the first time for what they really were. Many accepted their responsibility for it and repented. They were then forgiven, restored, and renewed to go on, humbly but confidently following their Lord. That is how the Lord Jesus persuades people to repent: by showing them what their lives are really like. It isn't done merely by sending them suffering, death, sorrow, and pain — the weapons wielded by the Euphrates angels. It is by exposing the sin in their hearts.

The Angel with a Little Scroll

Then I saw another mighty angel coming down from heaven. He was robed in a cloud, with a rainbow above his head; his face was like the sun, and his legs were like fiery pillars. He was holding a little scroll, which lay open in his hand. He planted his right foot on the sea and his left foot on the land, and he gave a loud shout like the roar of a lion. When he shouted, the voices of the seven thunders spoke. And when the seven thunders spoke, I was about to write; but I heard a voice from heaven say, "Seal up what the seven thunders have said and do not write it down."

Then the angel I had seen standing on the sea and on the land raised his right hand to heaven. And he swore by him who lives for ever and ever, who created the heavens and all that is in them, the earth and all that is in it, and the sea and all that is in it, and said, "There will be no more delay! But in the days when the seventh angel is about to sound his trumpet, the mystery of God will be accomplished, just as he announced to his servants the prophets."

Then the voice that I had heard from heaven spoke to me once more: "Go, take the scroll that lies open in the hand of the angel who is standing on the sea and on the land."

So I went to the angel and asked him to give me the little scroll. He said to me, "Take it and eat it. It will turn your stomach sour, but in your mouth it will be as sweet as honey." I took the little scroll from the angel's hand and ate it. It tasted as sweet as honey in my mouth, but when I had eaten it, my stomach turned sour. Then I was told, "You must prophesy again about many peoples, nations, languages and kings." (10:1-11)

. . . .

. . . another mighty angel . . . holding a little scroll, which lay open in his hand.

Is there any connection between this little scroll *(biblaridion)* and the previous scroll *(biblion)* that had seven seals? The first scroll was sealed tight when John first saw it; this scroll is wide open in the angel's hand. The

107

first scroll represents God's eternal plan for the world. This little open scroll represents the gospel.

This little scroll is not the New Testament, which is the written gospel, but the gospel itself irrespective of whether or not it is written — the good news that Jesus has risen from the dead, that he calls everyone to believe, repent, and be restored to godliness. This is not only the gospel as a set of ideas or as a recitation of facts; it is the power of God functioning in his Word. This vision shows us how the gospel fares in a world where God's wrath against sin is so evident.

He planted his right foot on the sea and his left foot on the land, and he gave a loud shout like the roar of a lion.

Picture the gospel in this posture relative to the world at large. The gospel covers land and sea. It thunders throughout the earth. It is the most decisive and powerful factor in the entire world, dominating over all other influences and voices. It is nothing less than the omnipotent presence of the Creator God himself — "him who lives for ever and ever, who created the heavens and all that is in them, the earth and all that is in it, and the sea and all that is in it" — who stands behind the gospel and gives it authority and power.

"Seal up what the seven thunders have said and do not write it down."

This might have been another major division of the book of Revelation had John written what the seven thunders said: seven churches, seven seals, seven trumpets, seven thunders, and seven bowls. But we will never know, for John did not write it down.

"There will be no more delay!"

Some older English translations say "time shall be no more." But the angel is not giving a metaphysical prediction that time itself will cease. Rather he is answering the impatient questions raised by all of us who wonder if and when God will keep his promise to destroy the destroyer. Recall the complaint of the souls under the altar: How long will it be until you judge the inhabitants of earth (see 6:10)? We all wonder from time to time whether any significant progress is being made in annihilating sin.

Wait no longer, there will be no further delay, John is told; it is going to happen right now. The visions John is about to describe show how God the creator uses the gospel, the work of Christ, to bring about the healing of the nations.

In terms of the actual process of history, we need to remember that it was in the fullness of the times that God sent his Son (Gal. 4:4). God postponed his judgment on the sin of the world until then. But with the coming of Jesus, God is beginning to exercise his final judgment, gradually eliminating sin and restoring righteousness. From our human point of view the process of redemption seems interminable, but God assures us that it all fits well within his timetable.

> *"But in the days when the seventh angel is about to sound his trumpet, the mystery of God will be accomplished, just as he announced to his servants the prophets."*

The sixth trumpet announces that the seventh trumpet will depict the final accomplishment of "the mystery of God," the mystery of how God will ultimately and eternally achieve the purpose he set forth when he created the world and man. God wants a human race in perfect harmony with the rest of the world, a human race without sin, without suffering, without misery, and without pain; a human race that perfectly images God himself as it goes about its task of dominating the earth and creating a civilization.

Now God has revealed how he plans to accomplish that goal: through Jesus Christ, the gospel, the church, and the Spirit. By means of Christianity God has begun the final step that will eventuate in the perfection of the human race. The visions of the seventh trumpet show in more detail how this is done. But for now, the sixth trumpet helps to set the stage by showing the initial stages of the process.

> *"Go, take the scroll that lies open in the hand of the angel who is standing on the sea and on the land."*

This is an interesting development in John's vision. For the most part in previous visions John is a spectator, watching as various angels and other beings take part in some dramatic activity. Now John himself is summoned to become a participant in his own visions. He is told to approach the mighty angel and ask him for the little scroll in his hand.

John can no longer just stand and watch. He is called to action, to participation. We, like John, cannot remain spectators in the process whereby God destroys destruction and redeems his people. Like John, all who follow Jesus as Savior and Lord are called to action, to participation.

"Take it and eat it. It will turn your stomach sour, but in your mouth it will be as sweet as honey."

Eat it. Eat the little scroll. John does so, and indeed it is sweet in his mouth but sour in his stomach (see Ezek. 3:1).

Our first experience of faith in the Lord Jesus is sweetness itself. It brings us the love of God and assures us that our faults are not decisive; it releases new and surprising energies of creativity and goodness. However, as the gospel is not only chewed but digested, certain other things happen which are not so sweet but are in fact sour.

Christians live in the joy, happiness, and love of Jesus Christ, but in doing so they encounter those who do not believe and live in him, those who represent a totally different lifestyle and do not easily tolerate a way of living that challenges the evils they have come to enjoy. They make trouble for God's people in varying degrees. The stronger the commitment to Jesus Christ, the more antagonism is elicited. Remember, Jesus Christ provoked the antagonism of not only the leaders of the people but eventually of the people themselves. The faithful followers of Christ must walk in his footsteps, carrying their cross with him. This is what John experiences in his vision when he eats the scroll and digests it.

Expand the vision to a broader level. See not only what John as an individual experiences, but what the entire Christian community as a whole experiences. Internally the church experiences the blessings of Christ as sweet and good, but as the church bears effective and powerful witness to the gospel it engenders conflict and opposition. Often new converts encounter ostracism in their own families, and newly formed Christian communities are discriminated against in non-Christian cultures. This is what John sees in his vision as he eats and digests the *biblaridion* in the angel's hand.

"You must prophesy again about many peoples, nations, languages and kings."

The term *prophet* is not usually employed when speaking about John. He is the apostle John or the disciple whom Jesus loved; rarely is he referred to as the prophet John. Yet his work is that of a prophet, and it always has been. A prophet is a person who brings the message of God. John, even after his "stomach turned sour," is commanded to continue the work of prophecy. The message of God must be brought to all peoples and languages, to all nations and governments.

The instruction John receives personally here must be understood as applying to the entire Christian community, the church. The gospel must continue to be spread abroad regardless of consequences, irrespective of opposition. This is the duty of the church.

The actual seven churches that John is writing to (Ephesus and the others) must see that this is one of the absolute conditions of their calling and of their existence. If they do not take part in the dissemination of the gospel, they will gradually degenerate, weaken, wither, and eventually die. They will lose their lampstand altogether. The church will die out. Each of these churches lives and dies by the gospel, and each must do its part regularly and perseveringly to expand the knowledge of Jesus Christ among its neighbors. The trumpet calls them to get involved and stay involved.

Two Witnesses

I was given a reed like a measuring rod and was told, "Go and measure the temple of God and the altar, and count the worshipers there. But exclude the outer court; do not measure it, because it has been given to the Gentiles. They will trample on the holy city for 42 months. And I will give power to my two witnesses, and they will prophesy for 1,260 days, clothed in sackcloth." These are the two olive trees and the two lampstands that stand before the Lord of the earth. If anyone tries to harm them, fire comes from their mouths and devours their enemies. This is how anyone who wants to harm them must die. These men have power to shut up the sky so that it will not rain during the time they are prophesying; and they have power to turn the waters into blood and to strike the earth with every kind of plague as often as they want.

Now when they have finished their testimony, the beast that comes up from the Abyss will attack them, and overpower and kill them. Their bodies will lie in the street of the great city, which is figuratively called Sodom and Egypt, where also their Lord was crucified. For three and a half days men from every people, tribe, language and nation will gaze on their bodies and refuse them burial. The inhabitants of the earth will gloat over them and will celebrate by sending each other gifts, because these two prophets had tormented those who live on the earth.

But after the three and a half days a breath of life from God entered them, and they stood on their feet, and terror struck those who saw them. Then they heard a loud voice from heaven saying to them, "Come up here." And they went up to heaven in a cloud, while their enemies looked on.

At that very hour there was a severe earthquake and a tenth of the city collapsed. Seven thousand people were killed in the earthquake, and the survivors were terrified and gave glory to the God of heaven.

The second woe has passed; the third woe is coming soon. (11:1-14)

. . . .

"Go and measure the temple of God and the altar, and count the worshipers there."

The personal involvement of John in his own vision continues. He has just eaten the little scroll, finding it bittersweet, and has been commanded to continue prophesying to the nations. Now he is told to measure the temple and count the worshipers.

God is telling him to observe the results of his prophesying. For us today this directive means something similar. We should become aware of the results of the church's continual prophesying throughout the centuries since Christ.

John was told very specifically to "measure the temple of God." In Old Testament times this duty was performed literally by Ezekiel (Ezek. 40), who preserved the measurements of the Solomonic temple that was destroyed by the Babylonians in 586 B.C. Ezekiel's purpose was to preserve this information for such time as it might become possible to re-build the temple.

A second temple, refurbished by King Herod, was destroyed in A.D. 70 when the Roman armies put down a Jewish revolt. This could conceivably have been the occasion for John to leave Jerusalem and emigrate to Ephesus, and it was surely in his mind when he saw this vision and heard the command to measure the temple. The purpose, then, of such a measuring was to preserve the dimensions for the future. Taken symbolically, it would mean discerning the spiritual dimensions of the temple of God, of the church.

This command is not guaranteeing an actual, literal rebuilding of the temple in Jerusalem. This too is a vision and must be understood symbolically. The literal temple in Jerusalem has been destroyed for a second time — a final time. Christ is now in the process of rebuilding the temple, beginning with his own resurrection and continuing with the addition of increasing numbers of people into that body. John is to understand that his work of prophesying contributes to the building of the body of Christ, which is the church and the temple of God, *the New Jerusalem* (Rev. 21:2).

> *"But exclude the outer court; do not measure it, because it has been given to the Gentiles. They will trample on the holy city for 42 months."*

The court of the Gentiles is not to be measured. And the Gentiles will desecrate the holy city for three and one-half years. All symbolic, of course. There was a long period of time between the destruction of Solomon's temple and the building of the second temple by Nehemiah. In John's day the city of Jerusalem was being trampled again.

In John's vision the "42 months" refers to this interim period, suggesting a transition period when Christianity was being salvaged out of Judaism.

The term *Gentiles* here refers to all who refuse Christ Jesus. In Old Testament times Gentiles (non-Jewish people) were not allowed to enter the inner courts of the temple, even if they converted to Judaism. From a Christian perspective the term means people who besiege Christianity. They may appear to have Christianity under their control, trampling the city of God for a while, but that will end. It will last only three and a half years. Do not take this figure literally. It is given as an indication that the

period when Christianity seems to be in direst trouble will be compara-
tively short.

> *"And I will give power to my two witnesses, and they will prophesy for
> 1,260 days, clothed in sackcloth."*

Who are these two witnesses? John has been told to continue his prophesying, but he is only one person. Now there are two. They are the witnesses of Jesus Christ; they are all who share the prophetic ministry of
the gospel, namely, every Christian believer. The "two witnesses" embody
the combined and cumulative testimony of all churches, of the whole of
Christianity itself.

What we are about to see, therefore, is a cross section of any given
moment in the history of the Christian church. The remaining events of
this part of the vision show how the church functions and what happens
to it as a result. The "1,260 days" are identical in length to the three and a
half years of the preceding verse, and refer to the same period of time.
The Gentiles may trample the holy city, but simultaneously the two witnesses go about their work. The opposition of the devil to the gospel may
go on, but he will not stop its spread. That is the significance of the time
references here.

> *If anyone tries to harm them, fire comes from their mouths and devours
> their enemies.*

It is difficult to visualize the church as a fire-breathing monster ready to
destroy its enemies. It is even more difficult to visualize Jesus as described this way.

What comes from the mouth of the two witnesses is the gospel, the
story of Jesus Christ. The gospel conquers the enemies of Christ by con-
verting them from enemies to friends.

Of course, not everyone who opposes Christ goes on to become converted, as did the apostle Paul, for example. The vision summons us to
view things in a larger dimension. It highlights the overall relationship of
Christianity to the non-Christian world. It tells us that the church universal carries a weapon able to conquer and destroy all opposition. That
weapon is the gospel of Christ Jesus. And the gospel will prevail in the
end, even though the battle may often seem in doubt.

These men have power to shut up the sky so that it will not rain during the time they are prophesying; and they have power to turn the waters into blood and to strike the earth with every kind of plague as often as they want.

The first reference, shutting up the sky, is to Elijah, who did this in his struggle with Jezebel and the prophets of Baal (1 Kings 17:1). The second, water turned into blood, is a reference to Moses, who did this when leading the Israelites out of Egypt (Exod. 7:17). The third reference, every kind of plague, is also to the ten plagues sent by God through Moses at the time of the exodus (Exod. 7–11).

The Christian church also has these powers, not literally as in the Old Testament instances but figuratively. Elijah and Moses did not possess these powers in their own humanity. Only God can restrain rainfall, only God can change water into blood and send plagues upon the earth. But God does this, as the Old Testament instances show, through his people.

Such are the powers of the church. The church does not exercise power in its own right, as if God transfers his divine sovereignty to people. No. No ecumenical council, no exorcist, no bishop or pope, no synod or consistory or minister, no board of directors ever has had or ever will have such innate power vested in it by God. God does, however, utilize human authorities and personages. He uses the church. He uses the proclamation of the gospel. He uses missionaries, pastors, believers, professors, evangelists, and teachers; he uses all who follow the Lord Jesus. He uses, in terms of the vision of John, his two witnesses.

Through the church in its variegated ministries God sends such influences into the world as he did in Old Testament times, but now they are directed specifically to the conversion of sinners, and in this way tend toward the destruction of the destroyer.

Now when they have finished their testimony, the beast that comes up from the Abyss will attack them, and overpower and kill them.

In the preceding trumpet blast the abyss yielded grasshoppers who metamorphosed into warhorses and were led by their king, Abaddon. Here a beast emerges from the abyss. These two accounts depict the same thing: anti-Christian forces, whether seen as many (locusts, horses) or as one (beast).

But what a startling and unexpected vision! The two witnesses go down not only to defeat but also to death. If the witnesses are the church, does the Christian church die? Does Christianity disappear? The beast attacks, overpowers, and kills them. This seems to conflict with what John told us previously, that the witnesses could devour their enemies.

There is no conflict. Look again to Jesus. He is the pattern, the paradigm. Jesus confronted the devil in the land of Judea. In that contest the devil attacked with all the powers available to him. He did not succeed in getting Jesus to bow down to him or to accept his guidance, so he had to resort to his only remaining weapon, death. He crucified Jesus. The beast that is Satan attacked Jesus, overpowered Jesus, and killed Jesus.

That is the pattern, and we must learn to see it repeated in the church. Jesus requires the church to walk in his footsteps, to carry its cross as it follows him. The cross entails crucifixion. The cross implies the devil attacking, overpowering, and killing. This happens in real life for all Christians, and for the churches to which John sent these visions.

The beast is always attacking, always using his powers to ruin and spoil and kill. He is always attacking against the church; against truth, justice, and righteousness; against wisdom and holiness, goodness and honesty; against trust and faith. He is always attacking against all the virtues of the Spirit that Christ mediates to us. The beast does indeed kill the two witnesses; he kills the witnessing function of the church.

The beast kills the witnesses in the same sense that it killed Jesus. The vision is about the climax of the gospel proclamation. Jesus' death came at the climax of his ministry. This death of the two witnesses comes "when they have finished their testimony."

When, in the judgment of God, the time has fully come for the church to have finished its witness — when, in other words, the church has compelled the entire human race as a whole to make its decision concerning God and his Son Jesus — then the end will come as the world makes the same decision as the Jews and the Romans made regarding Jesus: they will kill the church as they killed Jesus. This is the terrifying meaning of the vision of the death of the two witnesses.

> *Their bodies will lie in the street of the great city, which is figuratively called Sodom and Egypt, where also their Lord was crucified.*

Elsewhere Babylon is the symbol of the city of evil. Here it is Sodom, the city where Lot met his temptation (Gen. 13), and Egypt, where the ancient Israelites were enslaved (Exod. 1:11), and also Jerusalem, the city where the Lord was crucified (Luke 9:51). Imagine, Jerusalem! The Holy City, here called the great city, representative of the devil. It was, after all, in Jerusalem that the Lord was crucified.

> *For three and a half days men from every people, tribe, language and nation will gaze on their bodies and refuse them burial. The inhabitants of the earth will gloat over them and will celebrate by sending each other gifts, because these two prophets had tormented those who live on the earth.*

They will gloat, every people, tribe, language, and nation. They will gloat and celebrate. These are the very same categories of people that in the end will be saved! Understand it in the example of Jesus' crucifixion.

The crowds in Jerusalem hailed Jesus as their Messiah on Palm Sunday. The same people clamored for his crucifixion less than a week later. And still later, after the resurrection, many of the same people came to repentance and faith!

Here in the vision John sees crowds of people from all over the world rejoicing in the death of the two witnesses. It is a decision they themselves have made, and they are congratulating each other on their total rejection of Christianity. Their consciences have been tormenting them for ages because of the glaring light of truth shone on them by Christians. Now that pressure has been eliminated, and they celebrate their victory, gloating over the unburied carcass of the powerless church.

This vision is about the climax of the church's witness at some indefinite date in the future, but John wants his churches to see that similar forces are always operative in smaller, local aspects. They must expect comparable attacks and victories by the abysmal beast. We should not, like Jesus' original twelve disciples, despair or lose hope because of setbacks to the gospel. It all fits into God's pattern of redemption.

> *But after the three and a half days a breath of life from God entered them, and they stood on their feet, and terror struck those who saw them.*

The paradigm of Jesus is abundantly clear now. Just as Jesus rose from the dead on the third day after his crucifixion, so too these two witnesses in John's vision rise from the dead after three and a half days.

Jesus allowed the forces of the devil to do anything they wished to him. They did their worst: they put him to death. But Jesus calmly and quietly rose from the dead, demonstrating that the power of the devil was as nothing compared to that of God. The effect of Jesus' resurrection was to convince the people who witnessed it that they had been wrong in rejecting Jesus, so wrong as to have been opposing God himself. They repented and committed themselves to Jesus as Lord. Jesus became their Savior from sin. They began to follow Jesus' guidance for life, finding a righteousness that came as a result of this faith to replace the righteousness they had sought so disastrously before.

See John's vision in the same context. The people who gloat over the destruction of Christianity will see the error of their decision, after Christianity is revived by the power of God. They will repent and be saved, henceforth to live out their lives in submissive obedience to the will of the Creator. They will become functioning images of God.

There is a double dimension of meaning in this vision. Primarily it would refer to the climax of the church's witness at some distant date. But it would also have local and immediate importance for the churches to whom John sent these visions. Christian people, then and now, may take encouragement from this vision. The effect of our witnessing may not always be success; it may indeed be the opposite. As Christians we may be rejected instead of listened to. Yet we may be assured that Christ will find ways of resurrecting the gospel and the church even if, for the moment, things appear to be going badly. This is the local and immediate significance of this vision.

But this is a vision of humanity as a whole, just as the death of Jesus was a matter of the Jewish nation as a whole. A new Israel emerged out of the old Israel, and in John's perspective a new humanity will emerge out of the old humanity. As Paul would have put it, a new Adam emerges out of the old Adam. The overall course of humanity subsequent to this resurrection of the two witnesses will be in harmony with Christ and with God the Father. This is the larger meaning of the vision.

Then they heard a loud voice from heaven saying to them, "Come up here." And they went up to heaven in a cloud, while their enemies looked on.

This is a parallel to the ascension of Jesus, though the persons who witness it are not the disciples but rather the enemies. The significance that his ascension had for Jesus is the same significance that this ascension has for the two witnesses, that is, for the church.

Jesus, the man, had been completely and flawlessly faithful to his Father in heaven, to God. His ascension meant, for one thing, that he no longer had to engage in the battle against temptation and sin. He had fought that battle and had won. His resurrection symbolized that victory, and at the same time transported his human nature into a new level. His humanity emerged out of the fallen condition of Adam and into a new condition beyond even the possibility of temptation; he had conquered sin. Now, from heaven, he sends his Spirit to bring the rest of the human race through the same process he had undergone, and into the same condition of sinlessness he had now attained.

The vision of the two witnesses shows the church passing through the same stages that Jesus passed through: faithful witnessing to the truth of God the creator, willing submission to death, resurrection, and ascension. This process continues as the gospel spreads to the whole world and the whole world is gradually being challenged by it.

The ultimate destiny of humanity as a whole is to be what Jesus is, now in heaven, having passed through death, resurrection, and ascension.

> *At that very hour there was a severe earthquake and a tenth of the city collapsed. Seven thousand people were killed in the earthquake, and the survivors were terrified and gave glory to the God of heaven.*

In the "great city," the city of the devil, a powerful earthquake trembles. It brings down a tenth of the buildings and kills seven thousand citizens. The rest, frightened, give glory to God.

This is only a partial finale — a tenth of the city destroyed and only some of its citizens killed. The vision of the two witnesses is a vision of the process of history, not of its ultimate ending. There is a glimpse of the ending, but the emphasis is on the penultimate process, not the ultimate goal.

These survivors are citizens of the city of the devil, yet they give glory to God. If they are the devil's minions, how can they glorify God? Their praise to God is not out of faith in Christ, but out of fear of God's wrath. They are terrified to discover that God's power is so much more potent than that of their leader, the beast from the abyss. They recognize that

119

this is so, and in that sense give glory to God, but not because they repent, believe, or obey.

The second woe has passed; the third woe is coming soon.

The third woe will concentrate more on the outcome of the historical process, whereas the second woe examined more the development of the historical process, the pattern to be seen as the history of the church unfolds. The seventh angel will blow a trumpet, the issue of which will be the climactic woe to all the forces of evil in the world.

CHAPTER 9

The Seventh Trumpet

Revelation 11:15–14:20

The action of the seventh trumpet begins with voices summarizing what is about to happen: "The kingdom of the world has become the kingdom of our Lord and of his Christ, and he will reign for ever and ever" (11:15). This is the last trumpet. The vision describes the final climactic struggle between good and evil, showing how almighty God realizes his kingdom through Christ.

In this seventh trumpet vision John sees the birth of Jesus through the eyes of heaven, a woman giving birth to a son, and a great dragon waiting to pounce and devour him. When thwarted in this attempt, the dragon turns to make war on the rest of the woman's offspring — the church. The devil fails to seduce and destroy Jesus, so he tries again by attacking Jesus' followers. But he fails here also, since the entire number of 144,000 completely escapes his snares. And finally, after three angels make momentous announcements, John sees a vision of Jesus reaping the harvest of earth.

This is the sequence of the seventh trumpet:

1. Thematic prelude: The kingdom of God (11:15-18)
2. The woman, the child, and the dragon (11:19–12:6)
   War in heaven (12:7-16)
3. The dragon makes war against her offspring (12:17–13:18)
4. The 144,000 (14:1-5)

121

5. Three gospel angels (14:6-13)
6. The dual harvest of earth (14:14-20)

Thematic Prelude: The Kingdom of God

The seventh angel sounded his trumpet, and there were loud voices in heaven, which said: "The kingdom of the world has become the kingdom of our Lord and of his Christ, and he will reign for ever and ever." And the twenty-four elders, who were seated on their thrones before God, fell on their faces and worshiped God, saying: "We give thanks to you, Lord God Almighty, the One who is and who was, because you have taken your great power and have begun to reign. The nations were angry; and your wrath has come. The time has come for judging the dead, and for rewarding your servants the prophets and your saints and those who reverence your name, both small and great — and for destroying those who destroy the earth." (11:15-18)

．　．　．　．　．　．

"The kingdom of the world has become the kingdom of our Lord and of his Christ, and he will reign for ever and ever."

God has control over the way things go on earth. Christ will reign age after age, forever.

In accordance with Genesis 3, John understands that the course of human events from the beginning has been wrong: it has developed under the direction of the devil rather than according to the desire of God. The voices in heaven, which he now hears in the seventh trumpet, announce that that condition has been corrected. Control over human progress and destiny has now passed out of the devil's hands back into the hands of God, specifically into the hands of Jesus Christ, resurrected and ascended. God now has secured the ascendancy in human civilization, through Jesus his Son. "You have taken your great power and have begun to reign." The visions in this trumpet will demonstrate how Jesus assumes the ascendancy on earth.

"We give thanks to you, Lord God Almighty, the One who is and who was, because you have taken your great power and have begun to reign."

The twenty-four elders (representing both the old and new covenants) speak these words. From the perspective of heaven they see what is happening on earth. They see that Jesus has wrested control over human affairs from the devil, thus restoring that control to Almighty God. They understand the "Lord God Almighty" to be the same God of Israel, the one whose name was Yahweh (I AM), the one who *was* in old covenant times and who *is* still today in new covenant times. They perceive that God has exercised his "great power" in the death and resurrection of Jesus, and that through this ministry of Jesus the actual sovereignty of God has begun to take root within the human race as a whole.

"The nations were angry; and your wrath has come."

The Greek language shows a grammatical parallel between the wrath of the nations and the wrath (*orge* — anger, rage, hostility, animosity) of God. In Christ God has demonstrated once for all his opposition to the sinful decision of Adam and Eve, which has controlled human history from the beginning. That is God's wrath. And it elicited a response of wrath from the nations. Think of the anger people showed against Jesus while on earth. Think of the continuing anger people showed against Christians in the ancient world of the Roman Empire. Think of the opposition encountered by missionaries and new Christians in countries of non-Christian persuasion. The nations become angry when they are confronted by the gospel of our Lord Jesus Christ.

"The time has come for judging the dead, and for rewarding your servants the prophets and your saints and those who reverence your name, both small and great — and for destroying those who destroy the earth."

This is still part of the exhilarating commentary of the twenty-four elders. They are describing what is happening on earth as the result of the earthly ministry of Christ.

"The time has come." The interpretive clue for the entire book of Revelation is the effect the earthly ministry of Christ has on the course of temporal human affairs. The visions that John records look at this effect from a great variety of viewpoints. Accordingly, the "time" John mentions here is the time of Jesus' ministry, now completed on earth but continuing from heaven. In this statement John mentions three distinguishable facets of the effect of Christ and the gospel within the continuing affairs of human history.

1. "Judging the dead." In the past many people have lived faithfully according to the law of God, but they have not always been vindicated while living. Others have flouted the natural standards God has established in human life and have seemed to get away with it. Now, the elders say, through Jesus the time has come to demonstrate that the way of faithful obedience to God is the right way for the human race to go, and the way of sinful arrogance, the wrong way. Jesus makes that clear in his ministry. The ministry of Jesus, taken as a whole, makes that judgment.

This judgment is a matter of history, of actual events taking place on earth. It is the judgment of history.

2. "Rewarding . . . the prophets and . . . saints." This reward includes both the Old Testament people of God (represented by the prophets) and the New Testament church (saints), everyone who reverences God and lives accordingly. They are rewarded. The purpose for which they dedicated their lives is now in actual control through Jesus Christ. All who reverence God, whether or not they have a great human reputation, are rewarded now by the demonstrated victory of Jesus over the devil. Representing them, the twenty-four elders in heaven now see the faith of the saints vindicated as the power of Christ's Spirit begins to dominate human history. That is the reward as seen from heaven.

This vision does not address itself to the question of individual immortality or life in a world to come. It focuses on the impact of Jesus' earthly ministry on human affairs, showing that this success of Jesus is the visible reward — vindication, approval, recompense, justification, proof — of the life of faith which God's people have demonstrated.

3. "Destroying those who destroy." The time has come for the destruction of the devil and his legions. This too is one aspect of the ministry of Christ. The beginning of that destruction is demonstrated in the resurrection of Jesus himself, and the continuation of it is demonstrated in the salvation of people through the gospel.

The "time" therefore is a period of time. It has a beginning, it has a continuation, and it will have a future. What Christ has begun in his own personal life on earth he will continue by means of the gospel and the church until the final destiny is achieved. Human history since the time of Christ is the history of the progressive destruction — minimizing, lessening, depreciation, suppression, and ultimate elimination — of the forces of evil within human civilization. With Jesus the time for that narrowing has come, and it has continued ever since, everywhere the gospel has gone.

The Woman, the Child, and the Dragon

Then God's temple in heaven was opened, and within his temple was seen the ark of his covenant. And there came flashes of lightning, rumblings, peals of thunder, an earthquake and a great hailstorm.

A great and wondrous sign appeared in heaven: a woman clothed with the sun, with the moon under her feet and a crown of twelve stars on her head. She was pregnant and cried out in pain as she was about to give birth. Then another sign appeared in heaven: an enormous red dragon with seven heads and ten horns and seven crowns on his heads. His tail swept a third of the stars out of the sky and flung them to the earth. The dragon stood in front of the woman who was about to give birth, so that he might devour her child the moment it was born. She gave birth to a son, a male child, who will rule all the nations with an iron scepter. And her child was snatched up to God and to his throne. The woman fled into the desert to a place prepared for her by God, where she might be taken care of for 1,260 days. (11:19–12:6)

. . . .

John's vision of the seventh trumpet now shows in some detail how the things described by the twenty-four elders actually happen on earth.

John sees God's temple in heaven opened, and then a violent thunderstorm, complete with lightning and hail and earthquake — all symbols of the almighty power of God — now being unleashed on earth. God infuses his power into human life and history by sending his Son Jesus.

125

The thunderstorm symbolizes the catastrophic effect the coming of Christ has on human society.

A woman gives birth to a son, and a dragon seeks to devour the baby. His ploy fails. The dragon and his hosts then wage battle against Michael and his angels, seeking control of heaven. The dragon fails here also and is cast out. Thereupon he seeks to destroy the mother, and he fails again. The vision shows how the devil fails to thwart God's program of taking back his kingdom from the devil — a magnificent sequence of failures.

> . . . a woman clothed with the sun, with the moon under her feet and a crown of twelve stars on her head. She was pregnant and cried out in pain as she was about to give birth.

The sun, the moon, and the stars — these are symbolic of the entire physical universe. This woman represents the universal purpose of God for his creation, particularly for the human part of it. This woman may be seen in three dimensions: (1) as the universe itself (mother earth); (2) as the nation of Israel, whose purpose was to bring Messiah into the world; and (3) as Mary herself, mother of Jesus. From all three of these dimensions John is visualizing the pending birth of Jesus.

> Then another sign appeared in heaven: an enormous red dragon with seven heads and ten horns and seven crowns on his heads. His tail swept a third of the stars out of the sky and flung them to the earth.

Visualize the great symbols — the sun, the moon, and the stars — in the shape of a woman, paralleled by an equally enormous dragon so large as to sweep away a third of the stars of night. It is the face-off which sets in motion the great contest in which God begins to set things right in his world. As the serpent succeeded in seducing the woman in the first garden (Gen. 3), so now the same contest is being repeated on the broad universal scale of all humanity.

In the ancient world, when this was written, it may have been possible to identify the seven heads, the ten horns, and the seven crowns of this gigantic dragon. Now the significance is in the grotesqueness of this mythology. Such dragons do not exist in God's creation. This dragon is a symbol of the twisted, grotesque, repulsive, deranged, warped, hideous, distorted, unnatural demeanor of sin and evil.

> *The dragon stood in front of the woman who was about to give birth, so that he might devour her child the moment it was born.*

The dragon represents the satanic forces that have been in control of human life and civilization ever since the fall, as demonstrated in the story of Adam and Eve. This confrontation between the dragon and the woman represents the vast cosmic confrontation of godliness and sin. God is about to reclaim his creation from the control of Satan. Satan knows this and stations himself to prevent it from happening. He wants to stop it before it has a chance to get a foothold.

In more historical and concrete terms, this is a vision of the attempt of the devil to destroy Jesus by having him rejected by men, crucified and buried.

> *She gave birth to a son, a male child, who will rule all the nations with an iron scepter. And her child was snatched up to God and to his throne.*

This is the birth of Jesus seen in universal dimension. It is not only Mary who gives birth to a son; it is Israel as a nation, as well as humanity as a whole and the earth itself. This son is destined to rule all nations; in time all humanity will serve him willingly and well. The iron scepter is a symbol of royal authority. The destiny of the human race is to bring itself entirely and voluntarily under the gospel of Jesus Christ, thus attaining the goal intended by God from the beginning of creation.

The "child was snatched up to God." This refers to the perfect obedience of Jesus to his Father in heaven, uncontaminated morally and spiritually by Satan, an obedience rewarded by ascension into heaven and to the throne of God. The dragon, waiting ravenously to devour Jesus, fails because God protects him and keeps him faithful to the end. Jesus refuses to yield to temptation and sin; he chooses to obey God rather than the devil.

> *The woman fled into the desert to a place prepared for her by God, where she might be taken care of for 1,260 days.*

The son is caught up to heaven, and the mother finds safety in a desert oasis prepared by God.

The "1,260 days" (three and one-half years) have appeared in John's visions before (11:2-3) and will appear again (13:5). The figure is a symbolic representation of the remainder of human history, of the time until the gospel achieves its final purpose. The woman — understood in broad perspective as the people created and redeemed by God — will survive under the protection of God. The desert usually symbolizes hardship and death, but there are oases in it, so even if the woman must flee into the desert, it is nonetheless into an oasis of God's love and care. The people of John's churches may see themselves in this image. They live in an environment that is spiritually hostile, but even so they find a hospitable home, an oasis, in the love and care of God. So may all Christians find an oasis in the Lord Jesus, even though the satanic hostility with which we live may not be as obvious among us as it is in this vision.

War in Heaven

And there was war in heaven. Michael and his angels fought against the dragon, and the dragon and his angels fought back. But he was not strong enough, and they lost their place in heaven. The great dragon was hurled down — that ancient serpent called the devil, or Satan, who leads the whole world astray. He was hurled to the earth, and his angels with him.

Then I heard a loud voice in heaven say: "Now have come the salvation and the power and the kingdom of our God, and the authority of his Christ. For the accuser of our brothers, who accuses them before our God day and night, has been hurled down. They overcame him by the blood of the Lamb and by the word of their testimony; they did not love their lives so much as to shrink from death. Therefore rejoice, you heavens and you who dwell in them! But woe to the earth and the sea, because the devil has gone down to you! He is filled with fury, because he knows that his time is short."

When the dragon saw that he had been hurled to the earth, he pursued the woman who had given birth to the male child. The woman was given the two wings of a great eagle, so that she might fly to the place prepared for her in the desert, where she would be taken care of for a time, times and half a time, out of the serpent's reach. Then from his mouth the serpent spewed water like a river, to overtake the woman and sweep her away with the torrent. But the earth helped the woman by opening its mouth and swallowing the river that the dragon had spewed out of his mouth. (12:7-16)

. . . .

. . . war in heaven.

The combatants are Michael and his angels on one side and the great red dragon and his angels on the other. The location of this war, "heaven," is not somewhere off in space or in some nebulous unknown spot outside our experience. It is the warfare we all see every day between Christianity and its opponents. This war is not merely a war behind the scenes of history, it is specifically the conflict demonstrated continually within history.

The policies that control the affairs of any given government — greed, aggression, self-interest, military conquest, or humanitarian respect, cooperation, and peace — or the philosophies that control economic endeavor, educational goals, scientific research, technological utilization, and social practices are either godly or devilish. Either they enhance the welfare of the human race or they do not. That is the war seen by John in heaven, a battle whose lines are exposed, clarified, and defined precisely by the ministry of Jesus.

The great dragon was hurled down — that ancient serpent called the devil, or Satan, who leads the whole world astray.

This expulsion of Satan from heaven to earth is the antithesis of the ascension of Jesus to heaven. Satan had won the battle in the Garden of Eden as demonstrated in Adam and Eve, thereby ascending to a position of great power as controller over human life. Now he is cast out of that place he usurped at the beginning, cast out by the resurrection, ascension, and session of Jesus Christ. He no longer leads the whole world astray as he had done before Christ.

He was "hurled down" to earth. Satan is no longer in control — he is no longer in the position of victorious dominance (heaven) but is in the position of frustrated spoiler (earth).

129

"Now have come the salvation and the power and the kingdom of our God, and the authority of his Christ."

There is a dual reference here, first to the kingdom of God and then to the authority of Christ. It is a repetition of the voice described at the very beginning of this vision: "The kingdom of the world has become the kingdom of our Lord and of his Christ, and he will reign for ever and ever" (11:15). Do not casually equate God and Jesus. Do not transfer the attributes and qualities of God to the man Jesus. God and man are always two distinct and separate entities, even though we must see God functioning within the man.

Although Satan had usurped some control over the fortunes of the human race through the fall of Adam and Eve, this did not invalidate the creative authority of God. God created the world to function according to the laws he inserted within nature. Satan's control over mankind does not cancel these natural laws.

In similar fashion, God created moral law within the very constitution of humanity. When Satan persuaded Adam and Eve to violate this internal moral law, he did not thereby eradicate that law from human nature or cancel its jurisdiction. Satan obscured it. He spoiled it, corrupted it, poisoned it, polluted it, and in all respects ruined it. The result, since the Adamic beginning, is that God's moral law within each human being does not control the actual choices made, either by Adam and Eve or by the rest of the human race ever since. God's kingdom, even though not loved, embraced, or obeyed by people in actual life, remains, in this sense, real and definitive.

Into this world God sends Jesus. This man Jesus, God's only-begotten son, reverses Adam's choice; he obeys God rather than Satan. Jesus responds faithfully and truthfully to the moral law planted in all humans by his Father in heaven. Jesus lives the way God intended Adam and Eve to live. Jesus is the human being God intended in creation; he is man par excellence, the epitome of the human race, and the paradigm for all people everywhere. To use Paul's language, Jesus is the second man, the last Adam (1 Cor. 15:45-49).

The authority of Christ, the kingdom of Christ, has now come. But this kingdom must be seen as identical with the kingdom of God, which, though temporarily obscured by sin, is now resuming its rightful place in the life of Jesus and of his followers. What John sees is the kingdom of

God demonstrated in the kingdom of Jesus. It is "the kingdom of our God" that has become evident and real through "the authority of his Christ."

> *"For the accuser of our brothers, who accuses them before our God day and night, has been hurled down."*

The accuser of the brethren — an interesting name to give the devil! The devil is not only the adversary, not only the destroyer, not only the spoiler, but now also the accuser. The devil accuses Christians before the throne of God.

Visualize a court of law. The devil is the prosecuting attorney; God is the judge. He accuses us of the very things he has succeeded in persuading us to do! "Look how sinful these people are. They call themselves Christians, children of God, but look what they do. They are far from being what you, God, want them to be. Punish them. Make life hard for them. Have no mercy. They don't deserve anything good or pleasant."

But even worse, the accusations reverberate in our own consciences. The devil keeps reminding us of the willful, vicious, and wicked things we have done, and perhaps continue to do. "And you call yourself a Christian? God is ashamed of you. You're no good. Stop pretending you are a child of God and just abandon yourself to the wickedness which you know full well is in you."

This is one of the tactics the devil employs in the great battle he is waging against God and against his Christ. He wants to undermine our faith and thereby diminish the authority and kingdom of Christ. But this accuser has been hurled down from heaven; God pays no attention to him.

> *"They overcame him by the blood of the Lamb . . ."*

Christians can cope with this "by the blood of the Lamb." That is how they conquer. The blood of Jesus serves as the defense attorney, counteracting the accusations of the prosecutor, the devil.

The "blood of the Lamb," of course, refers to the crucifixion of Jesus. The death of Jesus was caused by the sin of the people who crucified him; it was sinful to nail Jesus to the cross. Jesus died *for* us, but he also died *because* of us. We sinfully put him to death. We are responsible for that godless deed.

131

But Jesus also died vicariously. He died *for* us also in the sense that he died *instead* of us. Our sins deserve punishment, but he accepted that punishment *for* us, *instead* of us. When we see this and believe it, we are dismayed that we have been responsible for crucifying the Christ of God. We are sorry for it and at the same time we learn something about ourselves, about our mentality, and about our orientation to life and to God, something that shows us the depth of human depravity even in ourselves. We repent and God assures us that he loves us and forgives us. We then respond in faith, following Jesus as our Lord and Savior. That is how the "blood of the Lamb" works.

Jesus' death is vicarious: he is our substitute. "With his stripes we are healed" (Isa. 53:5 RSV). We overcome the accusations of the devil, the prosecutor, because we know and believe that our guilt, though real, is forgiven by Jesus Christ, our Savior and Lord. We do not allow the accusations of Satan to undermine our faith and plunge us back into wickedness. We overcome through "the blood of the Lamb." This is how God the Father establishes his kingdom through the ministry of Jesus Christ.

> *"Therefore rejoice, you heavens and you who dwell in them! But woe to the earth and the sea, because the devil has gone down to you! He is filled with fury, because he knows that his time is short."*

What is the opposite of *heaven*? Most people would say *hell*. But John uses "the earth and the sea" as the opposite of *heaven*. Remember that the entire book of Revelation is symbolic and visionary, and ordinary language usages are not always what we expect.

Here John is talking about the contrast between where the Lamb of God reigns (Michael and his angels) and where the great red dragon reigns. John is describing the results of the death, resurrection, and ascension of Jesus. Jesus is casting Satan out of the domain in which he had been dominant. Beginning with the fall of Adam and Eve Satan had exercised dominance over human history. The coming of Jesus now changes this. Jesus ascends into that place of dominance and Satan is cast out. Jesus now controls human life. Destiny is no longer in the hands of evil, but in the hands of Christ. The Lamb who is a Lion has taken over the kingship of this world.

> *". . . his time is short."*

His time is not short as humans think of shortness, but short in the sense that his time of unchallenged control has been ended and that progressively his influence in human life and history will diminish, until at last it will be entirely eliminated. His eventual doom has been guaranteed. Through the gospel of Christ the power of good will gradually saturate human life, displacing the powers of evil, which have hitherto governed it. The dragon's time is short in the sense that in time his control will decrease to the vanishing point.

> *When the dragon saw that he had been hurled to the earth, he pursued the woman who had given birth to the male child.*

When the dragon discovers that he has lost the battle with Michael and the angels (i.e., that he failed to destroy Jesus), he pursues the woman, the mother.

The major thrust of this analogy is to Israel, seen as the mother of Jesus since Jesus is Israel's Messiah. This is the main intent, because the vision later distinguishes between "the woman" herself and "the rest of her offspring" (12:17). "The rest of her offspring" refers to all Christians. The vision suggests that the dragon first seeks to destroy the Jewish religion and then, after he is frustrated in this attempt, turns his destructive attention to Christianity.

During the first century A.D. the Roman authorities did not clearly distinguish Christianity from Judaism. Most early Christians were Jews, and the followers of Christ were regarded as a sect of Judaism. In time the majority of Christians came to be non-Jews, and it became clear that Christianity, though derived from Judaism, was not merely a branch of Judaism. Perhaps this is John's meaning when he says the dragon first attempted to destroy the woman and later turned his attention to the rest of her offspring. If so, then the attack on the "woman" would be anti-Semitism in all its hideous forms, whereas the attack on the "rest of the offspring" would be anti-Christianity also in all its menacing forms.

> *The woman was given the two wings of a great eagle, so that she might fly to the place prepared for her in the desert, where she would be taken care of for a time, times and half a time, out of the serpent's reach. Then from his mouth the serpent spewed water like a river, to overtake the woman and sweep her away with the torrent. But the earth helped the woman by*

133

opening its mouth and swallowing the river that the dragon had spewed out of his mouth.

The woman flies like an eagle to an oasis in the desert. The dragon sends a river of water to flood her out. But the dry desert absorbs the river and thus protects the woman.

The woman represents Judaism, and this is a picture of Judaism in post-Jesus history. Godless forces continually seek to destroy the Jewish people in irrational outbursts of anti-Semitic frenzy, but somehow they are protected in spite of it all, protected from destruction.

Actually, in terms of Western history, the oasis in which Judaism is protected is Christian civilization. There are constant anti-Semitic drives that originate within Christian culture, but they are also put down and opposed by that same culture. The Jewish faith has contributed nobly to that very culture of Christianity, becoming an essential part of its continuing virility.

The central focus of the dragon's fury is transferred away from Judaism to Christianity, which implies that the spear-point of God's work is now to be found in Christianity and not in Judaism, a perspective which John's vision shows us next.

The Dragon Makes War against Her Offspring

Then the dragon was enraged at the woman and went off to make war against the rest of her offspring — those who obey God's commandments and hold to the testimony of Jesus. And the dragon stood on the shore of the sea.

And I saw a beast coming out of the sea. He had ten horns and seven heads, with ten crowns on his horns, and on each head a blasphemous name. The beast I saw resembled a leopard, but had feet like those of a bear and a mouth like that of a lion. The dragon gave the beast his power and his throne and great authority. One of the heads of the beast seemed to have had a fatal wound, but the fatal wound had been healed. The whole world was astonished and followed the beast. Men worshiped the dragon because he had given authority to the beast, and they also worshiped the beast and asked, "Who is like the beast? Who can make war against him?"

The beast was given a mouth to utter proud words and blasphemies and to exercise his authority for forty-two months. He opened his mouth to blaspheme God, and to slander his name and his dwelling place and those who live in heaven. He was given power to make war against the saints and to conquer them. And he was given authority over every tribe, people, language and nation. All inhabitants of the earth will worship the beast — all whose names have not been written in the book of life belonging to the Lamb that was slain from the creation of the world.

He who has an ear, let him hear. If anyone is to go into captivity, into captivity he will go. If anyone is to be killed with the sword, with the sword he will be killed. This calls for patient endurance and faithfulness on the part of the saints.

Then I saw another beast, coming out of the earth. He had two horns like a lamb, but he spoke like a dragon. He exercised all the authority of the first beast on his behalf, and made the earth and its inhabitants worship the first beast, whose fatal wound had been healed. And he performed great and miraculous signs, even causing fire to come down from heaven to earth in full view of men. Because of the signs he was given power to do on behalf of the first beast, he deceived the inhabitants of the earth. He ordered them to set up an image in honor of the beast who was wounded by the sword and yet lived. He was given power to give breath to the image of the first beast, so that it could speak and cause all who refused to worship the image to be killed. He also forced everyone, small and great, rich and poor, free and slave, to receive a mark on his right hand or on his forehead, so that no one could buy or sell unless he had the mark, which is the name of the beast or the number of his name.

This calls for wisdom. If anyone has insight, let him calculate the number of the beast, for it is man's number. His number is 666. (12:17–13:18)

. . . .

Having failed in his war against Judaism (the woman), the dragon now makes war against Christianity (the rest of her offspring). The dragon employs two generals to conduct this campaign against the church: two unnatural beasts.

One beast, emerging out of the ocean, represents flagrant and open opposition; the other, coming out of the land, represents subtle and deceptive error. The first is the anti-Christian campaign waged by forceful and violent opposition, the second is the campaign waged with the tools of deception, ridicule, false philosophy, and unbelieving doubt. Enemies of the gospel are not only blatantly obvious, but also function godlessly and are hidden within the community of Christians. Christians must therefore wage intellectual, moral, and spiritual war against both these enemies, perceiving that anti-Christian forces may not always be open and obvious, but can be subtle and deceptive.

> . . . the rest of her offspring — those who obey God's commandments and hold to the testimony of Jesus.

"Her offspring" are identified by two qualifications: obedience to God and belief in Jesus. These should not be taken as two separate and parallel attributes. The phraseology describes people who come to a genuine obedience to God the creator by means of knowing and believing Jesus. Contrast this with the Jews of Jesus' day who insisted vociferously that they were the children of God, obeying the Torah faithfully and conscientiously, but who nonetheless clamored for the death of God's Son Jesus. Theirs was obedience without faith, and consequently was shown ultimately to be no obedience at all. On the other hand, faith in Jesus does and must result in obedience to God. One cannot claim to be a Christian without demonstrating in one's life that God is truly in control. Obedience to God and faith in Jesus go together. Both are important.

The First Beast

> And I saw a beast coming out of the sea. . . . The dragon gave the beast his power and his throne and great authority.

The dragon stands on the beach and summons up a grotesque creature out of the sea. "The sea" here refers to undifferentiated humanity, the human race as a whole without regard to any internal differences. Sometimes the sea may be peaceful, quiet, and calm. At other times it may be violent, restless, threatening, and stormy.

Now John sees, emerging out of the sea of humanity, a beast representing a great and powerful energy at work within the civilization of men. It is the incarnation of godlessness within human political and social structures, perpetuating the same destructive power as that depicted in Genesis 3. The serpent of Genesis 3 has become the great red dragon of Revelation 12, which in turn becomes the dreadful beast of the sea depicted in Revelation 13. It is the satanic, demonic, devilish power that flaunts its godlessness openly in defiant opposition to the gospel, to the church, to Christ, and to his Spirit.

John himself was feeling the effect of this beast in his banishment on the island of Patmos. In later centuries Christians would feel it much more severely in the great persecutions under such emperors as Decius and Diocletian. But wherever there is open and explicit opposition to Christ, there you see this beast from the sea at work.

> *He had ten horns and seven heads, with ten crowns on his horns, and on each head a blasphemous name. The beast I saw resembled a leopard, but had feet like those of a bear and a mouth like that of a lion.*

This may well be an allusion to Daniel 7, where four terrible beasts emerge one after another to terrify Israel: a lion, a bear, a leopard, and a nondescript monster. Here in John's vision these four monsters are combined into one, but with essentially the same meaning. This domineering beast has an appearance so threatening that Christians cower in fear before it. Who can resist, much less overcome, this unearthly brute?

> *"Who is like the beast? Who can make war against him?"*

Christians can easily become defeatist when thinking about the enormous power of godlessness in the structures of human culture and civilization. How could the ancient Christians make any real difference in the godless power exerted by Nero and Domitian and the other Roman emperors? How could they inject true godly life into the world when it was so totally dominated by idolatry, military control, coercion, slavery, and sheer godless power? How can Christians make a real difference in cultures like those of Islam, or Buddhism, or Hinduism, or primitive religions? How could sincere Christians resist the godless onslaught of Hitler and his Nazis prior to and during World War II? How do you go about making a government truly Christian? The odds against it seem so tremendous and impossible. Who can make war against this beast from the sea?

> And he was given authority over every tribe, people, language and nation. All inhabitants of the earth will worship the beast — all whose names have not been written in the book of life belonging to the Lamb that was slain from the creation of the world.

This authority is the same as that gained by the serpent in the Garden of Eden: the authority of wickedness, of godlessness. When Adam and Eve made their fatal decision, they committed the human race to a course of godlessness. Adam and Eve together are symbols of what the human race as a whole is like. "All inhabitants of the earth will worship the beast" in exactly the same sense that all humans are symbolized by Adam and Eve.

But this vision of John is now a Christian revelation. It adds a profound dimension to the understanding of Adam and Eve in the fall. It shows now that Jesus, the second man, the last Adam, reverses the fateful decision of Adam and Eve. Consequently all who believe in Jesus, all those whose names have been written in the Lamb's "book of life," escape this beastly demonic control. In Genesis terminology, they now eat of "the tree of life" (Gen. 3:22). The names written in the "book of life" are the same as those who eat of "the tree of life." They are those who through faith in the Savior Jesus Christ escape the clutches of sin and the dragon and the beast, and are therefore drawn into life as it was meant to be from the beginning.

That is the significance of the otherwise curious expression "from the creation of the world." Don't get confused by wondering how Jesus could have been crucified before the world was created. Understand simply that God's intention from the very beginning of human history was that the human race would develop into his intended pattern through the ministry of Jesus Christ. This is the way God planned it from the beginning. The human race must learn that the ways of violence, cruelty, power, disrespect, and sin do not produce life at its best. Jesus shows a better way. And not only does he show it, but he is the doorway into it. That was how God planned it from the beginning, "from the creation of the world."

> *He who has an ear, let him hear. If anyone is to go into captivity, into captivity he will go. If anyone is to be killed with the sword, with the sword he will be killed. This calls for patient endurance and faithfulness on the part of the saints.*

Christians must understand that being a godly person does not exempt them from the consequences of living in a hostile environment. In fact, being a Christian may exacerbate the problem. If Christians live by godly standards in a society that lives by godless standards, they will be noticed. They will be shunned, despised, discriminated against, even ostracized, and in many ways made to suffer for their beliefs. Followers of Christ may even be sent into exile, as John himself was, or killed with the sword, as thousands of Christians were later to discover. If you live for Christ, your property may be confiscated and you may be ostracized from society. These things may happen. Yet, in Christ you must be faithful and endure patiently. Being a Christian in a hostile environment is not easy, but it is the only way to eternal life.

The Second Beast

> *Then I saw another beast, coming out of the earth. He had two horns like a lamb, but he spoke like a dragon.*

The clue to the identity of this beast is the contrast between lamb and dragon. In some respects this beast resembles a lamb, very different from the beast of the sea. Jesus is the Lamb of God. This beast disguises himself with lamblike camouflage, imitating or impersonating Jesus, presenting himself as a counterfeit Jesus, one who brings an alternate way of salvation to people. But the net outcome of his speech is thoroughly demonic.

> *He exercised all the authority of the first beast on his behalf, and made the earth and its inhabitants worship the first beast . . .*

139

This counterfeit lamb functions in such a way that what he achieves is identical with what the first gross beast achieves. Both work against Christ and the gospel, one by blatant ridicule, open opposition, and violent persecution, the other by subtle deceit, false philosophy, and personality cults. The result is the same because people, if they succumb, are drawn deeper into the clutches of sin and evil. In John's terms, they are drawn into the delusions of the great red dragon that is the ancient serpent, Satan, the devil.

> *Because of the signs he was given power to do on behalf of the first beast, he deceived the inhabitants of the earth.*

If we examine the history of the world since the time of Jesus, we can find many illustrations of this insight. This subtle anti-Christian lamb has deceived the "inhabitants of the earth."

Perhaps the most widespread of these delusions is Islam. Islam presents an alternative way of salvation that has drawn millions of people into its web. This is not to say, of course, that everything in Islam is wrong. The commitment to one God, Allah, is of course very necessary. However, the parallel insistence that Muhammad is his prophet, from the point of view of John's vision, is the subtle pretense of a savior who is not God's Christ. A commitment like this, in spite of whatever benefits it might produce, does not result in the welfare of the human race that Christ Jesus brings as his salvation.

The same perspective is true for the hundreds of smaller sects and cults that claim to bring better life to people but only force them deeper into delusion. If they do not honor Jesus as the only Lord and Savior, sent by God to bring life to the world, then all of their attractions will ultimately fade away into failure. There always seems to be some great attractiveness, what John calls "signs," which persuades people to ally themselves with such movements. If such signs do not point unconditionally and unequivocally to Jesus, then we may be sure that this is the second beast from the earth at work.

There are also nonreligious examples of this second beast. In the twentieth century the two most glaring examples are Nazism and communism. Neither was based on the authority of Jesus Christ, and both caught up millions of people into their webs of deceit and falsehood. Both emerged out of countries that have had the gospel in their history for centuries.

Both presented to people the ideal of great prosperity, of righting the wrongs of human society. Both killed people by the millions in order to enforce their authority. And both resulted in abject and total failure. They demonstrate the way the second beast works: deceive people into thinking this is a better gospel by which to live and find prosperity and life.

> *He ordered them to set up an image in honor of the beast who was wounded by the sword and yet lived. He was given power to give breath to the image of the first beast, so that it could speak and cause all who refused to worship the image to be killed.*

This is one of the tactics this second beast employs. He sets up an image to the first beast, making it seem to come alive. This image is symbolic of some sort of organization. Again, look at Islam. It has become a highly organized and structured religion. And, for all their seeming informality, personality cults also have required commitments and patterns of behavior. Not just anyone can become a member of a religious cult. Members must agree to rules; they must make some kind of commitment, oath, or promise and then agree to live accordingly. This image comes alive, usually with the founder's charisma, and dominates the members' lives, sometimes even to the point of group suicide. Anyone who is a member but who turns against the movement is subject to exclusion, ostracism, and rejection. This is what John is seeing here.

> *He also forced everyone, small and great, rich and poor, free and slave, to receive a mark on his right hand or on his forehead, so that no one could buy or sell unless he had the mark, which is the name of the beast or the number of his name.*

The mark of the beast is symbolic, not a literal mark on your hand or head. But some kind of identification is made which certifies that a person is a member of a particular group and is entitled to the privileges and responsibilities associated with it. The picture is of an organization, either large or small, which exercises complete domination over its members, requiring total and complete subjection of the individual to the organization.

For example, the word *Islam* means "subjection," and even though this subjection is intended to be toward God (Allah), for all practical purposes it is to the doctrine and practices of the religion itself. Similarly, in communism and Nazism any person whose commitment to the movement was uncertain was soon in danger of elimination. Members had to be totally committed or they might actually be killed.

> *This calls for wisdom. If anyone has insight, let him calculate the number of the beast, for it is man's number. His number is 666.*

Do not misunderstand this number, 666; it is a symbol, just like the other number symbols in the book. Soon we will see the number 144,000. We have had several sevens and twelves. Three and a half years has appeared repeatedly. A thousand years will come up in chapter 20. These are all symbolic numbers, none to be taken literally.

Gematria is the practice of assigning a numerical value to each letter of a name, adding up the totals, and getting a number that is supposed to be significant. Followers of this believe that if you find a name that adds up to 666, you have discovered the antichrist. These numbers are just symbolic. Whatever process John had in mind, his meaning is no longer apparent to us today.

The number six is one less than seven. If seven were the symbol of perfect, complete goodness, then one less than that would be the symbol of imperfect, incomplete, partial goodness. It falls short of perfection. Do this three times, make three sixes, and the result is still the same. Three sixes still do not result in completion, in perfection. Seven, or 777, is a symbol of finality. No matter how many sixes you iterate, you will never get to seven.

Soviet communism promised utopia, but it did not produce it. Nazism anticipated the thousand-year Reich, but it did not achieve it. Islam strives for a progress, culture, and hope that it is unable to attain. The results of 666 do not reflect the wholeness and perfection of 777 that they hold out as a lure. If 666 is the number of the beast, the number of Christ would be 777.

The 144,000

Then I looked, and there before me was the Lamb, standing on Mount Zion, and with him 144,000 who had his name and his

Father's name written on their foreheads. And I heard a sound from heaven like the roar of rushing waters and like a loud peal of thunder. The sound I heard was like that of harpists playing their harps. And they sang a new song before the throne and before the four living creatures and the elders. No one could learn the song except the 144,000 who had been redeemed from the earth. These are those who did not defile themselves with women, for they kept themselves pure. They follow the Lamb wherever he goes. They were purchased from among men and offered as firstfruits to God and the Lamb. No lie was found in their mouths; they are blameless. (14:1-5)

.   .   .   .

. . . the Lamb, standing on Mount Zion, and with him 144,000 who had his name and his Father's name written on their foreheads.

This is all symbolism: the Lamb, Mount Zion, 144,000, foreheads. The Lamb of course represents Jesus and is a well-known metaphor. The literal Mount Zion is the highest of the hills on which the city of Jerusalem is built, and is often used as a symbol of the city itself or of its temple. The number 144,000 has been used by John previously (7:4) and represents all those who seek to obey God. The two names — the Lamb and the Father — signify ownership, as of slaves who may be branded somehow with the name of the master.

John now sees Jesus with 144,000 people standing on the highest hill in Jerusalem. He sees them protected from the onslaughts of the dragon and his two generals, the beasts from the sea and the earth. The dragon tried to destroy Jesus while on earth but failed. He tried to destroy the woman, Israel, but failed. He continues to try to destroy the rest of the woman's offspring, but fails again. John sees these people, the rest of the offspring (12:17), in the symbolic number of completion, safe with Jesus behind the walls of the city of God and of the Lamb.

The vision is designed to encourage the Christian people who read it. The monsters of hatred, persecution, discrimination, deceptive philosophy, and terrifying power may hound them. They may feel helpless in the face of insurmountable odds against the gospel and the church. But Jesus, through this vision given to John, wants them to take heart. What

143

seems impossible to us on earth is surely not impossible for God in heaven. Christ's people must remain faithful whatever the difficulties, trusting that the Lord will, in his own time and in his own way, use even that faithfulness to accomplish his purposes in the world. Those who trust in him are safe from the inhuman ravages of the dragon and his beasts. Stand with Jesus where he is, persevere in faithfulness; God will take care of the rest.

> *The sound I heard was like that of harpists playing their harps. And they sang a new song before the throne and before the four living creatures and the elders. No one could learn the song except the 144,000 who had been redeemed from the earth.*

In John's vision the 144,000 people are singing, and their singing resembles the sounds of a zither, a harp. They are the only ones on earth who are singing, because their song is the song of the redeemed.

All Christians — those now living, those who have lived in the past, and those who will live in the future — are singing in a vast choir scattered throughout the earth (but standing safe with Jesus where he is). Hear them as their very presence and witness in the world rises before the throne of God as a triumphant song of praise and a mighty doxology to the almighty Creator of the universe.

> *These are those who did not defile themselves with women, for they kept themselves pure. They follow the Lamb wherever he goes. They were purchased from among men and offered as firstfruits to God and the Lamb. No lie was found in their mouths; they are blameless.*

John describes these 144,000 people more closely. He gives four characteristics.

1. They did not defile themselves with women. Do not take this literally. Half of these people are women themselves. The metaphor is taken, very likely, from the custom of males in Greco-Roman society to worship their goddesses vicariously by visiting sacred prostitutes in the temple. The reference is not to the act of sexual union itself, but to the idolatry the pagan custom presupposes. The 144,000 therefore do not defile themselves with the rites of paganism. They are not idolaters.

2. They follow the Lamb. The way that Jesus lived on earth demon-

strates the way all Christians should live. He was faithful, without sin. He did what God wanted him to do, even when it led to hatred, enmity, and even death. But then he rose from the dead and ascended into heaven.

This life of Jesus, John now wants the people of his churches to see, is the paradigm of the life of every Christian. Jesus has led the way through life with all its problems and difficulties; he wants us all to follow him in his footsteps. The 144,000 are those people who follow him faithfully to the end, wherever faith in Jesus may lead them.

3. They are the firstfruits offered to God. The reference is to the old covenant law that required Israelites to bring the first samples of their harvest to the priests in the sanctuary. The symbolism now in John's vision is that of Jesus presenting to God the firstfruits of the harvest he is gathering. The 144,000 are this offering to God. If you wish to emphasize that where there is an offering of firstfruits there is also a later full harvest, then regard the 144,000 as those Christians living at John's day and the full harvest as those to be gathered in later generations. But do not make too much of this, since all are included in the numerical symbol of 144,000.

4. No lie is found in their mouths. Apart from Jesus, anyone who has ever lived has told a lie. Again, attend to the symbolism. They do not live a lie. They do not say they follow the Lamb when in fact they follow the beasts. They do not hypocritically claim to be Christians while living in such a way as to contradict their boasts. The 144,000 are those who not only profess Christ as Savior and Lord but also demonstrate this faith in their lifestyle.

Three Gospel Angels

Then I saw another angel flying in midair, and he had the eternal gospel to proclaim to those who live on the earth — to every nation, tribe, language and people. He said in a loud voice, "Fear God and give him glory, because the hour of his judgment has come. Worship him who made the heavens, the earth, the sea and the springs of water."

A second angel followed and said, "Fallen! Fallen is Babylon the Great, which made all the nations drink the maddening wine of her adulteries."

A third angel followed them and said in a loud voice: "If anyone worships the beast and his image and receives his mark on the forehead or on the hand, he, too, will drink of the wine of God's fury, which has been poured full strength into the cup of his wrath. He will be tormented with burning sulfur in the presence of the holy angels and of the Lamb. And the smoke of their torment rises for ever and ever. There is no rest day or night for those who worship the beast and his image, or for anyone who receives the mark of his name." This calls for patient endurance on the part of the saints who obey God's commandments and remain faithful to Jesus.

Then I heard a voice from heaven say, "Write: Blessed are the dead who die in the Lord from now on."

"Yes," says the Spirit, "they will rest from their labor, for their deeds will follow them." (14:6-13)

· · · · · · · ·

The First Gospel Angel

... he had the eternal gospel to proclaim to those who live on the earth — to every nation, tribe, language and people.

John, on behalf of Jesus, reminds us again and again that the gospel is for the whole world, for "every nation, tribe, language and people." Do not overlook this or misinterpret it. There is universalism in the gospel. Not a universalism that says all individuals are saved, but rather a universalism which says not only that the gospel is proclaimed to all people but also that the very essence of being human is included in the gospel. The gospel is that message which assures every person on earth that this is the only way to become what God intended human beings to be.

There is yet another dimension to this universalism. Jesus wants us to understand that the gospel is the harbinger of a time when all peoples will come to the obedience that God desires. If Adam represents the entire human race in its fallen condition, then Jesus as the second Adam represents the entire human race in its saved condition. Not everyone in the world today obeys God fully, not everyone is saved from the delusions

146

of the dragon and his associates. But John wishes us to understand that the gospel will prevail, given time. Just as Jesus overcame the devil, so too the human race will overcome. The remaining visions in this book of Revelation will show this aspect of God's plan more fully.

> *"Fear God and give him glory, because the hour of his judgment has come. Worship him who made the heavens, the earth, the sea and the springs of water."*

This is the message brought by the first gospel angel. He warns the entire human race that the time of God's judgment has come. This is written in the past tense, *has come*. Sometimes we think of God's judgment only in terms of the final judgment, a judgment at the end of time. Here, however, John reminds us that God's judgment has already come. It has come in the person of Jesus.

God gave up his only-begotten Son into the hands of the devil, who persuaded evil people to crucify him. God judged, however, that this crucifixion was wrong, and reversed it by raising Jesus from the dead. That is God's judgment. God has demonstrated in this most enigmatic way that religious activities are wrong if they are aimed against Jesus, if they harm Jesus, or if they seek to dismiss him from life. This is God's judgment, and this is what the gospel proclaims to everyone. All people are called to worship him who made not only them but also the entire universe. Worship the Creator, and do it as Jesus, our example, did. The hour of God's judgment *has already come* in the life, death, and resurrection of Jesus.

The Second Gospel Angel

> *"Fallen! Fallen is Babylon the Great, which made all the nations drink the maddening wine of her adulteries."*

Earlier in his visions John described the great red dragon and the two monstrous beasts he summons to his aid. Here he uses the name of Babylon to signify the city into which the beasts and the dragon seduce their victims, just as the ancient Babylonians carried captive Jews into the city. Babylon is the symbolic opposite of Mount Zion, of Jerusalem. If the 144,000 are safe with Jesus on Mount Zion, then those who live in Babylon represent their enemies, those who oppose Christ, the gospel, and the church.

The second gospel angel announces that Babylon has fallen. The angel repeats it twice: "Fallen! Fallen . . ." The gospel is meant to assure us that the powers represented by this fearful city have indeed met their match, and more than their match, in Jesus. His resurrection is the announcement that the powers of evil have been overcome. Overcome first by Jesus, then by all who come to him in repentance and trust and obedience.

"The maddening wine of her adulteries" is an arresting figure of speech, associating as it does the concepts of intoxication and adultery. Perhaps John is building on an implication that excessive use of wine sometimes results in the practice of adultery, especially in pagan temples. He surely is suggesting powerfully that what happens in that wicked city of Babylon is akin to severe intoxication, which produces behavior akin to adultery — all of it unnatural, destructive of human life and happiness, opposed to the best interests of human society. The misshapen beasts and the unnatural dragon all produce similar offspring among humans, people who distort and twist and spoil that which is best and good among us.

In the context of both gospel angels' messages, understand that this city built upon spiritual intoxication and violation of God's law is fallen, no longer the dominant force in human civilization. The gospel has brought something better, and that gospel will gradually penetrate to all nations, languages, and peoples, bringing life and goodness and joy to all.

The Third Gospel Angel

> "If anyone worships the beast and his image and receives his mark on the forehead or on the hand, he, too, will drink of the wine of God's fury, which has been poured full strength into the cup of his wrath. . . . There is no rest day or night for those who worship the beast and his image, or for anyone who receives the mark of his name."

This describes the inhabitants of Babylon. They drink the wine of God's fury, and they have no rest day or night. These two descriptions are of the same thing. God's fury on them is precisely that they can find no happiness or contentment in the unnatural lifestyle they choose.

God's fury is exactly the same as what he demonstrated in the death and resurrection of Jesus. In Jesus' resurrection God demonstrated that the decision of people to crucify Jesus was in complete and total opposition to his will. His fury is directed against that decision, so consonant with the sinful commitment of Adam and his descendants.

In Jesus' resurrection God is saying to the entire human race, "Your commitment is wrong; change it." God gives us no real peace or happiness so long as we choose godlessness over godliness. And in case we try to deceive ourselves, God forces us to see the true dimensions of our commitment when we see that we have rejected God's Son Jesus and have put him to death. This entire event of Jesus' death and resurrection is the expression of God's fury, of his complete disapproval of our commitment, of our being deceived by the serpent that is also the great red dragon.

"He will be tormented with burning sulfur in the presence of the holy angels and of the Lamb. And the smoke of their torment rises for ever and ever."

In the Middle Ages hell was often presented as eternal torment, and this passage was taken as its expression. Taken literally, it offers a picture of Jesus and the angels watching as people burned with everlasting fire but without burning up or dying. It is a picture of total, complete, and endless misery — with Jesus gloating in heaven.

Such an understanding violates the picture we get from the Gospels where love is the decisive characteristic of Jesus. A loving Jesus would not gloat through endless eternity over the torment of sinners in burning sulfur. God takes no pleasure in the death of anyone (Ezek. 18:32); neither does Jesus.

John wants us to understand by this image exactly what he says in the context: no rest day or night for those who live unnaturally. There is no peace, no contentment, no joy, no love, and no happiness. Don't think of this as in the future, beyond the grave, or beyond the end of history. It is now, in the present. Think existentially, of what life for an unbeliever is like. Everyone has experienced how miserable life can be, how stressful and pressurized daily existence can be. Christians know that in spite of this they can find contentment, forgiveness, acceptance, and new per-

149

spectives on life. They can live with a genuine personal peace of heart and soul. This peace cannot be attained by anyone living against the grain of human nature, against the human nature that God created and which God has demonstrated infallibly in his Son Jesus.

In this third gospel angel's message, do not see Jesus gloating over the eternal anguish of people in eternal fire, but see him now as he watches from heaven as people continue to resist the gospel, suffering under the delusions they accept from the dragon and the beasts. Jesus is not gloating; he is anguishing over their tenacity in sin. He wants them to get out of Babylon, to recognize that Babylon's day is past, and to come stand on Mount Zion with him. He wants them to come out of that doomed city where life is so miserable, and come with him where life is good and pleasant and peaceful.

"And the smoke of their torment rises for ever and ever."

This is not intended to describe existence after death, but the way things are in this world all the time. As long as you stay in Babylon, the smoke of your torment will continue. This is the way things are in this world forever.

This calls for patient endurance on the part of the saints who obey God's commandments and remain faithful to Jesus.

John is writing to specific churches about the hour of judgment and the fall of Babylon and the constant restlessness of the people. He is telling them that if they perceive conditions in the light of the gospel, they need only be patient, to endure whatever adverse circumstances there may be, to obey God before all else, and to remain faithful to the Lord Jesus. One individual Christian cannot do much to change the course of history, to bring about the decline and fall of the Roman Empire, to end the authority of organized godlessness, or to countermand the terror of the Third Reich. God will bring about his will in his own time. It is only necessary for us is to believe, to continue faithful obedience to God, patiently trusting him to use whatever means he chooses to promote his kingdom.

Then I heard a voice from heaven say, "Write: Blessed are the dead who die in the Lord from now on."

> *"Yes," says the Spirit, "they will rest from their labor, for their deeds will follow them."*

Remain faithful, John is told to write, and be blessed. Even if we die under persecution or other forms of stress, we are blessed.

The Christians of Asia Minor to whom John is writing may have tried to live faithfully, and may not have seen any hope of happiness. Many died without ever getting to live a truly good and happy life. They were persecuted all the time.

Yet they were blessed because they died in the Lord, that is, in faithful obedience to him. And we will be blessed if we remain faithful throughout the struggles of life. John reminds them of two things: (1) once we die, our struggle is ended, and (2) our deeds follow us. After we are dead we no longer have to struggle against injustice, discrimination, and ostracism. And what we have done during our lifetime continues to bear fruit in the following generations. The sons and daughters who follow us will receive the benefit of having our example and our training. Our deeds will follow us in the lives of generations to come, as the second commandment of the Decalogue explained long before, "showing love to a thousand generations of those who love me and keep my commandments" (Exod. 20:6).

There is a cumulative effect of the witness of individual Christians in history. The more Christians there are in any given society, the more influence they will bring to bear on the structures of that society. That influence will, under the Spirit of God, be progressive — perhaps not always obvious to our finite insights, but in God's plan — so that the world will slowly be brought under the sway of Christ and away from the control of the devil. The book of Revelation wants to show us how this works. It does not all happen at once. It takes time, as much time as only God knows. But the faithful and patient obedience of each individual Christian is important. Their deeds will follow them in an ever increasing crescendo of victory for the Lamb who has been slain and is now the Lion of God.

The Dual Harvest of Earth

I looked, and there before me was a white cloud, and seated on the cloud was one "like a son of man" with a crown of gold on his head and a sharp sickle in his hand. Then another angel came out of the temple and called in a loud voice to him who was sitting on the cloud, "Take your sickle and reap, because the time to reap has come, for the harvest of the earth is ripe." So he who was seated on the cloud swung his sickle over the earth, and the earth was harvested.

Another angel came out of the temple in heaven, and he too had a sharp sickle. Still another angel, who had charge of the fire, came from the altar and called in a loud voice to him who had the sharp sickle, "Take your sharp sickle and gather the clusters of grapes from the earth's vine, because its grapes are ripe." The angel swung his sickle on the earth, gathered its grapes and threw them into the great winepress of God's wrath. They were trampled in the winepress outside the city, and blood flowed out of the press, rising as high as the horses' bridles for a distance of 1,600 stadia. (14:14-20)

. . . .

These two harvests are simultaneous. Two things are going on at the same time in human life and civilization: first, the gospel is drawing many people into the kingdom of God; and second, the powers of sin and evil in human life are being decimated and destroyed. This vision of the twin harvests is a panoramic sweep of the entirety of human history after the infusion of Christian faith. This is what is always happening. Christ is reaping the earth by means of the gospel, and consequently the powers of the devil are being pressed out in the winepress of God's wrath. They are two sides of the same process.

Harvest Time: Facet One

> . . . seated on the cloud was one "like a son of man" with a crown of gold on his head and a sharp sickle in his hand.

This is another metaphor by which to understand the impact of Jesus upon life in this world. Here Jesus is seen seated on a cloud with a sharp sickle in his hand. The cloud is likely a reference to the ascension of Jesus

152

into the clouds; what John sees is the ascended Lord and what he is doing now. The sickle or scythe is another way of seeing how Jesus is working from heaven within our world.

> *Then another angel came out of the temple and called in a loud voice to him who was sitting on the cloud, "Take your sickle and reap, because the time to reap has come, for the harvest of the earth is ripe."*

When this book of Revelation was written, only about sixty years had passed since the time of Jesus' ascension into the clouds. It was at that time that this harvest began. The two causal clauses form a typical Hebrew parallelism, both identical in meaning: "the time has come . . . the harvest is ripe," both referring to what the apostle Paul earlier called the fullness of the times (Gal. 4:4).

> *So he who was seated on the cloud swung his sickle over the earth, and the earth was harvested.*

It was an angel who came to Jesus on the cloud and conveyed the command to reap. Angels are messengers of God, and therefore what they say is a message from God. God is telling Jesus to reap the earth.

This command is built into the entire happening of Jesus' earthly ministry, now completed. The very fact of God sending his Son into the world is the command to prepare for the reaping of the harvest. It was by means of the sending of the Holy Spirit on the Day of Pentecost that Jesus obeyed this command. The Spirit of Jesus infused itself into the timid disciples and transformed them into dynamic representatives and witnesses of the Lord. As they did their work for the gospel, the harvest of the earth began.

Harvest Time: Facet Two

> *Another angel came out of the temple in heaven, and he too had a sharp sickle. Still another angel, who had charge of the fire, came from the altar and called in a loud voice to him who had the sharp sickle . . .*

This is the reverse side of the reaping of the earth that Jesus does. It also involves two persons, in this case two angels. One angel holds the sickle, as Jesus did in the primary facet, and the other issues the command from God. Both come from the temple in heaven, but the second one is the priest in charge of the fire on the altar of burnt offering.

In old covenant law the sacrifices that were consumed on the altar of burnt offering symbolized the forgiveness of sins. As the animal sacrifice is burnt completely, so too are the sins of the people forgiven completely. Something of this symbolism remains. Just as the animal is consumed on the altar, so too the evil within the human race is now to be consumed.

> . . . *"Take your sharp sickle and gather the clusters of grapes from the earth's vine, because its grapes are ripe." The angel swung his sickle on the earth, gathered its grapes and threw them into the great winepress of God's wrath.*

The imagery in John's vision is not of fire; it is of "the . . . winepress of God's wrath." The purpose of a winepress is to press the juice out of grapes, thus separating the valuable juice from the discarded pulp.

God's wrath is never against people as such, but against the sin that corrupts them. This is the other side of the gospel. In exact proportion as Jesus draws people into his kingdom, he is eliminating the domination of sin in their lives. Where righteousness lives, unrighteousness dies. Where Christ reigns, the dragon is unseated. Where obedience prevails, sin declines. Where Christ reaps his harvest, the grapes of God's wrath are also reaped.

> *They were trampled in the winepress outside the city, and blood flowed out of the press, rising as high as the horses' bridles for a distance of 1,600 stadia.*

"Outside the city" means outside the city of Mount Zion, mentioned earlier; it means exclusion. Lepers were banished from the city. All unwanted persons were sent away. Here the term suggests that what happens outside the city is outside the blessing of the gospel. God's blessing rests upon the holy city; his wrath is upon Babylon and all that is non-Jerusalem, that is, outside the city.

The grapes are trampled out and their juice runs like blood five feet deep for a distance of 180 miles, filling up the entire land of Palestine from north to south and east to west. Obviously this is figurative. John wishes us to visualize the entire land of Palestine covered by this flood of grape juice, and symbolically to visualize the entire earth purged of its sin. This is what the gospel and the Spirit will do — it will in time purge the entire earth of godlessness. John sees the entire panoramic sweep of human history after the time of Jesus in this dual vision of the reaping of the earth.

*   *   *

This ends the third major section of the book of Revelation, the seven trumpets. The first section, the seven letters, reminds us at the very beginning that John's visions are about real people in real churches in real history. This perspective suggests the basic interpretive clue for the entire series of visions: they are pastoral sermons intended to strengthen and encourage young churches to persevere in the faith.

The second section, the seven seals, encourages John's churches to read the signs of history in the light of the ministry of Jesus. They, and we, tend to read current events from our limited finite human standpoint. We are deeply involved in the give-and-take of making a living, surviving threatening circumstances, and solving immediate problems, so much so that we often become unable to see these same events from God's vantage point. The opening of these seals helps us rise out of the immediacy of our own little lives and gain a view of history that sees the risen Lord Jesus as the functional controller over all of history.

This third section, the seven trumpets, provides the perspective that conflict is inevitably generated wherever Christ challenges the control of Satan. Satan seeks to destroy Christ and his work, but fails. Christ seeks to destroy Satan and his work, and will succeed. The trumpets summon John's seven churches, as well as all churches, to do their part in this conflict, being patient and faithful in obedience, whatever the opposition.

Our world is the locale of this great conflict. The events of our history, at whatever point in time we may exist, all reflect in one way or another the great conflict between Christ and Satan. In it all, the resurrection and ascension of Jesus is the guarantee that ultimate success belongs to Christ. Satan has not conquered Jesus in the crucifixion; Jesus has conquered Satan in the resurrection. The implications of this victory are being worked out slowly, year by year, in the events that have occurred

155

and continue to occur ever since, in and through the actual churches of the Lord. History, after our Lord defeated Satan, is the progressive triumph of the gospel within the ongoing process of human culture.

Next is the fourth septet, the seven bowls, in which John will see the final battle and will envision its final results. Remember always that what John sees is thoroughly symbolic, providing perspective on actual human history, but not to be taken literally.

FOURTH SEPTET

The Seven Bowls

Revelation 15:1–22:7

Revelation 15 is a prelude to the action described in the remaining chapters. It sets the stage and provides the background for the angels who pour out seven bowls of God's wrath.

Interestingly, all seven bowls are poured out in quick succession, and all are described in chapter 16. In the previous sets, four seals were broken in quick succession, but the last three received more extensive explanation. The same is true for the trumpets: four are sounded in a group, and the last three are spaced farther apart. But here all seven bowls are poured out in one chapter.

The remaining chapters, 17 through 22, show the cumulative effect of all seven bowls. Each of the seven bowls affects some specific aspect of earth, but taken together they produce the final results described in the remaining chapters. They describe the action triggered by the pouring out of the seven bowls of God's wrath, as follows:

1. John sees a prostitute, representing Babylon, riding on a ferocious red beast. But the bowls of wrath have been poured out on Babylon, which means its authority has been ended.
2. John then sees the great multitude of Christ's servants in two relationships: first, as invitees to the wedding supper of the Lamb, and second, as soldiers following someone who rides a great white horse and engages the armies of the beast in battle.

3. Satan and his hosts lose the battle. Satan is bound and thrown into the abyss for a thousand years, after which he emerges to threaten again the city of the Lord.
4. Then, finally, the devil is thrown into the lake of fire — meaning total incapacitation — and only peace and joy and happiness remain for the followers of the Lamb.

This is the ultimate effect of the bowls of wrath. They are poured out on the forces of evil, destroying their influence over the affairs of human civilization. God's wrath is expended against all the powers of evil, leaving them not only frustrated but finally ineffective, so that shalom may prevail on earth and people may enjoy the perpetual benefit of life in a civilization which fully incarnates the image of God.

The picture, remember, is of the actual process of human life and civilization as time moves on from one year to the next. The book of Revelation gives us perspective on this process, assuring us that whatever shortfall we may be experiencing now, the future will be God's shalom accomplished by the ascended Lord Jesus. We must therefore learn to see our world in the light of this gospel. Christianity will ultimately prevail so that every knee will bow, every tongue will confess that Jesus Christ is Lord. The nations on earth will be healed. The kingdoms of this world will have become the kingdoms of our God and of his Christ.

CHAPTER 10

Seven Golden Bowls

Revelation 15–16

Prelude to the Bowls of Wrath

I saw in heaven another great and marvelous sign: seven angels with the seven last plagues — last, because with them God's wrath is completed. And I saw what looked like a sea of glass mixed with fire and, standing beside the sea, those who had been victorious over the beast and his image and over the number of his name. They held harps given them by God and sang the song of Moses the servant of God and the song of the Lamb: "Great and marvelous are your deeds, Lord God Almighty. Just and true are your ways, King of the ages. Who will not fear you, O Lord, and bring glory to your name? For you alone are holy. All nations will come and worship before you, for your righteous acts have been revealed."

After this I looked and in heaven the temple, that is, the tabernacle of Testimony, was opened. Out of the temple came the seven angels with the seven plagues. They were dressed in clean, shining linen and wore golden sashes around their chests. Then one of the four living creatures gave to the seven angels seven golden bowls filled with the wrath of God, who lives for ever and ever. And the temple was filled with smoke from the glory of God and from his power, and no one could enter the temple until the seven plagues of the seven angels were completed. (Rev. 15)

.   .   .   .

. . . seven angels with the seven last plagues — last, because with them God's wrath is completed.

With this fourth section of the book of Revelation we come to the visions which not only conclude this book but picture for us the processes which produce the ultimate goal (telos) of human history. The Bible describes it as the "completed wrath of God."

John has written elsewhere, "God is love" (1 John 4:16). Can the God of love also be the God of wrath?

Love is not to be understood as approval of everything that exists or happens. Love cannot approve of hate. Love cannot approve of that which destroys love. Love and hate are incompatible. God cannot approve of the devil, God cannot approve of godlessness, and God cannot approve of that which seeks to destroy God. The "wrath of God," therefore, is whatever God does to remove sin, evil, lovelessness, and godlessness from the world.

In more historical terms, God cannot approve of the crucifixion of Jesus, which is the attempt of Satan to destroy God. God cannot allow this to succeed; he brings Jesus back to life again. The resurrection and ascension of Jesus is evidence of God's wrath upon the sin of humans. After Jesus' resurrection the eleven disciples, and many others, repented of their sins related to his crucifixion and began to live in faithful obedience to God because of their faith in Jesus. This is how God removed sin and godlessness from their lives. And this is how the wrath of God works.

In much the same way, the death and resurrection of Jesus is a synopsis of history as a whole. What we see here in the bowls of wrath is the same process as the death and resurrection of Jesus, but encompassing the entire human race as an entity. The death of humanity, pictured in Genesis 3, is now reversed as the gospel pervades the society of mankind, eventually resulting in the elimination of evil altogether.

John wants his churches in Asia Minor to see this development in process, and from his island retreat he wishes us also in our times to see the same development with two millennia of progress behind it.

The idea of plagues is reminiscent of the ten plagues sent by God through Moses upon Egypt at the time of the exodus (Exod. 7–11). There the purpose of the plagues was to persuade Pharaoh to let the Israelites leave Egypt. In a somewhat different dimension we may say those ten plagues were God's way of eliminating the evil of the slavery of his chosen people. Here in Revelation seven plagues are sent upon the enemies of God for the purpose of eliminating the evils enslaving all people.

And I saw what looked like a sea of glass mixed with fire . . .

The "sea of glass" was mentioned earlier in 4:6, where it was "clear as crystal." Here it is "mixed with fire."

In chapter 4 the sea of glass is situated before the throne of God, and would therefore represent the human race as God created it and will ultimately redeem it: clear as crystal, with no contamination whatever. In chapter 15 the sea of humanity is polluted by sin, but it is also the scene of purifying fire. Don't stumble over how fire and water can be mixed — these are symbols only. Actually, submitting sand to intense heat creates glass; perhaps John is visualizing this process as symbolic of what is happening to the human race. The fire of the gospel is turning the sand of our race into the glass that will ultimately become clear as crystal.

. . . standing beside the sea, those who had been victorious over the beast and his image and over the number of his name.

This could be reminiscent of the exodus story as well. Just as the liberated Israelites stood on the far shore of the Sea of Reeds, so too these victorious people emerge to stand beside the sea in triumph over the beast and his entanglements. While this is a prelude to the vision of the seven angels with their bowls of wrath, the symbolism also continues from the previous vision of the seven trumpets, namely, the beast that stood on the shore, his image, and the number 666. Chapter 15 is a transition vision to be connected both to the previous vision and to the next.

They held harps given them by God and sang the song of Moses the servant of God and the song of the Lamb: "Great and marvelous are your deeds, Lord God Almighty. Just and true are your ways, King of the ages. Who will not fear you, O Lord, and bring glory to your name? For you alone are holy. All nations will come and worship before you, for your righteous acts have been revealed."

These people are Christians, people whose lives continually celebrate victory over the beast. The music and singing is John's way of describing this celebration. People who know themselves to be redeemed by the blood of the Lamb and live peacefully and contentedly in that knowledge, they are the ones who are singing and playing harps. Christians know this now, already in this life — right here, right now, today — because they see what the resurrection and ascension of Jesus means for human life and destiny. An irresistible force has been introduced into the mainstream of human civilization, and this force will slowly but surely reduce its enemies to helplessness. As a gradual process to be completed far off into the future, we see all nations coming to worship God through the power of the gospel. We are able to see this because God has revealed his righteous acts in and through the career of Jesus Christ.

> *After this I looked and in heaven the temple, that is, the tabernacle of Testimony, was opened. Out of the temple came the seven angels with the seven plagues.*

John explains that the temple he sees is the "tabernacle of Testimony"; it is neither the temple of Solomon nor the second temple as refurbished by King Herod. John sees the old tabernacle, a tent of cloth that sheltered the two tables of the law after the time of Moses. Perhaps John is continuing his oblique references to the time of the exodus, this ancient tabernacle having been constructed shortly thereafter.

But John is very specific. The seven angels emerge out of this desert tabernacle. In the previous vision the mother of the child finds safety in the desert. Now from this desert and its shelter comes the final outpouring of God's wrath on everything that ruins, destroys, and corrupts his divine creation.

> *They were dressed in clean, shining linen and wore golden sashes around their chests. Then one of the four living creatures gave to the seven angels seven golden bowls filled with the wrath of God, who lives for ever and ever.*

The symbolism is of the priests and Levites in early Israelite history. These priests go about their duties in the tabernacle, offering burnt offerings and supervising the other rituals required in the law. Another divine agent intrudes suddenly into their rituals, giving each of the priests a golden bowl filled with burning incense, which they are to pour out as a sacrificial libation on the ground.

The function of these Old Testament priests in general is to supervise the rituals that symbolize the forgiveness of sin and the gratitude of those whose sin is forgiven. Now in John's vision of the seven bowls of God's wrath, the ultimate ritual is about to begin. Sin is not only to be forgiven, it is to be eradicated, its effectiveness destroyed forever.

> *And the temple was filled with smoke from the glory of God and from his power, and no one could enter the temple until the seven plagues of the seven angels were completed.*

The burning incense from these seven bowls fills the tabernacle with smoke. This smoke represents the glory and power of God. Just as the glory and the power of God overwhelm the tabernacle in John's vision, so too the entire world is saturated with the power of God.

The impossibility of anyone entering the tabernacle does not mean that no one can be saved. It means that we must let God do his work when, where, and how he chooses. We must never presume to tell God what to do. That is his territory. His glory and his power are enough for us to see, and we may live in that vision day after day and year after year.

Chapter 16 will show us what happens when the priests pour out their libations on the earth, that is, how God's wrath functions as it eliminates ungodliness.

The Seven Libations

Then I heard a loud voice from the temple saying to the seven angels, "Go, pour out the seven bowls of God's wrath on the earth."

The first angel went and poured out his bowl on the land, and ugly and painful sores broke out on the people who had the mark of the beast and worshiped his image.

The second angel poured out his bowl on the sea, and it

turned into blood like that of a dead man, and every living thing in the sea died.

The third angel poured out his bowl on the rivers and springs of water, and they became blood. Then I heard the angel in charge of the waters say: "You are just in these judgments, you who are and who were, the Holy One, because you have so judged; for they have shed the blood of your saints and prophets, and you have given them blood to drink as they deserve." And I heard the altar respond: "Yes, Lord God Almighty, true and just are your judgments."

The fourth angel poured out his bowl on the sun, and the sun was given power to scorch people with fire. They were seared by the intense heat and they cursed the name of God, who had control over these plagues, but they refused to repent and glorify him.

The fifth angel poured out his bowl on the throne of the beast, and his kingdom was plunged into darkness. Men gnawed their tongues in agony and cursed the God of heaven because of their pains and their sores, but they refused to repent of what they had done.

The sixth angel poured out his bowl on the great river Euphrates, and its water was dried up to prepare the way for the kings from the East. Then I saw three evil spirits that looked like frogs; they came out of the mouth of the dragon, out of the mouth of the beast and out of the mouth of the false prophet. They are spirits of demons performing miraculous signs, and they go out to the kings of the whole world, to gather them for the battle on the great day of God Almighty.

"Behold, I come like a thief! Blessed is he who stays awake and keeps his clothes with him, so that he may not go naked and be shamefully exposed."

Then they gathered the kings together to the place that in Hebrew is called Armageddon.

The seventh angel poured out his bowl into the air, and out of the temple came a loud voice from the throne, saying, "It is done!" Then there came flashes of lightning, rumblings, peals of thunder and a severe earthquake. No earthquake like it has ever occurred since man has been on earth, so tremendous was the quake. The great city split into three parts, and the cities of the nations collapsed. God remembered Babylon the Great and gave her the cup filled with the wine of the fury of his wrath. Every island fled away and the mountains could not be found. From the sky huge hailstones of about a hundred pounds each fell upon men. And they cursed God on account of the plague of hail, because the plague was so terrible. (Rev. 16)

.   .   .   .

The First Bowl

The first angel went and poured out his bowl on the land, and ugly and painful sores broke out on the people who had the mark of the beast and worshiped his image.

The vision of the first bowl clearly builds on some of the visions of the seven trumpets, for it is there that the mark of the beast (13:16) and the image of the beast are first mentioned. These visions of the bowls, therefore, are not entirely new visions unrelated to the previous ones, but rather they expand on them.

The "ugly and painful sores" are reminiscent of the plagues preceding the exodus of Israel from Egypt. Understand this in a larger dimension. The way of wickedness and sin, symbolized by the mark of the beast and the worship of its image, is negative, unproductive, and deceitful, bringing sorrow, shame, and failure instead of the glowing prosperity it falsely promises. You don't get to genuine life via the devil. Follow him, as Adam and Eve discovered, and you get the opposite of what he promises. Receive the mark of the beast on your forehead and you get "ugly and painful sores." That is the symbolism here.

The Second Bowl

The second angel poured out his bowl on the sea, and it turned into blood like that of a dead man, and every living thing in the sea died.

Again reminiscent of the plagues sent upon Pharaoh and Egypt prior to the exodus, this plague is upon the saltwater seas and oceans. It bears much the same significance as the previous plague. Follow Satan and discover to your surprise that instead of sailing through cooperative seas, you are forced to sail through bloody seas. Nothing works out as promised.

The Third Bowl

The third angel poured out his bowl on the rivers and springs of water, and they became blood. Then I heard the angel in charge of the waters say: "You are just in these judgments, you who are and who were, the Holy One, because you have so judged; for they have shed the blood of your saints and prophets, and you have given them blood to drink as they deserve." And I heard the altar respond: "Yes, Lord God Almighty, true and just are your judgments."

This bowl of wrath affects the fresh water of springs and rivers, the source of drinking water. They too become blood. The angel in charge of the waters interprets the meaning, and the punishment fits the crime: you have shed the blood of godly people, and now you are forced to drink blood as your punishment. The altar itself responds, yes indeed, God is doing this exactly right.

But this is symbolism; we need to know what this looks like in real life as we experience it year after year. How are the rivers and springs of water turned into blood in our times?

Strategies based on godlessness do not produce the desired results. The rivers and springs represent the philosophies and policies we follow to gain a good life. If these policies require us to be dishonest, deceitful, greedy, or vengeful — in other words, immoral — in our behavior and work, then the ultimate result will be disappointing. This is not always seen clearly on an individual level, or immediately on a national level. But the principle is inviolable: If we seek a good life by unjust means, we will fail. If we seek the water of life by being godless, we will achieve not sweet water but blood.

The Fourth Bowl

The fourth angel poured out his bowl on the sun, and the sun was given power to scorch people with fire. They were seared by the intense heat and they cursed the name of God, who had control over these plagues, but they refused to repent and glorify him.

This is another in the series of plagues, all of which combine to make the same point. Wickedness does not work. You must repent of that lifestyle and through faith in Jesus Christ adopt a godly lifestyle.

The purpose of these seven plagues is to bring people to see that a wicked way of life does not produce the results they want, and therefore that they should repent and change their ways. But the plagues do not have this result; rather, as in the case of Pharaoh earlier, they intensify their hatred of God. They blame God for making their lives miserable. They curse God for the things that happen as a result of their own wicked choices. They do not achieve their goals by the methods of godlessness, so they blame it all on God, cursing him for making life so miserable.

The Fifth Bowl

The fifth angel poured out his bowl on the throne of the beast, and his kingdom was plunged into darkness. Men gnawed their tongues in agony and cursed the God of heaven because of their pains and their sores, but they refused to repent of what they had done.

One of the plagues delivered by Moses was darkness. This fifth apocalyptic plague is clearly the same, with the addition that it resulted in agony, pain, and sores. And just as Pharaoh refused to let the Israelites go, so too these followers of the beast refuse to repent and do what is right.

The Sixth Bowl

The sixth angel poured out his bowl on the great river Euphrates, and its water was dried up to prepare the way for the kings from the East. Then I saw three evil spirits that looked like frogs; they came out of the mouth of the dragon, out of the mouth of the beast and out of the mouth of the false prophet. They are spirits of demons performing miraculous signs, and they go out to the kings of the whole world, to gather them for the battle on the great day of God Almighty.

"Behold, I come like a thief! Blessed is he who stays awake and keeps his clothes with him, so that he may not go naked and be shamefully exposed."

Then they gathered the kings together to the place that in Hebrew is called Armageddon.

Several allusions to the ten plagues of Moses are woven into this angel's plague. The Euphrates replaces the Nile. The water of the Red Sea dried up for the Israelites to cross over; here the water of the Euphrates dries up for the kings of the East to cross over. This latter reference is probably reminiscent of the Assyrian and Babylonian kings who invaded Israel and Judah and deported them.

The dragon, beast, and false prophet come from the previous vision of the seventh trumpet (Rev. 11). The frogs are an element from one of Moses' plagues. But here the frogs represent demonic spirits performing spectacular deeds. These sensational events have the effect of consolidating the great variety of godless people into a vast army mobilized to do battle against God Almighty and against his Christ. The army assembles at Armageddon.

Injected into the middle of this description is a pastoral counsel to Christians, specifically to John's parishioners in the churches on the mainland of Asia Minor. Be careful in your daily life, John is saying. Don't let your faith become lax and inoperative, and take your part faithfully in the ongoing battle against the devil and his hosts. The advice is, of course, still valid for us today. That battle is still going on, and we are all part of it every day of our lives.

The reference to Armageddon is to the mountain of Megiddo, part of the Carmel chain in western Palestine. People who interpret the book of Revelation literally consider this to be a prediction that there will occur a final climactic war at this place in Palestine. That explanation is completely unwarranted. The book of Revelation is symbolic throughout, and certainly here as well. Many military battles did occur at that location in Palestine, and perhaps that is why John selects that locale as the symbol here for the great climactic battle between the powers of Satan and the powers of Christ. However, we need to see this battle as the ongoing struggle between these forces, which takes place constantly throughout history.

We may expect, in the light of these visions of John, that this spiritual and moral battle will gradually progress toward a climax in the future. This is what John intends us to understand; the battle which John's contemporaries were fighting in the first century continues on even now in the twenty-first century. It will continue until some unknown date in the future when all of mankind will have to be mobilized on one side or the other in some form of showdown requiring a choice to be made by the human race as a whole.

The Seventh Bowl

> *The seventh angel poured out his bowl into the air, and out of the temple came a loud voice from the throne, saying, "It is done!" Then there came flashes of lightning, rumblings, peals of thunder and a severe earthquake. No earthquake like it has ever occurred since man has been on earth, so tremendous was the quake. The great city split into three parts, and the cities of the nations collapsed. God remembered Babylon the Great and gave her the cup filled with the wine of the fury of his wrath. Every island fled away and the mountains could not be found. From the sky huge hailstones of about a hundred pounds each fell upon men. And they cursed God on account of the plague of hail, because the plague was so terrible.*

This shows the climax of the great spiritual battle for the allegiance of mankind. A voice from the throne of God says this is it; now it is finally to be accomplished; what has to be done is now about to be done.

A violent thunderstorm combines with an unprecedented earthquake to shake the city of this world, splitting it into three parts — God is pouring out his final wrath on this upstart Babylon. The satellite cities collapse. Islands and mountains, objects of the landscape by which people chart their position, all disappear, so that people have no sure reference points anymore. Crushing hailstones fall. And people still do not learn their lesson from God. They continue cursing him for the troubles they have to endure.

Read this all symbolically, like an extended parable designed to cast light on actual life and history but not to be taken literally. The elements of this final plague of judgment are always present in God's actions in the world, but now in this seventh bowl we are shown them in their final configuration. Symbolically, the combat of history reaches its climax, Babylon is destroyed, all its satellites are powerless, and its citizens are tormented but unrepentant.

The absolutely final disempowerment of these godless entities, together with the absolutely final restoration of the human race into the perfection of the kingdom of heaven, has not yet occurred. These visions will come in the next several chapters. They will reveal in more detail how this final combat works out and what its consequences look like.

The seven angels are pouring out their libations upon the earth; God is handling the problem of sin and evil in the world in his own sovereign way. Christians may wonder why so much evil happens around them and to them, why there are so many people doing wicked things, why otherwise innocent people suffer so severely for things other people do. The temptation is to think that God is not really in control. Yet he is.

There is a constant outpouring of God's wrath upon the earth. This wrath requires time to achieve its purpose — people do not immediately repent when things go wrong in their lives. God's purpose is that the entire human race will repent, abandon sin, and achieve God's righteousness. All humans need to do this together, but it takes time, centuries of it, millennia of it, in order to move closer and closer to the telos God envisions. That is why the apostle John interjects from time to time the admonition to endure and be patient. It won't all happen in our lifetime.

CHAPTER 11

A Beast, a Prostitute, and a City

Revelation 17–18

The Beast

One of the seven angels who had the seven bowls came and said to me, "Come, I will show you the punishment of the great prostitute, who sits on many waters. With her the kings of the earth committed adultery and the inhabitants of the earth were intoxicated with the wine of her adulteries."

Then the angel carried me away in the Spirit into a desert. There I saw a woman sitting on a scarlet beast that was covered with blasphemous names and had seven heads and ten horns. The woman was dressed in purple and scarlet, and was glittering with gold, precious stones and pearls. She held a golden cup in her hand, filled with abominable things and the filth of her adulteries. This title was written on her forehead: MYSTERY BABYLON THE GREAT THE MOTHER OF PROSTITUTES AND OF THE ABOMINATIONS OF THE EARTH. I saw that the woman was drunk with the blood of the saints, the blood of those who bore testimony to Jesus.

When I saw her, I was greatly astonished. Then the angel said to me: "Why are you astonished? I will explain to you the mystery of the woman and of the beast she rides, which has the seven heads and ten horns. The beast, which you saw, once was, now is not, and will come up out of the Abyss and go to his destruction. The inhabitants of the earth whose names have not been written in the book of life from the creation of the world will be astonished when they see the beast, because he once was, now is not, and yet will come.

"This calls for a mind with wisdom. The seven heads are seven hills on which the woman sits. They are also seven kings. Five have fallen, one is, the other has not yet come; but when he does come, he must remain for a little while. The beast who once was, and now is not, is an eighth king. He belongs to the seven and is going to his destruction.

"The ten horns you saw are ten kings who have not yet received a kingdom, but who for one hour will receive authority as kings along with the beast. They have one purpose and will give their power and authority to the beast. They will make war against the Lamb, but the Lamb will overcome them because he is Lord of lords and King of kings — and with him will be his called, chosen and faithful followers."

Then the angel said to me, "The waters you saw, where the prostitute sits, are peoples, multitudes, nations and languages. The beast and the ten horns you saw will hate the prostitute. They will bring her to ruin and leave her naked; they will eat her flesh and burn her with fire. For God has put it into their hearts to accomplish his purpose by agreeing to give the beast their power to rule, until God's words are fulfilled. The woman you saw is the great city that rules over the kings of the earth." (Rev. 17)

. . . .

One of the seven angels who had the seven bowls came and said to me, "Come, I will show you the punishment of the great prostitute . . ."

It is one of the bowl angels who now guides John in this vision. What John now sees is a further articulation of what the bowls of God's wrath accomplish. This is not an addendum to the previous visions; it is an elaboration of them. Specifically, the angel wants John to see how the wrath of God functions in "the punishment of the great prostitute."

172

The visions in these next two chapters show in more detail what happens to the powers of evil when the final wrath of God is poured out on them. A woman symbolizes these powers of evil, the great prostitute, riding on a scarlet beast. At the same time, this woman also represents the great city, symbolic of Babylon, in which the human race has dwelt since the fall of Adam and Eve.

. . . a scarlet beast that was covered with blasphemous names and had seven heads and ten horns.

This beast was first described in 13:1, which in turn goes back to Daniel 7. The many "blasphemous names" suggest that this beast represents all the varieties of sin which humans are capable of committing. Name all the sins in the world, and they are all written on this monster of seven heads and ten horns. He represents the sum total of sin and evil.

"The seven heads are seven hills on which the woman sits. They are also seven kings. Five have fallen, one is, the other has not yet come; but when he does come, he must remain for a little while. The beast who once was, and now is not, is an eighth king. He belongs to the seven and is going to his destruction."

In dreams we often combine elements that do not make much sense in real life; they are related to real things but do not combine to be realistic. Major elements in dreams often change without rational sequence. John's visions are like that also. First John sees this woman sitting on a grotesque beast, and then without warning she is sitting on seven hills. And then immediately she is sitting on seven kings. The imagery changes rapidly, but the meaning remains basically the same. The beast merges into hills and then into kings. All represent the powers of evil within the cultural, collective, sociopolitical life of the human race.

In John's time these powers were cemented in the enormous authority of the Roman Empire, symbolized here by the seven hills on which the city of Rome was built. Perhaps John is thinking of the Caesars who were deified after they died, some of whom actually demanded religious worship of themselves as gods even before they died. In those days the empire demanded that its citizens give ultimate and absolute allegiance to the government, thus replacing God with Caesar. Caesar is lord.

173

Everything about the Roman Empire was not an incarnation of evil. There were many good things which later Christian civilization salvaged from the Greco-Roman civilization it replaced. The basic question John raises with this vision is: Who rules in this culture? If it is man who is absolute, man who is the measure of all things, then it cannot be God the creator who rules. That is what John sees in this vision. The great prostitute, not God, sits supreme over contemporary Rome.

John wants his readers to see clearly what is happening in the contemporary world in which they live, but what he sees must also apply to other times and other places. John wants us all to test whether God or the scarlet beast rules over our contemporary culture.

Even more importantly, John wants us to understand that the coming of Christ into the world, and his continuing ministry from the clouds, means that the beast on which the woman sits is vanquished, no longer residing supreme over the world where Christ reigns.

If you miss this point when you read the book of Revelation, you will have missed the entire thrust of the book. Christ has dethroned the dragon, the beasts, the prostitute, Satan, not just theoretically or behind the scenes but in real life and in real history. The history of Christianity is therefore the history of the dethronement of evil within human civilization and the enthronement of Jesus Christ in actual time and space. This insight is the heart of John's visions.

The "seven kings" — five in the past, one in the present, and one in the future — are difficult if not impossible to tie down to actual historical events. They could be individual persons or entire empires, as in the prophecy of Daniel. Presumably John had something definite in mind, but scholars who have investigated the connection do not seem to agree on anything definite. The seven kings are simply and symbolically the ongoing forces affecting life and happiness everywhere.

"The ten horns you saw are ten kings who have not yet received a kingdom, but who for one hour will receive authority as kings along with the beast."

Ten kings will reign for one hour each. Obviously this is not to be taken literally. There is an ongoing process of history in which Christ gradually overcomes the power of Satan. Kingdoms and empires rise and fall, but in the end all yield to the irresistible power of Christ in the gospel, the church, and the Spirit. The kingdom of this world is becoming the kingdom of our God and of his Christ.

> *"The beast, which you saw, once was, now is not, and will come up out of the Abyss and go to his destruction. The inhabitants of the earth whose names have not been written in the book of life from the creation of the world will be astonished when they see the beast, because he once was, now is not, and yet will come.*
>
> *"This calls for a mind with wisdom."*

"The beast . . . once was, now [he] is not, and [in the future he] will come up out of the Abyss and go to his destruction." Curious phraseology indeed! Here is the beast, the incarnation of Satan. John sees the beast's past, present, and future.

Contrast this with John's description of God in earlier passages (1:4, 8; 4:8). John describes God the Father as "him who is, and who was, and who is to come" (1:4). He sees God in the present, in the past, and in the future. God is the eternal unchanging one, the same God who existed in the past with our forefathers, who lives now with us, and who will live forever with our descendants. He is Yahweh, the great I AM.

In this passage John is contrasting the devil with God. The devil may have been dominant over human life since the fall of Adam and Eve — that is the past. But now one man has overcome him, namely, Jesus. In the present the devil "is not": his domination over human life is broken. Yet the angel predicts that a time will come when the devil will make a comeback — the devil "will come up out of the Abyss" into which the resurrection of Jesus cast him. John expands on this in a later vision (chap. 20).

> *"They will make war against the Lamb, but the Lamb will overcome them because he is Lord of lords and King of kings — and with him will be his called, chosen and faithful followers."*

John sees the combined forces of the evil one making war against the Lamb, not vice versa. He does not see the Lamb making war against the kings who incarnate the powers of the beast. The position of John, his perspective, is that rightful authority belongs to God and to the Lamb, not to Satan and his cohorts. God is always the one who takes the origi-

175

nal initiative, and Satan is the one who is reactionary, seeking to destroy what God has done.

In this vision the powers of evil are attacking the Lamb, not the Lamb attacking them. In Genesis perspective the serpent has been attacking God from the very beginning. Now, in Revelation, this attack is not only being repulsed but totally annihilated.

It is of great importance to recognize, with John, who is in attendance along with the Lamb. They are "his called, chosen and faithful followers." This is the church as defined by the Apostles' Creed: one, holy, catholic, the communion of saints. At any given point in history, since the resurrection of Jesus, there are places where the gospel of the Lord Jesus has taken root. That particular time and place in history is the locale of John's vision. All kinds of attacks against the church, both overt and subtle, take place, but the Lamb not only protects his churches but leads them in defensive battle, the results of which are typified, foreshadowed, and guaranteed in his own death and resurrection.

"He is Lord of lords and King of kings" — this summarizes the entire result of Jesus' ministry. There is no power on earth or in heaven that is superior to his. His resurrection from the dead assures us of this. The lords and kings of this world cannot compare with him in actual authority. This is not an idle boast. Don't defer the situation to an indefinite future, tacitly conceding that it is not true in our world. It is true in our world. Jesus is Lord of lords and King of kings in the Americas, in Europe, in Africa, in Asia, in China, and throughout the entire world. Not *will be*, but *is*. Now. Here today, in the present. The book of Revelation is given to us precisely to enable us to see this.

> *"The waters you saw, where the prostitute sits, are peoples, multitudes, nations and languages."*

The dream changes. Now the prostitute sits, not on a beast, not on seven hills, not on seven kings, but on "the waters." Recall that these waters, elsewhere called the seas, represent the people of the world.

But whether the woman sits on a beast, on seven hills, on seven kings, or on the waters, it all refers to the same thing. Ever since the fall of Adam and Eve the devil has presided in usurped authority over the nations of the world. The human race has given its moral allegiance to sin rather than to rightness. John continues to see these visions in the broad panoramic sweep of universal history and global dimensions.

> *"The beast and the ten horns you saw will hate the prostitute. They will bring her to ruin and leave her naked; they will eat her flesh and burn her with fire."*

The beast hates the prostitute! Remarkable! You would think the dragon, the beast, and the prostitute would be in a high degree of mutual cooperation. But John sees the beast turn against the prostitute!

In its moral application, John means to suggest that sin becomes its own worst punishment. A man digs a pit and falls into it. A man sets a trap and is caught in it himself. A man practices deceit and it comes around to harm him. John wants us to see that evil cannot sustain itself. Turn to drugs and eventually the habit will kill you. Cheat other people and sooner or later you will be found out and will lose whatever you might have gained. Build your life on moral quicksand and eventually it will wash away, leaving you with emptiness. All of this and more is what John sees when he sees the beast hating the woman, eating her flesh, and burning her with fire. Sin is deadly, parasitic, feeding on itself and thus destroying itself.

> *"For God has put it into their hearts to accomplish his purpose by agreeing to give the beast their power to rule, until God's words are fulfilled. The woman you saw is the great city that rules over the kings of the earth."*

Even more remarkable! What God has put into the hearts of the beasts is precisely "his purpose"! We must never think that Satan, whether in the guise of a dragon or a beast or a prostitute, ever acts on his own independent authority. Satan is not on a level with God. There are not two equal and eternal powers at war in the universe, good and evil. God remains in absolute control of all things, even after the fall of Adam.

This perspective has given Christians a challenge which we often either refuse to face or solve only superficially. Can it be that what Satan does is put into his heart by God? If what Satan does is evil, how is it possible that God puts this into his mind and wants him to act on it? John says that God agrees "to give the beast their power to rule, until God's words are fulfilled." Does this suggest that God is the author of sin?

Think of Satan as somehow fitting within the sovereignty of God, and therefore that Satan, in spite of appearances to the contrary, is actually serving the cause of God. We often refer to the devil as a fallen angel (Luke 10:18; Rev. 12:12). An angel is a messenger of God, and Satan never loses that character. Whatever Satan does somehow contributes to the furtherance of God's purposes.

God persuades humans to make the right choice by allowing us to make the wrong choice. We obey Satan rather than God, and then we must take the consequences, while confronting the realization that our own choice has brought about such awful results. Jesus' crucifixion is the epitome of it all. After the resurrection the people perceived how utterly wrong the decision was to crucify him; only then could they see what should have been done. As Christians we can choose to repent and we can resolve to live in Christ.

God created human beings with the capacity to choose between what is good and what is bad — moral choices. God does not make this choice for us; he insists that humans make that decision themselves. Choosing *good* will result in beneficial things happening, whereas choosing *bad* will result in detrimental things happening. Jump off a cliff and you will die; stand back and you will live. Be careful how you hunt an animal for food and you will succeed; be careless and you will be mauled. God created nature and nature's laws to provide success for doing things the way nature requires and failure for doing things that are incompatible with nature.

This is true on all levels of human choice. Success or failure may not always be immediately apparent; it may take years or, in the case of empires, centuries to recognize. But in God's time all will become clear. John in this vision sees the empire of Satan imploding. It cannot sustain itself in the long run because it is in violation of the laws God himself imposed on the nature of man and man's culture.

Extend this insight to the universality of the human race. God is leading the body of humanity century by century to perceive what happens when we make wrong choices, showing us how to repent of them and how to make better choices.

This is the theology of time and history that the book of Revelation wishes us to acquire. John wants us to understand the forces operative within our world and our history, and to choose the way of truth, which is at the same time the way of nature — not just as individual Christians, not just as the church, but as human beings in a redeemed race, as the body which is not only the body of humanity but is becoming the body of Christ. Humans must learn to resist the blandishments of the prostitute upon the waters of the nations and to follow the Lord Jesus into the full culmination of God's purpose. The human race is slow to learn. It usually learns by trial and error, but we are gradually realizing that the way of sin brings negative consequences, as we see the results of sin bringing disappointment and ruin, as we see our heroes, the beast and the prostitute, fighting to their mutual destruction. In God's grace we *are* learning.

The Woman

The woman was dressed in purple and scarlet, and was glittering with gold, precious stones and pearls.

The woman's clothing and jewelry present a facade of glamor and desirability, which represent everything in the ungodly way of life that is attractive. It bears exactly the same meaning as the blandishments of the serpent in Genesis 3 when he seduced Eve and Adam to choose the wrong lifestyle. The serpent did what he could to make "the tree of the knowledge of good and evil" (Gen. 2:9) desirable and attractive. The devil continues to do this everywhere, falsely persuading people that they hold their fortunes and happiness in their own hands. Wherever people think they can find the good life without recognizing the final authority of God, there you see this alluring woman with her tempting demonic finery.

She held a golden cup in her hand, filled with abominable things and the filth of her adulteries.

After Eve and Adam consented to taste the fruit of the forbidden tree, they immediately encountered a wide variety of disappointment and sorrow. Closer inspection of this glamorous witch, looking into the cup she holds, shows the filth and slime and squalor that she really brings. Again, the meaning is the same as that of the story of the fall in Genesis 3, which describes the sad and disillusioning results of the human choice to disregard God's instruction.

179

This title was written on her forehead: MYSTERY BABYLON THE
GREAT THE MOTHER OF PROSTITUTES AND OF THE ABOMI-
NATIONS OF THE EARTH.

The word *mystery (musterion)* is probably not a part of the title itself, but
rather an adjective modifying the term *title,* thus: "This mysterious title
was written on her forehead: . . ." The title identifies the woman, just as in
some of John's other visions the names written on the characters identify
them.

This woman is Babylon, the great city that spawns wickedness
throughout the earth. Whatever evils exist in human life and culture are
traced back to this mother of all prostitutes. The name Babylon, of
course, alludes to the Babylon of Old Testament times. The Babylonians
carried off the Jews into captivity, and thus it becomes the symbol of the
ultimate enemy of God's people.

I saw that the woman was drunk with the blood of the saints, the blood of
those who bore testimony to Jesus.

While still on earth Jesus summoned his followers to bear their cross after him. Here John sees it happening in his vision. The blood of the saints
follows the blood of the Lamb. The same ungodly forces which seduced
Eve and Adam into sin and nailed Jesus to the cross now continue their
unscrupulous work against the followers of Christ.

John, of course, wants to reassure his parishioners back on the mainland; he wants to encourage and strengthen them in their Christian commitment. This vision of the great prostitute gulping the blood of the
saints does not appear to encourage them. In fact, one might suspect it
had the opposite result, frightening them.

They, and all Christians, must continually keep their eyes fixed on
Jesus. If Jesus had to go through this treatment before he could enter
heaven, then surely he will help us go through it also. There is no
other way into resurrection except by death. We need to focus on Jesus
and maintain our loyalty and faithfulness even when it seems coun-
terproductive. John's parishioners in Ephesus and the other cities may
be undergoing persecution and martyrdom, but John assures them it
is a path Jesus has trod himself. Keep your eyes fixed on him, follow
him.

When I saw her, I was greatly astonished. Then the angel said to me: "Why are you astonished?"

"Greatly astonished," completely amazed, thoroughly surprised, maximally bewildered! John wondered with great wonder when he saw this woman drinking herself into intoxication with the blood of Christian people.

How do you react when you see powerful hostile forces outlawing Christian faith, destroying churches, ridiculing Christian perspectives, and generally putting Christianity down? You may wonder why God permits this to happen. Can't God stop this? You don't understand why such terrible things are permitted to occur. If you've ever felt this way, then you know how John felt when he saw this evil woman gorging herself on the blood of the *saints (hagion)*, God's holy ones.

The messenger angel then asks John why he is so surprised. To the angel, who sees things as they should be seen, there is no surprise in this sight of the woman gorging herself on the blood of the saints. Are you surprised to see Jesus on the cross? Jesus' blood fits into God's purpose, so also does the blood of the saints. The following visions will show why such orgies are to be expected, why they are an integral part of the strategy God uses to turn the tables on the woman herself.

The City

After this I saw another angel coming down from heaven. He had great authority, and the earth was illuminated by his splendor. With a mighty voice he shouted: "Fallen! Fallen is Babylon the Great! She has become a home for demons and a haunt for every evil spirit, a haunt for every unclean and detestable bird. For all the nations have drunk the maddening wine of her adulteries. The kings of the earth committed adultery with her, and the merchants of the earth grew rich from her excessive luxuries."

Then I heard another voice from heaven say: "Come out of her, my people, so that you will not share in her sins, so that you will not receive any of her plagues; for her sins are piled up to heaven, and God has remembered her crimes. Give back to her as she has given; pay her back double for what she has done. Mix

181

her a double portion from her own cup. Give her as much torture and grief as the glory and luxury she gave herself. In her heart she boasts, 'I sit as queen; I am not a widow, and I will never mourn.' Therefore in one day her plagues will overtake her: death, mourning and famine. She will be consumed by fire, for mighty is the Lord God who judges her.

"When the kings of the earth who committed adultery with her and shared her luxury see the smoke of her burning, they will weep and mourn over her. Terrified at her torment, they will stand far off and cry: 'Woe! Woe, O great city, O Babylon, city of power! In one hour your doom has come!'

"The merchants of the earth will weep and mourn over her because no one buys their cargoes any more — cargoes of gold, silver, precious stones and pearls; fine linen, purple, silk and scarlet cloth; every sort of citron wood, and articles of every kind made of ivory, costly wood, bronze, iron and marble; cargoes of cinnamon and spice, of incense, myrrh and frankincense, of wine and olive oil, of fine flour and wheat; cattle and sheep; horses and carriages; and bodies and souls of men.

"They will say, 'The fruit you longed for is gone from you. All your riches and splendor have vanished, never to be recovered.' The merchants who sold these things and gained their wealth from her will stand far off, terrified at her torment. They will weep and mourn and cry out: 'Woe! Woe, O great city, dressed in fine linen, purple and scarlet, and glittering with gold, precious stones and pearls! In one hour such great wealth has been brought to ruin!'

"Every sea captain, and all who travel by ship, the sailors, and all who earn their living from the sea, will stand far off. When they see the smoke of her burning, they will exclaim, 'Was there ever a city like this great city?' They will throw dust on their heads, and with weeping and mourning cry out: 'Woe! Woe, O great city, where all who had ships on the sea became rich through her wealth! In one hour she has been brought to ruin! Rejoice over her, O heaven! Rejoice, saints and apostles and prophets! God has judged her for the way she treated you.'"

Then a mighty angel picked up a boulder the size of a large millstone and threw it into the sea, and said: "With such violence the great city of Babylon will be thrown down, never to be found again. The music of harpists and musicians, flute players and trumpeters, will never be heard in you again. No workman of any trade will ever be found in you again. The sound of a millstone will never be heard in you again. The light of a lamp will never shine in you again. The voice of bridegroom and bride will never be heard in you again. Your merchants were the world's great men. By your magic spell all the nations were led astray. In her was found the blood of prophets and of the saints, and of all who have been killed on the earth." (Rev. 18)

·　·　·　·　·　·　·

After this I saw another angel coming down from heaven. He had great authority, and the earth was illuminated by his splendor. With a mighty voice he shouted: "Fallen! Fallen is Babylon the Great!"

Take a long objective look at the coming of Jesus Christ into this world. Prior to his coming there were millennia of development in Egypt, Mesopotamia, Greece, and Rome — and also in China, India, Africa, and the Americas. Now Jesus' life, death, and resurrection affect the totality of human life and history, the ongoing process of actual human civilization.

This is what John now sees and hears in his vision of the angel with "great authority" who illuminates the whole earth "by his splendor." The angel announces "with a mighty voice," a voice that all earth must hear, that "Babylon the Great" is fallen (16:19). He is announcing that the powers of evil, which have incarnated themselves within the structures of human civilization, have now been overcome and destroyed. The sole authority of Satan over the history of the earth is now broken. By rising from the dead and ascending into heaven, the Lamb of God has taken authority away from Satan and is now calling all humans to follow him. What this splendid angel announces is exactly what the gospel of Jesus Christ announces.

"She has become a home for demons and a haunt for every evil spirit, a haunt for every unclean and detestable bird. For all the nations have drunk the maddening wine of her adulteries. The kings of the earth com-

mitted adultery with her, and the merchants of the earth grew rich from her excessive luxuries."

The nations of earth have had ample time to try out the blandishments of Satan. They have found that a good life for all people does not come by following the precepts of the devil. Instead human civilization has become a gathering place for every evil spirit; people have become inebriated, losing their human sensitivities, by drinking the wine provided by the great prostitute.

Humans must now learn to see all of this previous human experience concentrated, encapsulated, focused on the way they have treated God's Son. Jesus represents all that is good and right and noble and true and divine, and we put him to death. We rejected all those virtues for their opposite. But Jesus doesn't stay dead. He rises from death, and with him rise truth and justice and goodness. And not only do these things rise with Christ, they ascend with him into the position of authority and power. They ascend to the throne, to the power, to the controlling forces of life. Jesus has become "King of kings and Lord of lords" (19:16).

In the light of Christ's resurrection and ascension, therefore, we are enabled to see the sordid, disgusting, revolting conditions that sin and evil have produced in our civilizations. There is something better, and Christ the Lamb of God brings it. That is what this angel wishes us to see and hear.

> *Then I heard another voice from heaven say: "Come out of her, my people, so that you will not share in her sins, so that you will not receive any of her plagues; for her sins are piled up to heaven, and God has remembered her crimes."*

Come out of Babylon, for Babylon has fallen. People will continue to live there, seeking their welfare and happiness in ungodly ways. But if you want to be a child of God, if you want to establish a new civilization where righteousness and justice prevail, then you must get out of Babylon. This is symbolic, of course. John is telling us to stop living by the standards of wickedness, do "not share in her sins," repent of them, and become a follower of the Lamb.

> *"Give back to her as she has given; pay her back double for what she has done. Mix her a double portion from her own cup. Give her as much tor-*

ture and grief as the glory and luxury she gave herself. In her heart she boasts, 'I sit as queen; I am not a widow, and I will never mourn.'"

Pay her back double; exact double punishment. Is this what God wants Christians to do? Punish our enemies *double* what they deserve?

This "voice from heaven" is not telling Christians to treat their enemies twice as poorly as they themselves have been treated. Rather the voice means to tell us what is happening as the house of Babylon falls. Its inhabitants suffer much worse conditions when they choose to remain instead of getting out.

God has not decided to take his anger out on them in unusually harsh ways. He has created nature in such a way that no one can get away with evil. People will suffer desperately if they choose to go against nature and against the laws God has put there. God created the world to function according to the norms he built into the universe. Go against these norms and you can't possibly succeed. That is what this "voice from heaven" is saying.

But to the end this Babylon of evil insists, in spite of reality, that she is *queen* — that she is ruler over the earth, that she holds her destiny in her own hands, and that she will never mourn or become a homeless widow. The resurrection of Christ has demonstrated that she is entirely wrong — she cannot escape that fact. But reality does not faze Satan, the prince of evil, so he/she maintains the illusion that sin is the way to go, not obedience.

"Therefore in one day her plagues will overtake her: death, mourning and famine. She will be consumed by fire, for mighty is the Lord God who judges her."

In these visions Babylon and the prostitute coalesce into one. Do not take the phrase "in one day" in a literal sense, for all is symbolic in John's visions. You might, however, consider it to be symbolic of the day of Christ's resurrection. The heavenly speaker sees the destruction of Babylon, the elimination of sin and evil from human life, as if it happens all of a sudden, in one day. Take our total human history after the time of Christ and condense it into one day. This is the angel's message.

For God "a day is like a thousand years, and a thousand years are like a day" (2 Pet. 3:8). The expressions of time and duration in these apocalyptic visions are symbolic. Understand that the ultimate destruction of Babylon is assured, guaranteed by the blood of the Lamb. The powers of evil will bring only misery, "death, mourning and famine," and this will be their own undoing. This is how the Lord God judges her: by calling his own people out of her and letting those who chose to remain destroy themselves.

> *"When the kings of the earth who committed adultery with her and shared her luxury see the smoke of her burning, they will weep and mourn over her. Terrified at her torment, they will stand far off and cry: 'Woe! Woe, O great city, O Babylon, city of power! In one hour your doom has come!'"*

The symbolism here presupposes the kind of imperial order that existed in the Roman Empire of John's time. There were many kings throughout the empire who owed allegiance to the emperor in Rome. The ancient world had been governed like that for centuries, sometimes by Nineveh, sometimes by Babylon, sometimes by Egypt, and now by Rome. The figure of speech was much clearer then than it is now with empire rule all but disappeared.

John in this vision sees (or rather hears the voice describing) the fall not only of Babylon itself, but also of all its satellite kings. This city upon which all other cities depend can no longer function. Babylon, symbolic of the empire of evil, is collapsing. The civilization that depends on the authority of sin is disintegrating. This way of life which depends on the wrongdoing of its leaders must pass away, and in its place must come a civilization which incorporates into its institutions the principles of justice, truth, honesty, faith, trust, love, and all the virtues of godliness. John is told to see this happening now as the result of Jesus' ministry from heaven.

In the centuries since John wrote this book, we, from the vantage point of the twenty-first century, may see a very clear example of how this has actually happened in western Europe. In the Dark Ages Greco-Roman civilization was thoroughly devastated. Barbarian tribes of northern and eastern Europe spilled over the empire's borders and went on a rampage of destruction. After the worst was done, the only surviving authority in the area was the church, headquartered in Rome and administered by the bishop of Rome (the pope). The barbarian tribes were converted to Christianity and then, in an astonishing burst of constructive (as opposed to previous destructive) energy, civilization was rebuilt, this time on Christian foundations rather than on pagan ones.

What we now know as Western civilization is the result, a civilization that is trying hard to incorporate Christian virtues into its very soul. The city of Babylon, in this case the Roman Empire, has fallen; Christians have come out of her; and a new city of God is being rebuilt. It is not the work of a day or a year, or even of a century or a millennium. It will be the work of perpetuity, Christians striving closer and closer to the goal of the divine telos. Wherever we see a deliberate rejection of wrongdoing in public affairs, replaced by a deliberate acceptance of justice and righteousness in public life, there we see examples of the ruin of Babylon.

> *"The merchants of the earth will weep and mourn over her because no one buys their cargoes any more — cargoes of gold, silver, precious stones and pearls; . . . and bodies and souls of men. . . . They will weep and mourn and cry out: 'Woe! Woe, O great city, dressed in fine linen, purple and scarlet, and glittering with gold, precious stones and pearls! In one hour such great wealth has been brought to ruin!'*
>
> *"Every sea captain, and all who travel by ship, the sailors, and all who earn their living from the sea, will stand far off. When they see the smoke of her burning, they will exclaim, 'Was there ever a city like this great city?' They will throw dust on their heads, and with weeping and mourning cry out: 'Woe! Woe, O great city, where all who had ships on the sea became rich through her wealth! In one hour she has been brought to ruin!'"*

First all "the merchants of the earth" and then "every sea captain" weep and mourn because the great city has been brought to ruin. The source of their livelihood and prosperity is being destroyed. How will they make a living?

This is not a rejection of merchandising or transportation. The picture is symbolic of commercial activity that depends on the city of evil, Babylon. When the economic vitality of any civilization, small or large, depends on ingrained evil presuppositions, then it is wrong and needs to go down to ruin. This is what John sees happening in the visions of the seven bowls.

Perhaps the most dramatic recent example of how this happens is the collapse of Soviet communism. The philosophy on which that system was based, professedly atheistic, could not sustain itself and collapsed under the pressure, both internal and external, calling for a better way.

> " 'Rejoice over her, O heaven! Rejoice, saints and apostles and prophets! God has judged her for the way she treated you.' "

This does not advise rejoicing in the pain of someone you hate. These visions are designed, remember, to encourage the faith and perseverance of the harassed Christians in the churches served by John. They must not think their present suffering is symptomatic of ultimate defeat. They must not think that the authorities that now make life so difficult for them will win out in the end, and that Christ will lose.

On the contrary, they must understand that present sufferings must be endured, as in the case of Jesus himself, so that in the future the cause of righteousness and godliness will prevail. They must see the end. They must see the city of evil burning and collapsing, perhaps not in their lifetime but when the time is right in God's timetable. They must learn to rejoice *now* in the success of the gospel *then*.

> Then a mighty angel picked up a boulder the size of a large millstone and threw it into the sea, and said: "With such violence the great city of Babylon will be thrown down, never to be found again. The music of harpists and musicians, flute players and trumpeters, will never be heard in you again. No workman of any trade will ever be found in you again. The sound of a millstone will never be heard in you again. The light of a lamp will never shine in you again. The voice of bridegroom and bride will never be heard in you again. Your merchants were the world's great men. By your magic spell all the nations were led astray. In her was found the blood of prophets and of the saints, and of all who have been killed on the earth."

This passage is a further confirmation of the previous one concerning the merchants and sea captains. Economic trade is thrown into consternation, and now internal culture is ravaged.

Ungodly civilization collapses because it has consistently rejected the way of truth, goodness, and justice. It has made martyrs of people who agitated for honesty and integrity; it has squelched all attempts to institute conditions that lead to prosperity, inventiveness, happiness, and progress. This is opposing the way of godliness, rejecting the way in which God wishes his people to live, despising the way Christ has come to establish. In this sense the civilization of godlessness sheds "the blood of prophets and of the saints" and of all who wish to create genuinely good and godly conditions in life.

The great boulder thrown by the angel into the sea is a symbol of what God has done by sending his Son into the world. The sea, as always in Revelation, represents the human race as a whole. Jesus has come into our human civilization and functions as this great boulder, disturbing and eventually destroying the ingrown habits of evil that propel contemporary civilization. In order for a good culture to come into existence, the old evil culture must be eliminated. This is what Jesus has come to do.

*   *   *

Take a moment again to review the processes that the book of Revelation presents to us.

First are the seven churches. Christ's strategy as he rules from heaven is to first establish groups of believers in various communities. This is how he interjects his Spirit, the spirit of godliness and truth and justice, into the existing human society. It is done, of course, by the preaching of the gospel, the telling of the story of Jesus himself, culminating in his resurrection and ascension.

Second are the seven seals. Jesus wants us to see that he, now in heaven, is indeed in operative control of how events on earth develop. There are operative forces of which we often are not aware. But Jesus wants us to know that the faithfulness of people in the churches does have a cumulative and massive effect on the way history develops. Jesus opens these seals so that we may glimpse how he uses us and the gospel to bring about his reclamation of human life.

Third are the seven trumpets. Here we see and hear the summons to action. The trumpets sounded by Christ's angels resound throughout the earth. They are intended to show us how the gospel challenges the seemingly irresistible forces of evil incarnated in human culture. The trumpets set the stage for the great conflict between incompatible ways of life. And they assure us that the spiritual battle we are in, though often very discouraging, is nonetheless being conducted precisely as Christ wants it to be. He had to go to the cross in order to accomplish his mis-

189

sion before he could rise again to assume his status of "King of kings and Lord of lords" (19:16). Jesus wants us, hearing the trumpets, to know that we too are expected to take up our cross and follow him, to sit with him on his throne.

Fourth are the seven bowls. These show us what happens when the battle between Christ and Satan is engaged. They show us the ultimate and eventual defeat of Satan and the breaking of his hold on human civilization. We must see our own history and our own contemporary conditions in the light of these bowls of God's wrath. We must see that the pouring out of the bowls is a history-long process, not producing its results in a day or a century or a millennium. And we must be encouraged to persevere in our present awkward civilization in which the battle is still being waged. We must see the end result and work patiently and faithfully in our own times, trusting that the Lord is indeed in control and will in time bring all things to their appointed end of full and complete godliness.

CHAPTER 12

Final Victory

Revelation 19–20

The last four chapters of Revelation, 19 through 22, are an in-depth look at what happens when the seven bowls of God's wrath are poured out on the earth. John sees the results in terms of spiritual warfare and its outcome.

The beast, represented by "the kings of the earth and their armies," makes war on "the rider on the horse" (19:19), who is Christ, and his armies, namely, Christians. This is not to be understood as a literal battle to be fought at some indeterminate date at the end of time. Rather it is a battle being fought every day and every year, every century and every millennium. Christian people everywhere are forever engaged in this momentous battle against sin and the devil.

The devil wants us to be intimidated by the enormity of his power as displayed daily in human life and civilization. He wants us to cringe in fear and in defeat, ceding control of society to him. He wants us to withdraw from the battle, contenting ourselves by futile protests from the sidelines. The devil would like nothing better than for Christians to withdraw into monasteries and permit the ruthless and undisciplined powers of evil to control public life. He wants us to say, "This is not a Christian civilization; this is the devil's world, let him have it; Christ is not Lord, the beast is."

Do not, however, miss the encouragement this vision provides. John sees the final victory for Christ and his armies, the defeat of his enemies, and their plunge into the lake of fire. If you see this only as something to happen suddenly and miraculously, far off into the future, then you miss its significance. John wants his own parishioners to take comfort from this vision, and with them, all Christians everywhere. The battle we are all engaged in is never in doubt; its outcome is assured. Just as surely as Jesus rose from the dead, so surely is this battle being won.

What is happening even now in our world is part of that battle. It may appear that evil is gaining control in our country. Such appearances are illusory. Christ, with his armies of Christians following him, is in the process of securing his victory. It cannot fail. We must continue to fight the good fight of faith without wavering, without doubting, and without fear. There is no place for pessimism, only for rejoicing!

Rejoicing in Heaven

After this I heard what sounded like the roar of a great multitude in heaven shouting: "Hallelujah! Salvation and glory and power belong to our God, for true and just are his judgments. He has condemned the great prostitute who corrupted the earth by her adulteries. He has avenged on her the blood of his servants." And again they shouted: "Hallelujah! The smoke from her goes up for ever and ever."

The twenty-four elders and the four living creatures fell down and worshiped God, who was seated on the throne. And they cried: "Amen, Hallelujah!"

Then a voice came from the throne, saying: "Praise our God, all you his servants, you who fear him, both small and great!"

Then I heard what sounded like a great multitude, like the roar of rushing waters and like loud peals of thunder, shouting: "Hallelujah! For our Lord God Almighty reigns. Let us rejoice and be glad and give him glory! For the wedding of the Lamb has come, and his bride has made herself ready. Fine linen, bright and clean, was given her to wear." (Fine linen stands for the righteous acts of the saints.)

Then the angel said to me, "Write: 'Blessed are those who are invited to the wedding supper of the Lamb!'" And he added, "These are the true words of God."

At this I fell at his feet to worship him. But he said to me, "Do not do it! I am a fellow servant with you and with your brothers who hold to the testimony of Jesus. Worship God! For the testimony of Jesus is the spirit of prophecy." (19:1-10)

. . . .

. . . a great multitude in heaven. . . . The twenty-four elders and the four living creatures . . . "you his servants, you who fear him, both small and great!"

The first part of this chapter must be understood in connection with what is described previously in chapter 18, namely, the fall of Babylon, which in turn is the defeat of the beast and the woman sitting on his back. Everybody is watching as this happens. The kings of earth and the merchants of earth, all symbolizing dependence on the kingdom of evil, wail and moan because their power and prosperity are taken away. But the reaction in heaven is the complete opposite. There we see and hear only rejoicing and hallelujahs to the Lamb.

Note the three groups mentioned: (1) the great multitude in heaven, namely, the sum total of all God's people; (2) the twenty-four elders and four living creatures, whom we met much earlier in these visions (chap. 4); and (3) God's servants now living on earth, namely, Christians.

We cannot conclude that godly people who have died continue to be conscious of what is occurring here on earth, any more than we can conclude that there are literally twenty-four elders and four living creatures around the throne of God in the court of heaven. These are visions and are therefore symbols. What John sees and hears is symbolic throughout.

We must think of our saintly forebears as a choir in heaven rejoicing with us over the fall of Satan. Their lives of faithfulness and godliness are being justified, vindicated in the great victory of Jesus Christ that is even now being extended into subsequent history. We are conscious today of carrying on the fight our predecessors in faith have so nobly fought. The focus of John's vision is always on his parishioners, encouraging them in the struggle against sin. Keep that focus in mind constantly as you study these chapters.

"Hallelujah! For our Lord God Almighty reigns."

This is what our lives as Christians must communicate. How common it is for us as Christians to bemoan what is happening in our world. We see crime and injustice, we see squalor and self-indulgence, we see dishonesty and deceit — we have eyes for what the devil does but sometimes fail to see that in the midst of all this evil there is a still more powerful force at work, the force of God himself. We need to train ourselves to see how God reigns in the actual world in which we live. We need to see how the city of this world, Babylon, is being overthrown, and how the great prostitute who rides the beast is being unseated.

Our lives, including our perspectives on current events, must be one great hallelujah to "our Lord God Almighty" who reigns even now in our world through the resurrection of Jesus Christ. Ours must be the optimism of knowing that in spite of any appearances to the contrary, our world is being progressively brought under the control of God by means of the gospel, the church, and the Spirit of Christ.

> *"For the wedding of the Lamb has come, and his bride has made herself ready."*

Strange symbolism! A lamb about to get married! And the bride is there ready for the ceremony!

Think first in terms of what John intended his original readers to see in this symbolism. They must see Jesus, of course, as the Lamb of God, the one who was slain but now lives also as "the Lion of the tribe of Judah" (5:5). They must also see the symbolism of "the wedding of the Lamb" in terms of ancient Jewish tradition as modified by Christian faith.

In the Old Testament the relationship between God and his people was occasionally represented in terms of marriage (Isa. 54:5-7; Hos. 2:19), and in the New Testament writings the relationship between Christ and the church was sometimes described in the same way (Matt. 22:2-14; Eph. 5:32). John is urging his people to see themselves as the bride of Christ. They must view their entire lives as preparation for the wedding ceremony.

> *"Fine linen, bright and clean, was given her to wear."* (Fine linen stands for the righteous acts of the saints.)

Christians need to prepare themselves for the marriage ceremony. They must receive from God the wedding garment of freshly laundered linen.

This description is symbolic, but the NIV explains it as "the righteous acts of the saints."

Think seriously about what this means. To employ the analogy that occurs next, that of warfare, these wedding garments are precisely the weapons whereby the prostitute is toppled and Babylon is razed. These wedding garments are the same as those forfeited by Adam and Eve when they refused God's instructions in the Garden of Eden. When people believe in Jesus Christ, they turn away from the ways of sin toward the ways of righteousness. When this happens, the dominance of the devil over them is ended and the dominance of God replaces it. This is what John sees as the wedding garment, the "fine linen" that stands for "the righteous acts of the saints."

Pursue the vision further. See how this affects human culture and history. As more and more people receive this wedding garment, the control of the beast over society diminishes. Evidence of the beast's presence, of course, does not disappear immediately, but there is a process taking place, the end result of which John sees as the total disempowerment of the woman, the beast, and the devil himself. The evidence of the wedding garment in our civilization is the extent to which righteousness and justice and truth are incorporated into the institutions and daily life of any given country.

> *Then the angel said to me, "Write: 'Blessed are those who are invited to the wedding supper of the Lamb!'" And he added, "These are the true words of God."*

There is a difference between a bride at a wedding and her guests, but this is a vision, and therefore symbolic. In this case all of the guests *are* the bride. The entire church is the bride.

It is important to connect the idea of being blessed with attendance at the wedding ceremony. The wedding garment is a gift received when you are invited. The blessedness is not just in being there, but in acquiring the gift of God's righteousness, of being enabled to live according to the guidelines of God rather than the guidelines of the devil. Blessedness consists of living a life in which the goodness and glory of God is evident, in which we image the nature of God himself and of his express image Jesus Christ. Make no mistake about this, the angel adds, "these are the true words of God!"

At this I fell at his feet to worship him. But he said to me, "Do not do it! I am a fellow servant with you and with your brothers who hold to the testimony of Jesus. Worship God! For the testimony of Jesus is the spirit of prophecy."

Another strange and unexpected event: John begins to worship the angel who tells him this good news. But the angel forbids him to do so, affirming that he himself is also a servant of God, just as John is.

Note that John's aborted attempt to fall at the feet of the angel is identical with worship. The Greek word is *proskunesai*, which is literally to get on one's knees before someone. It is the same word the angel uses later when he says, "Worship God." Also of interest in this verse is the phrase translated "testimony of Jesus." In the original Greek the phrase is "martyr of Jesus." But the Greek word *martyr* is "witness," the "witness of Jesus." In English we use the word to mean someone who is killed for the sake of Christ, but that is not what it originally meant. It meant a person who bore witness to Jesus.

The angel is saying that the story of what Jesus did is the essence of the message that is brought from God. There is no end to what humans might say or do, but at the very heart of it all is the life and work and teachings of Jesus.

Jesus himself, including everything he ever said or did, is the essence of what it means to be human. He is man par excellence. He *is* humanity, not only at its best but also as its *only* criterion. He is the standard, the paradigm, the exemplar of what God intends the entire human race to become. Jesus is the express image of God; he is what Adam was created to be but failed to exemplify. That, in the words of this angel, is "the spirit of prophecy."

That is the message being brought to the world. Jesus is the incarnation of the word (logos) of God, the incarnation or demonstration of the message God is sending to us.

The Army of Heaven

I saw heaven standing open and there before me was a white horse, whose rider is called Faithful and True. With justice he judges and makes war. His eyes are like blazing fire, and on his

196

head are many crowns. He has a name written on him that no one knows but he himself. He is dressed in a robe dipped in blood, and his name is the Word of God. The armies of heaven were following him, riding on white horses and dressed in fine linen, white and clean. Out of his mouth comes a sharp sword with which to strike down the nations. "He will rule them with an iron scepter." He treads the winepress of the fury of the wrath of God Almighty. On his robe and on his thigh he has this name written: KING OF KINGS AND LORD OF LORDS. (19:11-16)

. . . .

I saw heaven standing open and there before me was a white horse, whose rider is called Faithful and True.

John has been told that the message God is sending into the world is the witness of Jesus. Immediately thereafter he sees a vision in which this message is personified by a horse and its rider. This vision shows us what the message of Christ, which is the gospel, accomplishes as it penetrates the social fabric of human life.

The description of the rider given here is "Faithful and True." The description is to be contrasted with the treachery and falseness of the devil, his beasts, and the prostitute. What this rider represents is what is right and true for the human race. What the devil shows us in the glamor and glitter of evil is what Jesus once called the "broad . . . road that leads to destruction" (Matt. 7:13). Follow this rider on the "white horse" and you will find the truth about being human. This rider is faithful. He will not delude you with false pretenses and claims as his opponent has done ever since Adam.

With justice he judges and makes war. His eyes are like blazing fire, and on his head are many crowns.

This is how we need to see Jesus. Not just as a man who lived two thousand years ago and vanished into the clouds, but as Jesus our Lord as he rides triumphantly into human history and continues to wage the war of justice and truth within the structures of human civilization. "Eyes . . . like blazing fire" because he sees everything, penetrating every disguise of evil. "Many crowns" because he conquers everywhere he goes. This is what he has been doing ever since he ascended into heaven.

> *He has a name written on him that no one knows but he himself. He is dressed in a robe dipped in blood, and his name is the Word of God.*

"No one knows" his name, but "his name is the Word of God." Strange! An invisible name is written on him, but his bloody robe tells us that this rider is the same person as the incarnate Logos (Word of God) who died on the cross.

There is an unknown name and a known name. The unknown name that only Jesus knows is the power in Jesus himself that is invisible, the power of the Spirit of God. Even though this power is invisible, a "name . . . that no one knows," Jesus does make this power available to us. That is what makes his name knowable to us as "the Word of God."

This is a way of saying the invisible power of God comes to us also by means of the gospel. Jesus is the Word of God incarnate, and when the gospel penetrates our lives, we too incarnate that Word of God. Christ in us becomes the power by which we live, for we too bear his name in this way.

The power of God the creator is the source for the entire life and career of Jesus. Jesus continually did the will of his Father in heaven, without flaw, without defect, without sin. The invisible Spirit is the power enabling Jesus to become the perfect human being that God intended when he created Adam. That is the name that "no one knows but he himself."

However, the message of the gospel is that Jesus does enable us to share in his life and power. Jesus is our mediator between God and man. He himself represents the fullness of the deity as functioning in human life and existence. We hear the message, we believe it, and we follow him. On the one hand his name is unknown; on the other hand it is the message God wants us to hear, "the Word of God."

> *The armies of heaven were following him, riding on white horses and dressed in fine linen, white and clean.*

Don't make the mistake of thinking these "armies of heaven" are angels. They are the multitudes of people who believe in Jesus and follow him daily into the spiritual battle he himself masterminds. They are the sum total of all Christians, people who believe in Jesus and serve him in the daily affairs of ordinary human life. Remember, "the fine linen, white and clean," in which these soldiers are dressed is "the righteous acts of the saints." The army of heaven is the church, comprised of all who follow the "Word of God" in living justly and honorably and truthfully.

> *Out of his mouth comes a sharp sword with which to strike down the nations. "He will rule them with an iron scepter." He treads the winepress of the fury of the wrath of God Almighty.*

The rider on the white horse is prepared to engage in battle. The "sword" with which he fights is not in his hand but in his "mouth." It is the power of the *message* rather than the power of the literal sword that achieves victory. The message of the gospel, as proclaimed by the church throughout the earth, is the sword of the Spirit, which is the word of God.

The "iron scepter" quotation comes from Psalm 2:9. John wants his readers who are of Jewish descent to know that Jesus fulfills the Old Testament prophecies which they so highly prize. Jesus is the authentic Messiah who establishes the rule of God within the human race.

At the same time, what Jesus has done, and what he continues to do from heaven in and through the gospel, is to "tread" out the evil from the human race. This is what the gospel does: it enforces the wrath of God in such a way that goodness and righteousness replace sin and evil. This is what is happening progressively and cumulatively as time moves on and the cultures of man absorb increasing influences of the word of God.

> *On his robe and on his thigh he has this name written: KING OF KINGS AND LORD OF LORDS.*

John writes that there is yet another name, this one written on his coat and on his leg: "King of kings and Lord of lords." This is not just an empty and meaningless name. It defines the identity of the ascended Jesus Christ. Precisely because he died, rose from the grave, and ascended into the clouds, Jesus has attained the position of highest authority in the human race. There is no lord, prince, king, emperor, president, or prime minister whose power exceeds that of Jesus in this present world. No other person in the history of the world has ever done what Jesus has done. No other man submitted to death and then overcame it by resurrection. There is no authority or power present in this entire world of human beings that can even approximate the overwhelming power and authority of our Lord Jesus Christ. He is the greatest of all *kings* and the ruler of all *lords*.

The Battle's Outcome

And I saw an angel standing in the sun, who cried in a loud voice to all the birds flying in midair, "Come, gather together for the great supper of God, so that you may eat the flesh of kings, generals, and mighty men, of horses and their riders, and the flesh of all people, free and slave, small and great."

Then I saw the beast and the kings of the earth and their armies gathered together to make war against the rider on the horse and his army. But the beast was captured, and with him the false prophet who had performed the miraculous signs on his behalf. With these signs he had deluded those who had received the mark of the beast and worshiped his image. The two of them were thrown alive into the fiery lake of burning sulfur. The rest of them were killed with the sword that came out of the mouth of the rider on the horse, and all the birds gorged themselves on their flesh. (19:17-21)

. . . .

And I saw an angel standing in the sun, who cried in a loud voice to all the birds flying in midair, "Come, gather together for the great supper of God, so that you may eat the flesh of kings, generals, and mighty men, of horses and their riders, and the flesh of all people, free and slave, small and great."

The great battle is about to begin, and the angel summons all the scavenger birds to forage in the carnage that is about to occur. Surprisingly, the angel calls it "the great supper of God." Humans are invited to the wedding feast of the Lamb, but birds are invited to "the great supper of God"! Can you envision the hawks and eagles and vultures and condors descending on a great battlefield after the slaughter? Pecking away at the

200

flesh of the dead and wounded? The "great supper of God" is for the birds of prey!

Don't push this part of the scene too far. The importance of this invitation is in emphasizing the results of the battle itself that is soon to be described. The battle will result in total and abject defeat for the armies of Satan.

> *. . . the beast was captured, and with him the false prophet who had performed the miraculous signs on his behalf. With these signs he had deluded those who had received the mark of the beast and worshiped his image.*

The several items in these sentences — the beast, the false prophet, the miraculous signs, the mark of the beast, the image of the beast — all come from earlier visions. What we see in this vision has continuity with what John has seen in previous visions.

There is a continuous story going on in the four major divisions of the book: the churches, the seals, the trumpets, and the bowls. The sequence of these four divisions is significant. John begins with the churches in the actual circumstances they experience daily. He continues by showing them how the mission of Jesus opens up the meaning of life and history. Then, in more detail, he describes the confrontation Christ initiates against the powers of godlessness. And finally now, in the bowls, he describes the results of that confrontation.

To understand Revelation, you must understand the structure of the book and the philosophy of history that it incorporates. The continuous process of history, and Christ's part in that history, must be realized and embraced. Christ came into our history, he died and rose again, and he ascended into heaven. It is possible to trace what Christ has been doing from heaven in the actual happenings of the world in the last two thousand years. Revelation was given to us to help us and guide us in our understanding of God's work throughout history.

> *The two of them were thrown alive into the fiery lake of burning sulfur.*

"The two of them" refers to "the beast . . . [and] the false prophet," characters introduced earlier. Their fate is different from "the rest of them," which would have to refer to the others mentioned in the previous sentence, "those who had received the mark of the beast and worshiped his

201

image." The latter were all killed and the birds gorged themselves on their flesh. But the beast and the false prophet "were thrown alive into the fiery lake of burning sulfur."

In the next chapter the "lake of fire" is identified as the "second death" (20:14). In subsequent visions John sees the devil being thrown into this lake of fire (20:10), "death and Hades were [also] thrown into the lake of fire" (20:14), and finally all whose names were not "written in the book of life" (20:15) joined them in this fiery sea. But here in this vision the beast and the false prophet "are thrown alive into the lake of fire." They are thrown in alive, and they remain alive. God keeps them alive because, for all their perversity, they remain essential parts of his creation.

Go back to Genesis 3. There the devil was the tempter in the guise of a serpent or dragon. The devil's function in the scheme of God was to compel humans to exercise their decision-making potential. Human beings are held responsible for their decisions while animals are not. The capacity for making decisions is one of the facets of our human imaging of God. That is where the devil fits in. He represents the possibility of wrong decision making on our part.

If the devil did not exist, there would be no possibility for humans to make wrong choices. The devil represents the negative side of human will. If he dies or is totally annihilated, then human beings no longer have the possibility of choosing right from wrong, hence they are no longer responsible for their choices and thus have ceased to be distinctively human.

In this vision the devil's associates are cast alive into the lake of fire. The significance is not that they cease to exist or cease to represent the possibility of human evil, but that their influence in human life is expunged. Just as Jesus obeyed his Father in heaven flawlessly while on earth, so now John also sees the entire human race in flawless obedience to the Father. That is the meaning of this vision. This is the goal toward which the gospel is working.

The rest of them were killed with the sword that came out of the mouth of the rider on the horse, and all the birds gorged themselves on their flesh.

"The rest of them" means the various elements in the empire of evil, not necessarily people but the institutions and characteristics of evil within human civilization. The entirety of human life and culture is cleansed and purified. All the effects of the beast and the false prophet are killed, eliminated from human life completely. The gospel, which "is the sword that came out of the mouth of the rider on the horse," is the means by which this is accomplished.

If, as a Christian, you are at all interested in the study of history, this is what you must look for. Look to see how the gospel has been working ever since the ascension of the Lord Jesus into the clouds. Look to see the process whereby the gospel is slowly but steadily purifying and cleansing human life. Look to see how the cohorts of the devil are being overwhelmed. The battle is still being waged, but its outcome is shown to us in this vision. Look to see how the battle is progressing, knowing beforehand whither it is destined to go.

Satan Bound

And I saw an angel coming down out of heaven, having the key to the Abyss and holding in his hand a great chain. He seized the dragon, that ancient serpent, who is the devil, or Satan, and bound him for a thousand years. He threw him into the Abyss, and locked and sealed it over him, to keep him from deceiving the nations anymore until the thousand years were ended. After that, he must be set free for a short time. (20:1-3)

.   .   .   .

He seized the dragon, that ancient serpent, who is the devil, or Satan, and bound him for a thousand years.

The integrating and intriguing feature of this passage is the symbol of a thousand years. Satan is "bound . . . for a thousand years," and the witnesses of Jesus come to life and "[reign] with Christ a thousand years" (20:4).

These two items of John's vision, the binding of Satan and the reigning with Christ, are the reverse complements of each other. To say that Satan is bound is to say also that Christians are freed to reign with Christ. To say that believers reign with Christ is to say that Satan is bound. If Christ reigns in us and we therefore reign with him, then Satan does not reign in us — he is bound.

This vision is symbolic, not literal. The book of Revelation is symbolic throughout. It is not appropriate to lift passages out of it here and there for nonsymbolic interpretations, as has often been the case. The idea of "a thousand years," or millennium, comes of course from this chapter (and nowhere else in the Bible), where the term is employed six times. This term, along with everything else in John's visions, is symbolic and means an indefinitely long period of time, nothing more.

The various things John sees happening during this thousand-year period are the things which define its meaning, not the number itself.

Hence the "thousand year" period means the time during which people turn to Christ in faith and the power of Satan over human civilization is being diminished. As more and more people are persuaded by the gospel and learn how to live in obedience to the Lord, their influence within human society also grows. And as the power of truth and righteousness grows, the influence of the devil is increasingly exposed for its illusory promises and sorry results, and his influence wanes. As long as this process continues, so long the thousand years continues.

. . . to keep him from deceiving the nations anymore until the thousand years were ended.

Satan is bound, but his influence in human life is not completely eliminated. Only his ability "to deceive the nations" is ended.

Think of human civilization as a whole, the nations taken as a whole, the entire human race engaged in the God-given process of subduing the earth as images of God himself. With the fall of Adam and Eve, Satan began to deceive the world. But now Jesus has come and overcome the power of Satan. People now have a choice; they no longer need be deceived. Wherever people or nations come under the domination of Jesus Christ, there they are undeceived, there the power of Satan over them is bound. He is not yet totally eliminated, but his power is significantly diminished.

That is what the thousand years means in Revelation 20. It is that period of human history during which the nations are undeceived because they have come under the authority of Jesus Christ, and consequently they are continually reducing the power of Satan in their national life.

204

After that, he must be set free for a short time.

This is highly unexpected! Satan set free once again after he has been bound? The successes of the gospel within human civilization lost once again to evil?

We must think always in terms of actual history, in terms of the crosscurrents which push nations one way or another. For two thousand years now the gospel of our Lord Jesus Christ has been penetrating the nations of the world and modifying their national character. It is still continuing to expand into new territories, and many peoples still remain to be evangelized. In the meantime the gospel continues to sanctify the national institutions of the longtime Christian countries. We do not know how long this process will continue.

What John is showing us in this enigmatic statement, that Satan will once again "be set free for a short time," is that the onward expansion of the Christian faith, together with its corollary improvement of society, will eventually come to a halt, challenged by the revived forces of godlessness.

Just what form this challenge will take in the future we have no way of knowing for certain. But there are hints regularly in contemporary history — Nazism, for example. The country where Protestantism was born, one of the leading cultural countries in the world, somehow recoiled from its Christian heritage and opted for its godless opposite. Another example is the emergence of communism in the Soviet Union. The Orthodox Church had been leavening that culture for centuries, but the Soviet Revolution rejected it and sought to reinvent its civilization on atheistic grounds. Neither of these godless states has endured.

Visualize this godless reaction to the gospel and to a just civilization on a worldwide scale. The atheistic powers within the world will unite and acquire incredible power, such that will threaten the very existence of the entire Christian world. This is the prognosis John is showing us in this vision of Satan unbound.

The First Resurrection

I saw thrones on which were seated those who had been given authority to judge. And I saw the souls of those who had been beheaded because of their testimony for Jesus and because of the word of God. They had not worshiped the beast or his image and had not received his mark on their foreheads or their hands. They came to life and reigned with Christ a thousand years. (The rest of the dead did not come to life until the thousand years were ended.) This is the first resurrection. Blessed and holy are those who have part in the first resurrection. The second death has no power over them, but they will be priests of God and of Christ and will reign with him for a thousand years. (20:4-6)

. . . .

I saw thrones on which were seated those who had been given authority to judge.

In his vision John sees that there are other thrones upon which other judges sit, others to whom God has delegated his "authority to judge."

Take a long and comprehensive view of history and the progress of civilization. There is always a tension between right and wrong. Everyone has a sense of outrage when treated unjustly or when deceived, a sense of wrongness. Everyone therefore has some sense of how things should have been done, a sense of rightness. But when it comes to defining rightness and wrongness in terms of actual social policy, matters become muddled and confused. Often totally contradictory policies are advocated as being the right way to react or respond in any given controversy. No one can really tell in the long run which will prove to be the best policy. So who will be the "judge" of such things?

This is the arena in which to decipher the meaning of John's vision. Only God knows what is the best policy for humans to follow in their evolving cultures. Only God can show and teach and encourage the way of rightness. Further, God has already done this showing and teaching and encouraging in the person of his Son Jesus Christ. Jesus is the incarnation of that eternal rightness which God desires for the entire human race. So who then are the persons to whom "authority to judge" has been given?

It is not given to individual persons, or church officials, or political leaders. It is rather given to all Christians who take their allegiance to Jesus Christ seriously and live by it. John here sees the cutting edge of civilization honed by the gospel. The right direction for people and nations to go is determined by following God, by following Christ, and by joining with the millions of others who follow in faith.

The judgment as to what is right and wrong in human civilization is determined by God and Christ as incarnated in the combined body of the church universal. The overall combined thrust of Christianity within the ongoing civilizations of the human race is in the direction of godliness. Christianity, taken as a whole, is therefore what John sees sitting on thrones in heaven, judging and pointing out the direction the will of God should take the human race.

> *And I saw the souls of those who had been beheaded because of their testimony for Jesus and because of the word of God. They had not worshiped the beast or his image and had not received his mark on their foreheads or their hands. They came to life and reigned with Christ a thousand years.*

This is a vision of Christianity in the past — all Christians, all godly people who have lived in the past, not merely those we designate as martyrs. It is all people who have lived in faith until they died, all who refused the mark of the beast because they had the mark of Christ. John sees their souls as having come to life and reigning with Christ for this thousand years.

He wants us to see their souls, their faith, and their obedience continuing to live powerfully in those who follow after them as the Christians of today. The faith of the past is living on into the present. The soul of the past comes to life in the soul of the present, and in this way they reign "with Christ a thousand years."

Many believe Jesus will establish his kingdom in Jerusalem for a literal millennium. They have many spirited discussions among themselves about details of this belief. But the book of Revelation is told to John in visions. It is symbolic throughout and must not be deciphered literally, certainly not here in chapter 20.

> *(The rest of the dead did not come to life until the thousand years were ended.)*

"The rest of the dead" are all the people who lived in the past but are not included in the previous reference, those who have received the mark of the beast and have lived accordingly.

207

They do not come to life during the thousand-year period. Coming to life means living in Christ, and thus coming to dominance, that is, coming to reign. But Christ reigns during this thousand-year period, together with those who follow him. The dragon and the beast do not reign where Christ reigns; hence the rest of the dead, who are the beast's followers, do not reign either.

After the thousand years, however, when Satan is released again for a little while, then the "rest of the dead" will come to life for a while too. That is, their evil, their soul, their intent, their commitment will be resurrected temporarily.

> *This is the first resurrection. Blessed and holy are those who have part in the first resurrection. The second death has no power over them, but they will be priests of God and of Christ and will reign with him for a thousand years.*

If there is a "first resurrection," there must also be a second resurrection. John writes that people "who have [a] part in the first resurrection" are "blessed and holy." This is something larger than any given individual, something of which a person may become a part, some great movement of history.

"The first resurrection," accordingly, is the wave of resurrection that has been washing through human history as a result of the resurrection of Jesus Christ. It is the movement of people coming alive all over the world from the death of sin. See the great awakening of the human spirit produced in human society and history. See it happening wherever the gospel of Jesus Christ goes. Become part of that revitalization of human life through faith in the Lord and be joined with others in Christ for that entire period as the gospel chains the serpent in the depths of the abyss (20:1-3).

John is writing to his parishioners: if you are part of this event, you need not worry about some fearsome power of evil gaining control over you; you will, as a matter of fact, be a "priest of God" for this entire period of a thousand years. Accordingly, understand the first death to be the death that is sin, the death represented by the fall of Adam and Eve, the death that has gripped human civilization since the beginning. The "second death" would be the finalization of that first death, represented in these visions by "the lake of burning sulfur" (20:10). If you are part of the first resurrection, that is, if you truly believe in Jesus and follow him faithfully, you need not worry that some dread unseen forces of evil will ultimately claim you. You are safe as a "priest of God and of Christ." You will reign, not Satan.

It is important to understand that the first resurrection is not merely one person believing in Jesus and being born again, being regenerated. Rather it is a description of what happens on earth as a result of Jesus' resurrection. It is the expansion of Christianity, it is church history, and it is the power of the Spirit of Christ improving human civilization. It is the rescue of human life as a whole from the domination of evil and the progressive sanctification of humanity. It is the reversing of the decision of Adam and Eve and the redemption of the human race. It is the healing of the nations. You can be part of all of that if you believe in Jesus and follow him.

Satan Released

When the thousand years are over, Satan will be released from his prison and will go out to deceive the nations in the four corners of the earth — Gog and Magog — to gather them for battle. In number they are like the sand on the seashore. They marched across the breadth of the earth and surrounded the camp of God's people, the city he loves. But fire came down from heaven and devoured them. And the devil, who deceived them, was thrown into the lake of burning sulfur, where the beast and the false prophet had been thrown. They will be tormented day and night for ever and ever. (20:7-10)

．　．　．　．　．　．

When the thousand years are over . . .

The danger of dispensationalism and millennialism is that they do not relate to contemporary life and history. John is writing in the late first century for the edification and encouragement of his readers there on the mainland of Asia Minor. Modern millennialists, however, take these visions of John and project them into some indefinite future, interpreting the thousand years as some curious and enigmatic period of time, which is for all practical purposes unrelated to what is going on in history right now. John's visions become obscure, abstract, and mysterious. People argue about details of the vision, which have no bearing whatever on the way they live in this present world. John did not have such speculations in mind, nor did Jesus when he provided these visions to John.

The "thousand years" (20:3) is not a period of time postponed to some indefinite future. It is now! It is the period of time during which Jesus reigns with his disciples and the devil is bound. It describes what the gospel does in human life and history, what has been happening ever since Jesus ascended into heaven.

> . . . Satan will be released from his prison and will go out to deceive the nations . . .

But John also sees the thousand years as ending. This does not mean that Jesus ceases to reign, but that the success of the gospel on earth becomes seriously challenged and compromised, so much so that Christianity appears to have ceased to function as the controlling perspective of human life and civilization. That is what John means when he says Satan will deceive the nations (20:3).

John's vision does deal with the future, but not in the way millennialists suggest. For them, both the beginning and the ending of the thousand-year period are in the future. For John, however, the beginning of the thousand-year period is in the past: it is the ascension of Jesus and the pouring out of his Spirit on Pentecost. That is when the thousand-year period began.

But the ending is still in the future. John's vision of Satan unleashed to deceive the nations is a warning to us that the time will come when the successful advance of Christianity will be reversed, a time in which the nations of the world will combine to reject the way of God and of Christ. Human life and civilization will revert to anti-Christian ungodliness.

> They marched across the breadth of the earth and surrounded the camp of God's people, the city he loves.

This vision is baffling. Christians do not want to believe it. They prefer to think the church of Jesus Christ will just keep on rolling over all opposition, defeating all the powers of evil until at last the human race will be entirely Christianized. But here John sees the nations of the world, having been deceived by Satan again, besieging the city of God. John sees the people of the world, long hospitable to Christianity and deeply indebted to it, now turning against the Lord and trying hard to destroy the Christian church. This is a disturbing and enervating vision, one not easily understood.

In the light of the cross of Jesus Christ, the disciples were confident. Jesus, worker of miracles that he was, could easily defeat any enemies who opposed him. Jesus' death came as a most disillusioning blow to their hopes and expectations. Nobody now would sit on his left and on his right when he came into his kingdom. Judas would not become secretary of the treasury. Peter would not become vice president. They would all retire into oblivion, their dreams shattered beyond repair. They did not yet understand, even after Jesus rose from the dead. Till the very end, even after the resurrection, they expected him to set up the throne of David in Jerusalem. "Are you at this time going to restore the kingdom?" they asked him (Acts 1:6).

Jesus informed his disciples that they would have to take up their cross, just as Jesus did his (Matt. 16:24). This information is not limited to individual persons. It is addressed also to the church as a whole. The church must take up its cross, not just symbolically but in reality, just as Jesus did. Taking up the cross does not mean just carrying some heavy burden; it means being crucified. Each Christian must carry his or her cross as an individual all the way to death, whatever form that may take.

And now in this vision John sees the church as a whole carrying its cross, being crucified just as Jesus was, surrounded by the hosts of sin and evil, its very existence threatened. But remember, it was only through death and subsequent resurrection that Jesus accomplished what he did in human life and times. What he accomplished prior to his crucifixion was penultimate, not final, a good beginning but not sufficient. The disciples did not understand what it was all about until a long time afterward.

We should see the history of Christianity in the same light. What is occurring now in our history and in our culture is also penultimate; it is not final, not ultimate. It is necessary and indispensable preparation, just as Jesus' preresurrection ministry was necessary and indispensable. It is preparation for something much better, something which must come afterward.

211

In our world, saturated as it is in many parts by the gospel, we see wonderful effects within civilization: in science and technology, in research and education, in communications and travel, in the fine arts, in all areas of human endeavor. Yet for all this glorious advance of life, we still see massive and intimidating expressions of evil: poverty, injustice, crime, greed, violence, hate, and all the rest. The good we are seeing and experiencing is not enough. It is positive and it must continue — the evolution of life and the advance of culture — but it is not enough. What must happen is that Christianity must not only expose the difference between the two basic lifestyles, it must eliminate the evil lifestyle altogether.

The stronger Christianity becomes in any given culture, the stronger the opposite powers of evil become as well. That, you will recall, is the stage depicted by the opening of the seven seals on the scroll in God's hand. One of the functions of the gospel as it operates through the church is to expose the difference between good and evil in human life and civilization. But merely exposing the difference is, of course, insufficient. Good must prevail and evil must be annihilated.

But fire came down from heaven and devoured them.

What this vision is showing us, therefore, is that the way to final victory is precisely by following Jesus' steps, taking up our cross, and being crucified — not just as individuals, but as a body. Christianity must set its face, as Jesus did, to go to Jerusalem, to be put on trial, to be judged unfairly, and to be executed. It must do this in the full confidence that there is resurrection beyond this death, triumph beyond this defeat. Christianity cannot achieve its goal except via the same cross that Jesus bore. Just as the powers of death were overcome when Jesus rose from the dead, so too Christians may be assured that "fire [will come] down from heaven" and destroy the enemies of the church.

In terms of actual history this vision is showing us that some great crisis, comparable to the crisis that Jesus instigated among the Jews, must occur in the human race as a whole. It must be a crisis in which the human race must make a decision, just as the Jewish people had to make a decision. Which way will we go, the way of godlessness or the way of Christ? The Jews ratified the Adamic choice when they crucified Jesus. The whole human race will make the same choice when it rejects Chris-

212

tianity. But Jesus secured the reversal of the crucifixion when he rose from the dead, and we are promised that Jesus will secure the reversal again when he sends fire from heaven to consume the opposition.

> *And the devil, who deceived them, was thrown into the lake of burning sulfur, where the beast and the false prophet had been thrown. They will be tormented day and night for ever and ever.*

This is the final outcome of the great battle in which Satan makes his last great counterattack on the Lord Jesus and his church. The nations have been consumed by fire from heaven — that is, opposition to Christianity has been obliterated — and now the devil himself is thrown into the lake of fire to join his captains, the beast and the false prophet.

"They will be tormented day and night for ever and ever." They are not uncreated or annihilated; rather they are tormented, forever rendered innocuous, without influence or power.

Precisely because humans are fully human, and as such, images of God, we must exercise our ability to choose, to decide between good and evil. In this vision of the triumph of the rider on the white horse and his followers, John is seeing the human race reversing the decision of Adam and Eve, choosing to obey God the creator rather than to disobey. The choice is always there. Jesus in his lifetime always chose obedience to his Father in heaven. He is the same human being as we are, except for sin.

Now John is seeing the entire human race doing what Jesus did, choosing the way of pure obedience, without any sin whatever. But for the choice to be real, the alternative must still exist. So the serpent, the devil, Satan, continues to exist forever, but in the lake of fire, in the torment of knowing himself to be without influence at all in human affairs.

That is the goal of Christianity in this world, a goal that is the same as that of Jesus himself, and of God himself. God wants a human race working to subdue the world as his image. He wants his people to develop civilization in such a way that it incorporates all that is right and good and just and holy, without sin or evil to corrupt and ruin the happiness and shalom that is God's intent. This is what John sees happening after this great battle of Armageddon.

Final Judgment

Then I saw a great white throne and him who was seated on it. Earth and sky fled from his presence, and there was no place for them. And I saw the dead, great and small, standing before the throne, and books were opened. Another book was opened, which is the book of life. The dead were judged according to what they had done as recorded in the books. The sea gave up the dead that were in it, and death and Hades gave up the dead that were in them, and each person was judged according to what he had done. Then death and Hades were thrown into the lake of fire. The lake of fire is the second death. If anyone's name was not found written in the book of life, he was thrown into the lake of fire. (20:11-15)

. . . .

Then I saw a great white throne and him who was seated on it.

The vision shows a standard courtroom of those days, and this is the same throne with the same person seated on it that John saw previously in chapter 4. John sees God seated on the throne, ruling and judging all creation. The same God who, through Jesus, supervises and directs the course of human history is now also functioning as ultimate judge.

God is always the judge. He is not postponing his judgment until some undetermined date in the future, the end of the world, as people like to think of it. No indeed! He is constantly functioning as judge of what goes on in the world. He judged Adam and Eve in the Garden of Eden. He judged the world in the time of Noah, and the Sumerians when they built the Tower of Babel. He judged Israel and Judah when they turned to idolatry, sending them into exile.

Notice particularly how God judged the Jews when they put Jesus to death. The people judged that Jesus was an imposter, but God judged otherwise. The evidence of this judgment of God is precisely the very real historical event of Jesus' resurrection.

God executed his judgment by raising Jesus from the dead. Jesus' resurrection is, accordingly, God's judgment that the people who put him to death were wrong, and everyone who accepted that judgment repented and was forgiven.

What we need to see, therefore, is that God's judgment is constantly taking place in the actual affairs and developments of human history. We speak of the final judgment. And indeed God's judgment is final in the sense that it is decisive, ultimate, conclusive, and unalterable. But surely it is not reserved only for some nebulous date in the future. It is current and constant.

Earth and sky fled from his presence, and there was no place for them.

It is not clear just what purpose this observation serves in John's vision. It suggests that no extraneous things will enter into God's judgment to alter his objective and impartial determinations. God cannot be bribed or sidetracked by anything in heaven or earth.

And I saw the dead, great and small, standing before the throne . . .

Everyone who has ever lived John sees standing before God. With John we should see that all of human history is constantly being paraded before the throne of God, and that God is helping us to analyze and comprehend our own human history. John wants us to see from the perspective of God himself how to discern what in our past has been decisive in forming the movements that are now coming to their climax in the struggle of good versus evil. Every person, great or small, stands before God to be judged.

. . . and books were opened. . . . The dead were judged according to what they had done as recorded in the books.

The books (plural) are simply the record of how people lived. Did they live according to the will of God or did they not? God judges people "according to what they had done."

God does not judge anyone unfairly, unjustly, or arbitrarily. You simply have to consult the actual record of how they lived to discover what God's judgment is. God doesn't change anything in the record of our lives, nor does he overlook anything. Everyone gets treated exactly as the record shows.

215

Another book was opened, which is the book of life. . . . If anyone's name was not found written in the book of life, he was thrown into the lake of fire.

The other book (singular) is the "book of life." This book functions alongside the other books. It contains the names of those who escape the fate of being thrown into the lake of fire.

"The lake of fire," you will recall, symbolizes the elimination of evil as a force within human life and culture. The only people thrown into this lake of fire are those who represent the function of sin within human life. Before God can fully establish his kingdom on earth, that is, before the human race can become perfect, everything evil and contaminating has to be eliminated. This is what John now sees in the vision of people whose name is not found in "the book of life." If they are not in the book of life, they are in the book of death, that is, in the lake of fire.

Does this serve to bypass what is recorded in the books (plural), namely, the record of what each of us has done? It would seem that if the "book of life" is the decisive factor in this process of judgment, then the books (plural) are not. The answer to that problem is to be found in asking how one gets his or her name into that book of life. That happens by believing in Jesus Christ and by living accordingly. And that very belief and obedience is, as you will recognize, also an act recorded in the books (plural).

Recall again that John wants to strengthen the people back in the seven churches on the mainland. He wants them to see that if they continue to believe and obey the Lord Jesus to the end, their names will be written in "the book of life" and they will not perish in "the lake of fire." The books which they are writing each day will show that they have lived in faithfulness, living in the forgiving and enabling grace of God as mediated to them by the Lord Jesus. Their names will then be transcribed into that other book (singular), "the book of life."

But there is a broader focus to this vision than merely what happens to each of us as individuals. There is also a perspective that shows us what factors are decisive in the way human history develops. What triumphs in the end? What enables the human race to shed the tyranny of evil and throw off the chains of wickedness with its developing civilization? Which way must we go as a human race to push on toward the goal of having a perfectly just and good society?

We must go the way that writes our names into the book of life. The individuals whose names are in that book are the only people who do not perish. Everything else is dumped into the lake, which represents ineffectiveness, irrelevancy, impotence, and meaninglessness.

The only way for the world to achieve the kind of society we all want is the way of faith in the Lord Jesus. Everything else will ultimately be judged worthless. That is what we must see in the broad dimension of God's purpose and the way of God's judgment.

The lake of fire is the second death.

"The lake of fire" is permanent exclusion from the life of God's world. "The second death" is, accordingly, being finally cast into irrelevance with respect to how the world runs. Christians do not have to worry about that. Their names are written in the "book of life" so that the "second death" cannot touch them. The first death, though the term is not used, would mean the life of sin. When, in the end result, sin is eliminated, so too is the first death. When that condition is achieved in its finality, as this vision shows us, then "the lake of fire [which] is the second death" will represent the permanent exclusion of sin from human life.

*   *   *

Chapters 19 and 20 show the final battle between Christ and the devil, what is sometimes called the battle of Armageddon. It is, of course, not a literal pitched battle of guns and ammunition, tanks and warplanes, or battleships and bombs. It is a battle for the heart of the human race. To whom will we give allegiance in the end, to sin and evil or to obedience and goodness? Will we as a human race continue to wallow in the misery of Adam's fall, reaffirming his decision year after year, or will we somehow manage to escape that fate and return to the God who created us and loves us in spite of ourselves?

In these two chapters John sees this final battle and its final outcome, the glorious victory of Christ and the total defeat of Satan. The entire process of human history after the ascension of Jesus is the gradual development of that final battle, moving inexorably to the conclusion once for all decided by Jesus himself.

The next two chapters, 21 and 22, depict the glory of the new city of

God toward which our present life and history is moving. The old city, Babylon, has fallen. Now the new city, Jerusalem, will be established, symbolically of course!

CHAPTER 13

The City of God

Revelation 21–22:7

A New Heaven and a New Earth

Then I saw a new heaven and a new earth, for the first heaven
and the first earth had passed away, and there was no longer any
sea. I saw the Holy City, the new Jerusalem, coming down out of
heaven from God, prepared as a bride beautifully dressed for her
husband. And I heard a loud voice from the throne saying, "Now
the dwelling of God is with men, and he will live with them. They
will be his people, and God himself will be with them and be
their God. He will wipe every tear from their eyes. There will be
no more death or mourning or crying or pain, for the old order
of things has passed away." (21:1-4)

. . . .

*Then I saw a new heaven and a new earth, for the first heaven and the
first earth had passed away . . .*

After the visions of the final victory of Jesus Christ in the previous chapter, John now receives visions that show the kind of life that victory produces. He sees it as "a new heaven and a new earth." Clearly this parallels
Genesis 1, in which the first heaven and the first earth are described.

But what is *new* about this heaven and earth? It is not new in the sense that the old creation is dissolved and an altogether new planet is created to replace it. The newness means that the human race has gotten a new start on life.

The old life is the life of Adam, a life of sin, wickedness, and the curse. The new life, represented by the new heaven and earth, is a new beginning of obedience, holiness, justice, righteousness, and imaging of God. All satanic influence in human life is now eliminated. Humans choose to obey God rather than the devil. Christ has redeemed the human race. "The kingdom of the world has become the kingdom of our Lord and of his Christ" (11:15). The nations have been healed (22:2). That is what is new — the condition into which the battle of Armageddon, with its defeat of Satan, has ushered the human race.

> . . . *and there was no longer any sea.*

The sea has been a symbol of humanity throughout the book of Revelation. Now John tells us there is no sea.

The term *sea* refers to humanity as it existed prior to the final victory of Christ and his followers; it is used to describe fallen humanity. That humanity is no longer in existence. Fallen humanity has become, through the ministry of Christ, redeemed humanity. If indeed John would have described the sea at all now, he probably would have seen it as perfectly clear, smooth, placid, a thing of beauty and peace, rather than as wild and tumultuous and dangerous. It would be exactly as he saw it in the throne room in chapter 4.

> *I saw the Holy City, the new Jerusalem . . .*

In the new heaven and the new earth the human race works out its new orientation, its new commitment of obedience to the Creator. The concept of city suggests the human community living in mutual cooperation, the actual civilization or culture that we produce.

This city is holy; the people in it function perfectly as images of God. They follow precisely the command given to humans in the very beginning: the ongoing task of subduing the earth and having dominion over it. The perfect obedience of Jesus himself is extended to become the perfect obedience of people as a whole. Human holiness is the perfection of obedience within the ordinary and common ventures of life. This human civilization expresses its newness in the holiness with which it conducts the work assigned by the Creator God.

This city is called "the new Jerusalem," perhaps in contrast somewhat to the old Jerusalem, but more so in contrast to Babylon. Babylon has always been, among ancient Jews and early Christians, the symbol of the civilization of ungodliness and sin. Jerusalem has always been the symbol of the opposite, the civilization built upon the law of God. The old Jerusalem, however, had crucified Jesus and hence had to be renewed also. John now sees a "new Jerusalem," a new "holy city" in which righteousness dwells.

. . . coming down out of heaven from God . . .

Much is made in some Christian communities of this passage. They draw an incorrect implication that, since it comes down from heaven, it is in no way a product of human effort, not built by humans but by God. They suggest that God prefabricated this city by an act of sheer and undeserved grace, with no human work in it at all.

This is a wrong understanding of the vision. Grace does not suggest an act of God entirely separate from any human activity. Grace is precisely that act of God by which he enables humans to act rightly. Divine grace is not one area of reality and human obedience another. For Christians to insist that their life depends on the grace of God does not mean they are treated as stones, objects to be manipulated by God.

On the contrary, grace is the Spirit of Christ showing its effect precisely in the new obedience people give to God. It is not a question of either/or; it is an affirmation of both/and. Grace is that power of God which produces obedience on the part of Christians. The grace of God is seen in the honesty, truthfulness, goodness, love, and faithfulness of living human beings who believe in Jesus Christ.

When we see with John that the "holy city" comes "down out of heaven from God," it should remind us that we live as Christians only by the power of God manifested in Jesus Christ and channeled to us by the Holy Spirit. John's vision of the "new Jerusalem" assures us already here and now that the obedience we humans now show but poorly will someday become complete and entire, with no alloy of sin or evil. This comes to us from heaven, that is, through Jesus Christ and the inner working of the Holy Spirit in the lives of people.

It is in that sense that the holy city comes "down from heaven." The ongoing civilization John envisions is not therefore one which God prepares entirely apart from actual people and then invites us into, but a city which God by his grace enables *us* to build as we fulfill the responsibilities which he has created within us.

> *. . . prepared as a bride beautifully dressed for her husband.*

The city is described as a bride prepared for her husband. A bit later an angel will say to John, "Come, I will show you the bride, the wife of the Lamb" (21:9). The new Jerusalem, in John's vision, is the bride of the Lamb. This would seem to be a rather odd and inappropriate analogy.

Think of the people who are citizens of this holy city. They, taken together, are the wife of the Lamb — not the brick and mortar of a city, but people; not walls or streets or houses, but living, breathing citizens.

During previous times, before the final battle and judgment, this bride could be described as the church. We, living today, are familiar with that analogy, and surely the Christians of John's day would have been also. But in this new heaven and new earth, the new holy city has expanded to encompass the entire human race. Every evil thing has been exorcised; all sin has been eliminated, and only righteousness and holiness remain. The church and humanity have melded together. Christ has thrown the devil into the lake of fire. All that is left of humanity is good and perfect. This new purified humanity is what John sees as the bride of Christ.

> *And I heard a loud voice from the throne saying, "Now the dwelling of God is with men, and he will live with them. They will be his people, and God himself will be with them and be their God."*

Men, of course, does not mean male as opposed to female, but human as opposed to nonhuman. "The dwelling of God is with men." Does this imply that God did not dwell with men previously, during the period of the old Jerusalem and Babylon or with John and the churches during the first century? Does God not dwell with us now in the twenty-first century?

God always dwells with men, in the sense that God is omnipresent, as stated in Psalm 139, where there is no place in heaven and on earth where God is not. But that is not what John hears this angel say. The angel is not affirming the omnipresence of God with men (which is always the case, even with wicked people), but he is affirming a more intimate relationship connoting love and obedience on the part of the people. John sees God dwelling with men, not now as judge and punisher, but as loving and faithful Creator. His grace, inserted into the human race by Jesus Christ, has produced its intended effect, the redemption of the race, and now God no longer places a curse upon us because there is no longer any sin to curse.

People will no longer be experimenting with evil options in life, but God himself will "be their God." They will have heard the devil's temptations, as Adam did and as Jesus did, and they will have resisted them as Jesus did. They will obey their Father in heaven exactly as Jesus did, and God will be with them in exactly the same way he was with his Son Jesus.

"He will wipe every tear from their eyes. There will be no more death or mourning or crying or pain, for the old order of things has passed away."

This latter clause describes the newness of the holy city, the new Jerusalem: "the old order of things has passed away," the old order of human civilization and history. All of that previous order of things was dominated by sin and evil. Now that order of things is gone, and a new order of human life is in place.

God "will wipe every tear from [our] eyes." Pain and suffering, as the by-products of sin, will be nonexistent. Recall that after the fall of Adam and Eve God placed a curse on everything: Eve, Adam, and the serpent. Or, looked at from our created point of view, sin brought its own punishment as a result of the way God created the world to function. Now sin is banished and consequently its effects are gone.

But does this really include death, besides tears, mourning, crying, and pain? Is death really a consequence of sin? Is not death a part of the natural order of creation which God fixed in the beginning? Trees sprout from seeds, grow, and after a certain number of years, die. Animals are born, live their terms, and die. Is this not also true for humans? Can death be traced to human sin rather than to the natural order? The answer depends on your definition of death.

God told Adam and Eve that the day they eat of the Tree of the Knowledge of Good and Evil, they will die (Gen. 2:17). The answer to the question of whether death is the consequence of sin or the result of natural processes depends on what that original pronouncement by God means.

In this vision God is referring to moral death, not physical death. Adam and Eve did not die physically the very moment they sinned, but they did die morally. Making the wrong moral choice for Adam and Eve was the same as committing themselves to the control of the devil, and that is the way of death. There is no future along that path, as now the book of Revelation is showing us. The future, that is, true and genuine life, is only in obedience to God. It is no accident that the Tree of Life is mentioned not only in Genesis but also in this last section of Revelation. The death which will exist no more in the holy city is most surely moral death, spiritual death.

God's Summation

He who was seated on the throne said, "I am making everything new!" Then he said, "Write this down, for these words are trustworthy and true."

He said to me: "It is done. I am the Alpha and the Omega, the Beginning and the End. To him who is thirsty I will give to drink without cost from the spring of the water of life. He who overcomes will inherit all this, and I will be his God and he will be my son. But the cowardly, the unbelieving, the vile, the murderers, the sexually immoral, those who practice magic arts, the idolaters and all liars — their place will be in the fiery lake of burning sulfur. This is the second death." (21:5-8)

. . . .

He who was seated on the throne said, "I am making everything new!" Then he said, "Write this down, for these words are trustworthy and true."

God is "making everything new." This newness is the same newness as that of the new heavens and the new earth and the new Jerusalem (21:1-2). God is speaking directly to John in the vision. God himself assures John that what he sees and writes down for the benefit of the churches is "trustworthy and true." The final and total significance of these visions, once we really sense what they mean about our lives and history, is stupendous.

Actual events happening every day and every year do not seem to support a vision that Christ is gaining the victory over sin. Many people, including, sadly, many Christians, are pessimistic about the course of human history, seeing the progress of civilization being not the progress of truth, justice, and righteousness but its opposite, the progressive clutch of Satan over the affairs of our societies. They do not see history as pointed by the gospel in the direction of "the holy city," so they find some other way to bypass the claim of these visions in the book of Revelation. John, however, is quoting God when he writes that these visions "are trustworthy and true." We must see as John sees, that they are true representations of what is going on in our life and times and history.

> *He said to me: "It is done. I am the Alpha and the Omega, the Beginning and the End."*

What is "done" is exactly what John has been describing in his visions: the process by which the kingdom of this world has become the kingdom of God, by which the human race has been brought to reverse its original decision. It is the process of history during which the gospel of our Lord Jesus Christ has penetrated and claimed more and more of earth's humans until at last the church and the human race have become identical.

God was there at the beginning when he created the world — he is the Alpha. God is there now at the conclusion of this process — he is the Omega. "The Beginning and the End" is not merely some other name for God; it is a philosophical description of the origin and the destiny of human life. We originated with God, and we are destined to culminate in God. And the process of human history is the process whereby we move from one to the other.

> *"To him who is thirsty I will give to drink without cost from the spring of the water of life. He who overcomes will inherit all this, and I will be his God and he will be my son."*

God is still speaking here. In this speech God is addressing people in John's time and in our time, not people in the future new Jerusalem. He is addressing people on their way toward the new Jerusalem. If you know yourself to be thirsty, God will give you something to drink, namely, "the water of life," emphasis on the word *life*. God will give you life.

We all want life. And everyone wants to live life as it ought to be lived: with happiness, contentment, love, truth, and justice, and everything that goes into the idea of life at its best. That is what we want and that is what God is promising to give us. It costs us nothing, but we must be able to overcome. To overcome means to persevere to the end in faith and obedience against all temptations. To overcome means to overcome sin, to never deny the Lord by the way we live our lives.

God wants the Christians in Smyrna, in Laodicea, and elsewhere to see the vast dimensions of what is really going on in the plan of God. They, and we, must take instruction from these visions, and from that instruction, courage and renewed conviction. And from that renewed conviction we must pursue steadfast obedience in the faith. God promises us we "will inherit all this" — the holy city and the new Jerusalem in which God is our God.

Those who overcome will be sons of God. That does not mean we become God or are deified. It means we become the creatures God originally intended all humans to be. It means we become the images of God described in Genesis 1 and which Jesus incarnated. We become God's *sons*, his reflections, his extensions, his images.

> *"But the cowardly, the unbelieving, the vile, the murderers, the sexually immoral, those who practice magic arts, the idolaters and all liars — their place will be in the fiery lake of burning sulfur. This is the second death."*

In the new Jerusalem, created by Christians through the Spirit of Jesus, there will be nothing that compromises goodness or diminishes justice. That is all in the lake of fire, still out there as an ominous presence but nonfunctional in the new city.

The New Jerusalem Profiled

One of the seven angels who had the seven bowls full of the seven last plagues came and said to me, "Come, I will show you the bride, the wife of the Lamb." And he carried me away in the

Spirit to a mountain great and high, and showed me the Holy City, Jerusalem, coming down out of heaven from God. It shone with the glory of God, and its brilliance was like that of a very precious jewel, like a jasper, clear as crystal. It had a great, high wall with twelve gates, and with twelve angels at the gates. On the gates were written the names of the twelve tribes of Israel. There were three gates on the east, three on the north, three on the south and three on the west. The wall of the city had twelve foundations, and on them were the names of the twelve apostles of the Lamb.

The angel who talked with me had a measuring rod of gold to measure the city, its gates and its walls. The city was laid out like a square, as long as it was wide. He measured the city with the rod and found it to be 12,000 stadia in length, and as wide and high as it is long. He measured its wall and it was 144 cubits thick, by man's measurement, which the angel was using. The wall was made of jasper, and the city of pure gold, as pure as glass. The foundations of the city walls were decorated with every kind of precious stone. The first foundation was jasper, the second sapphire, the third chalcedony, the fourth emerald, the fifth sardonyx, the sixth carnelian, the seventh chrysolite, the eighth beryl, the ninth topaz, the tenth chrysoprase, the eleventh jacinth, and the twelfth amethyst. The twelve gates were twelve pearls, each gate made of a single pearl. The great street of the city was of pure gold, like transparent glass.

I did not see a temple in the city, because the Lord God Almighty and the Lamb are its temple. The city does not need the sun or the moon to shine on it, for the glory of God gives it light, and the Lamb is its lamp. The nations will walk by its light, and the kings of the earth will bring their splendor into it. On no day will its gates ever be shut, for there will be no night there. The glory and honor of the nations will be brought into it. Nothing impure will ever enter it, nor will anyone who does what is shameful or deceitful, but only those whose names are written in the Lamb's book of life. (21:9-27)

.   .   .   .

One of the seven angels who had the seven bowls full of the seven last plagues came and said to me, "Come, I will show you the bride, the wife of the Lamb."

The identity of this angel is significant: "one of the seven angels who had the seven bowls full of the seven last plagues." It confirms to us that these visions are not to be interpreted separately from the bowls but as their *effect*. What we see here is also to be included in the meaning of the bowls.

And he carried me away in the Spirit to a mountain great and high, and showed me the Holy City, Jerusalem, coming down out of heaven from God.

John is "carried away in the Spirit." Physically he is on an island off the coast of Miletus in the Aegean Sea. Now, in his imagination, he flies to a mountain overlooking faraway Jerusalem, but close enough so that he is able to describe its various dimensions and features in minute detail. What follows is, of course, symbolic, not literal.

Its Glory

It shone with the glory of God, and its brilliance was like that of a very precious jewel, like a jasper, clear as crystal.

In Old Testament times the idea of the glory of God often connoted some visible manifestation, such as a cloud or a fire or some other tangible evidence. Here John sees this new city emanating an aura, a "brilliance," or shining, which is comparable to the finest jewel known. The whole city gives off an aura of awesome brilliance, reflective of the pure and loving presence of God within it.

Its Wall and Gates

It had a great, high wall with twelve gates, and with twelve angels at the gates. On the gates were written the names of the twelve tribes of Israel. There were three gates on the east, three on the north, three on the south and three on the west. The wall of the city had twelve foundations, and on them were the names of the twelve apostles of the Lamb.

John sees a multiplicity of twelve this time, not seven: twelve gates, twelve angels, twelve tribes, twelve foundations, and twelve apostles. Perhaps the arrangement of the twelve gates, representing the twelve tribes of Israel, is intended to allude to the arrangement of the tribes as they encamped in the wilderness after the escape from Egypt (Num. 2). Here now is a new city, of which the original tribes of Israel had been the forerunner and prophecy. What the original Old Testament camp of God had been intended to accomplish is now being achieved here in John's vision of the new city of God.

At the same time, however, the walls of the city rest on the foundation, not of the twelve tribes, but of the *twelve apostles* of the Lamb, that is, of the gospel which Christ Jesus entrusted to them. There is no essential conflict between Old Testament and New Testament, between Judaism and Christianity. Both are built into this new and glorious city of God. The historical continuity of God's purpose runs through the ancient Israel of Abraham, Moses, David, Isaiah, and the other Old Testament saints, and it continues on through Jesus, John, Peter, James, Thomas, and the others.

We are intended to see, therefore, that Christianity is the child of Judaism, continuing the work of God in rescuing the human race. The transition from old covenant Judaism to new covenant Christianity is not an ending and a new start, nor is it the beginning of parallel development. It is a continuation, a linear progress, a direct succession and development, a unified historical process in which the achievements of God continue to mature and evolve within the human race.

Its Dimensions

The angel who talked with me had a measuring rod of gold to measure the city, its gates and its walls. The city was laid out like a square, as long as it was wide. He measured the city with the rod and found it to be 12,000 stadia in length, and as wide and high as it is long. He measured its wall and it was 144 cubits thick, by man's measurement, which the angel was using.

The angel has a yardstick made of solid gold. Everything about this city is maximum, superlative, made of the best and finest materials, even down to its measuring stick.

The Greek measure 12,000 stadia translates into about 1,400 miles or 2,200 kilometers. The walls are 200 feet thick and 1,400 miles high. So the city measures out to a cube, one side of which is about the distance from Jerusalem to Rome, or from New York to Chicago. It towers up into the sky that distance also!

Obviously all of this is symbolism and cannot be taken literally. The cube shape of the city is reminiscent of the desert tabernacle, in which the room known as the Holy of Holies (or Most Holy Place) was a perfect cube. Once again, this is a clear reference to ancient Judaism. The symmetry of the cubic shape suggests a perfection of design, which urges us to see that it is God who is the architect. Just as God gave Moses the instructions for the desert tabernacle, so too in this epitome of the tabernacle God's design is the standard.

But there is still more to this symbolism. The perfect cube of the new city represents dimensions far larger than any city could possibly have. A city of such incredible dimensions represents the entire earth. God created the planet earth precisely for a habitat for the human race, and now John sees in this vision that entire habitat serviced by a perfect city. What he sees represents the human race, engaged in its regular and normal activities of making a living and constructing its civilization, and doing so in a holy, righteous, and just manner. The city is holy. The earth is subdued by a righteous people.

Its Decorations

> The foundations of the city walls were decorated with every kind of precious stone. The first foundation was jasper, the second sapphire, the third chalcedony, the fourth emerald, the fifth sardonyx, the sixth carnelian, the seventh chrysolite, the eighth beryl, the ninth topaz, the tenth chrysoprase, the eleventh jacinth, and the twelfth amethyst. The twelve gates were twelve pearls, each gate made of a single pearl. The great street of the city was of pure gold, like transparent glass.

The length of the city wall is 1,400 miles, and its foundation is constructed in twelve layers. Fourteen hundred miles times four walls equals

5,600 miles worth of each of these precious stones. Scholars are not able to identify with certainty all of the fine jewels mentioned here. Twelve huge pearls, carved into magnificent gates, are set into the walls, three on each side, 350 miles apart. Main Street is paved with translucent gold.

One hears occasionally of Christians who believe this literally and hope some day to walk on this street of pure gold. Don't go that route. All is symbolic. The point of this elaborate description of the city is that only the very best and finest of materials have gone into its making. No alloys, no imperfections, no defects, no seconds. And this in turn is symbolic of moral purity, sinlessness, perfect peace and joy, all that is good and fine, beautiful, true and just. Don't anticipate walking on gold; anticipate living in God's goodness and holiness.

Its Temple

> I did not see a temple in the city, because the Lord God Almighty and the Lamb are its temple.

In a city that large, stretching from Jerusalem to Rome, there would certainly have been room for a good-sized temple. But there isn't any in the new Jerusalem. God and the Lamb are its temple.

In ancient times a temple was considered to be a home for a god or goddess. It is where people could go to enter the presence of a particular god. But God does not need a home that is smaller than the city itself. The whole city is his home, so that God himself functions as the temple for the people. Live in this city and you automatically live in the presence of God. You don't have to go here or there to find God. God is his own temple.

The Lamb also is the temple — not just the Father but also the Son, Jesus, the Lamb of God who was slain on the cross and who rose again from the dead to become the Lion, the same Jesus who was born of the virgin Mary, who was crucified under Pontius Pilate, who rose from the dead, who ascended into heaven, and who extended his Spirit into the lives of the disciples. That Jesus is also the temple in this city.

Its Luminescence

> *The city does not need the sun or the moon to shine on it, for the glory of God gives it light, and the Lamb is its lamp.*

The city analogy continues here in John's vision. There is no sunshine or moonlight. The city of God does not need them. The luminescence, which is the aura of God in the city, provides all the light necessary for people to go about their duties. Nor does the city need electric lighting (lamps). The Lamb is the "lamp."

Recall that Jesus once said, "I am the light of the world" (John 8:12). He meant that the light of God's purpose for the human race is incarnated in him. He incarnates all that is right and good and true for the human race. If you live by his light, you will find the kind of life that God the creator wishes all of us to have. It is with that meaning that John in this vision sees Jesus as the lamp that gives light to this new civilization of God.

Its Function

> *The nations will walk by its light, and the kings of the earth will bring their splendor into it.*

It is interesting that John here talks about the "nations" and the "kings of the earth." Aren't they the ones who were allied with the beast and who gained their livelihood from Babylon? Aren't they the ones who were thrown into the lake of burning fire along with the beast? John now sees them doing business in the new Jerusalem.

John does not require us to think that no one works in this city. Many nations and kings do business in the new Jerusalem. Perhaps they once were deceived by the beast and did business with Babylon. But now that is all ended. They have been converted to the service of the Lamb. Now they do their business in righteousness, honesty, and justice. People engage in various occupations. Commerce continues. Travel and communications continue. Education, science, technology, and business continue. Communal life in this perfected world is such that a perfected human race lives in perfect harmony with God and nature. That is what it means that nations walk in its light and kings bring their splendor into it.

On no day will its gates ever be shut, for there will be no night there.

In the old Jerusalem the gates were shut on the Sabbath day, so that no one would be tempted to violate the day by doing business on it. That does not happen in the new Jerusalem. There is no Sabbath day shutdown. Every day is a Sabbath. All work is done in the spiritual peace and rest that the Sabbath always represented throughout earlier history.

There is no night there. Does this mean that the earth no longer revolves around its axis? The night is a symbolic night. It is the opposite of the symbolic day described earlier in the phrases "for the glory of God gives it light, and the Lamb is its lamp." If the day in this new Jerusalem is defined by the light of God and of the Lamb, then the night would be the absence of that light, which by definition cannot happen. The light of the Lamb cannot go out, no more than the glory of God can grow dim. Hence there is always light, always day in this city. There is "no night" there.

The glory and honor of the nations will be brought into it. Nothing impure will ever enter it, nor will anyone who does what is shameful or deceitful, but only those whose names are written in the Lamb's book of life.

This repeats and sums up much that has been said earlier. The picture is of shalom, a perfect peace in which all elements of human life and culture function as God intended. There are no serpent, no devil, no Satan, no beast, no image of the beast, and no prostitute who has access to this city. They are all in the lake of fire, effectively excluded from any and all commerce.

Through the grace of God in Jesus Christ human life has been redeemed in its entirety. People have chosen to serve the Lord. Through the process of history the human race has learned what is in its best interests and what is not. Its best interests lie in the path of flawless and unalloyed obedience to God.

Its Sustenance

Then the angel showed me the river of the water of life, as clear as crystal, flowing from the throne of God and of the Lamb down the middle of the great street of the city. On each side of the river stood the tree of life, bearing twelve crops of fruit, yielding its fruit every month. And the leaves of the tree are for the healing of the nations. No longer will there be any curse. The throne of God and of the Lamb will be in the city, and his servants will serve him. They will see his face, and his name will be on their foreheads. There will be no more night. They will not need the light of a lamp or the light of the sun, for the Lord God will give them light. And they will reign for ever and ever.

The angel said to me, "These words are trustworthy and true. The Lord, the God of the spirits of the prophets, sent his angel to show his servants the things that must soon take place."

"Behold, I am coming soon! Blessed is he who keeps the words of the prophecy in this book." (22:1-7)

．　．　．　．　．　．　．

Then the angel showed me the river of the water of life, as clear as crystal, flowing from the throne of God and of the Lamb down the middle of the great street of the city.

"The water of life . . . flowing from the throne of God and of the Lamb"; there is a constant and uninterrupted stream in the city. It flows through the middle of Main Street, easily available to all. Life itself, true life, flows from God by way of Jesus Christ the Lamb.

In the dry parts of Palestine streams run only during the spring of the year when the snowfall on the mountains melts, or when a rare rainstorm sends brief torrents down the dry riverbeds. But in the holy city the river is steady and always available. There is no shortage of water, no fighting over wells in remote oases. There is plenty for all.

On each side of the river stood the tree of life, bearing twelve crops of fruit, yielding its fruit every month.

234

It is not clear how one tree could grow "on each side of the river" — but these analogies should not be taken literally, nor should we insist on strict coherence in the visions. Dreams do not work that way. Suffice it to say that access to the tree is possible from both sides of the river.

The tree bears its fruit *monthly,* the significance being that there is always something there to eat, never any barren seasons, never any branches without food. God provides continuous nourishment to all.

The symbolism of the river and the tree completes the symbolism of Genesis 3, the Garden of Eden. Rivers surrounded the Garden of Eden, and it contained the Tree of Life. It also contained a Tree of the Knowledge of Good and Evil. The new Jerusalem has a Tree of Life but no Tree of the Knowledge of Good and Evil, whose equivalent would be the lake of fire outside the walls of the holy city. The time of temptation is past. The decision to obey God has been made. Now there is continued and open access forever to the Tree of Life.

The fruit of this tree is available every month. People live by this fruit. For them it is the source of life, not only physical life but holy life. The picture is of God providing all that is necessary for humans to live in such a way as to be the images of God we are intended to be, but also to do so in such a way as to preserve and guarantee the happiness and contentment of everyone else in the world. There is no longer any fruit offered by the devil.

And the leaves of the tree are for the healing of the nations.

In ancient times medicines were made by crushing leaves of certain plants or trees and making a salve of them, like the "balm in Gilead" (Jer. 8:22). But if there is no sin in the holy city, what wounds are there to be healed?

Again, this is symbolism. The nations of the world in John's day, as well as still in our day, need healing. The gospel goes into all the world, and its purpose is to bring the nations out of disobedience and into obedience, out of sin and into righteousness. This happens via the process of "the healing of the nations." The sickness from which they are healed is the sickness of sin, the sickness unto death.

On this Tree of Life there is not only food for the sustenance of the righteous but also healing balm for the sin-sick soul. The Tree of Life exists not only in the remote past in the Garden of Eden, and not only in the remote future in the holy city, but also now in our world as represented by the gospel of the Lord Jesus Christ. That tree has help even for those who, like Adam and Eve, have sinned. It heals by its leaves, then sustains daily by its fruit.

No longer will there be any curse.

Return to Genesis 3 also for this clause. From the human point of view, the choice of sin by Adam and Eve was a terrible curse for the human race to bear. From the divine point of view, that sin was the occasion for God pronouncing a curse upon the serpent, upon the woman, and upon the ground.

In the new Jerusalem, with its perpetual stream of living water and its ever-bearing tree of living fruit, the curse has finally been lifted. Sin has been removed. People no longer choose evil but consistently choose the path of righteousness. The human race has reversed its Adamic choice and has made its Christian choice. The curse is gone, lifted through the grace of God and of the Lamb.

The throne of God and of the Lamb will be in the city, and his servants will serve him. They will see his face, and his name will be on their foreheads. There will be no more night. They will not need the light of a lamp or the light of the sun, for the Lord God will give them light. And they will reign for ever and ever.

John has mentioned all of these items at one time or another in his earlier reports. Now John sees the servants of God and of the Lamb reigning for ever and ever.

This righteous civilization will continue to grow and develop forever. The human race will continue to put down the devil and his cohorts forever. Just as the Lamb of God overcame the powers that oppose God, so too, in following him, will his servants join him in that same overcoming. In that sense they will *reign* with him for ever and ever. The devil will not be the final victor over the human race. Goodness and righteousness and honesty and virtue will prevail.

The angel said to me, "These words are trustworthy and true."

John has come to the end of his visions. The bowl angel has a final confirmation to add. "These words" — that term includes all his visions — can be

236

relied on to be accurate. God wants his servants to see what is happening in the world, but in a way that newspapers and reporters cannot convey.

God wants, by means of these visions, to show us what is happening behind the scenes. He wants us to think not only in terms of political intrigue, economic changes, social upheavals, scientific advances, and the advance of civilization, but also in terms of the moral and spiritual dimensions of that life. God wants us to see the process of history as a conflict between godliness and ungodliness in human civilization. He wants us to see how ancient Israel, culminating in Jesus, forms the focal point of God's work in our world, and how that same process is now continuing by means of the gospel and the church.

The visions recorded here by John should have that effect on us. They should teach us how to evaluate what is going on in our world even now, not just what may happen at some indefinite time in the future. Jesus Christ has injected a great and powerful force into human history. The visions of the Apocalypse are designed to show us how that power works: through the church, highlighting the difference between two lifestyles, forcing confrontation, and producing a human civilization which is God's holy city, the new Jerusalem. These visions, the angel assures us, "are trustworthy and true."

> *"The Lord, the God of the spirits of the prophets, sent his angel to show his servants the things that must soon take place."*
> *"Behold, I am coming soon! Blessed is he who keeps the words of the prophecy in this book."*

"The things that must *soon* take place" is followed immediately by "Behold, I am coming *soon.*" These clauses ought not be separated. They go together as parallel sentences. The angel has shown John what "must soon take place," and this is identical with what is meant by "I am coming soon."

The crucial point is to determine what is meant by *soon*. In the Bible this word can mean such things as quickly, speedily, hastily, shortly, immediately, suddenly, easily, readily. It is an adverb suggesting not only time but also manner. It means that the action being described is not something far away or delayed till long into the future. On the contrary, it is an action that is taking place right now, immediately. It is something to be observed here and now in the present.

237

The angel is assuring John that the things he has seen must take place right now, immediately. These are existential events. Learn to see them happening all the time in your life and in your community and in your world.

Similarly with the statement "I am coming soon," *erchomai tachu*. *Erchomai* is in the present tense, suggesting continual action in the present. Jesus is assuring John that he is indeed coming now, coming in John's present world, coming by means of the gospel in the churches and the power of his Spirit. The meaning is identical with that of the previous sentence.

This is surprising — that 22:7 would mean anything other than the personal, physical, climactic, far-off-in-the-future second coming of the Lord Jesus as most of us have been taught all our lives. But that interpretation of this verse in Revelation 22 can hardly be justified on the basis of the actual Greek grammar and usage. Jesus is speaking of the present, not the future. He is already, even in John's time, in the process of coming.

*   *   *

This ends John's report of the visions. What remains in 22:8-21 is an epilogue, complementing the prologue in 1:1-8. What we have in these concluding verses, therefore, is *not* visionary and hence not to be interpreted symbolically.

It is important to bear in mind that the beautiful symbolic visions of the new world also cast their shadows backward into our present world. The new Jerusalem is a city in the making. It has been in the making ever since Jesus was on earth. It is indeed a vision of the destiny, or end of the process of history, the goal of our civilizing efforts. But as such it should be understood not as a sudden divine supernatural intrusion into our world, but as the gradual accomplishment of the gospel of Jesus Christ.

Jesus refused to set up an earthly kingdom while he was on earth. We certainly should not expect him to do so at any time in the future. On the contrary, we should take our point of departure from Genesis. What God intended when he created Adam and Eve he now shows us in this superb book of Revelation. What did not happen in Genesis 3 does happen in Revelation 21. It is the ministry of our Lord Jesus Christ that accomplishes it, first on earth and then continued from heaven.

We are summoned therefore to be churches, to recognize clearly how the life of Christ contrasts with the life of sin, to join faithfully and courageously in the holy warfare against the devil, and to be guided by the vision of a new heaven and a new earth.

CHAPTER 14

Epilogue

Revelation 22:8-21

I, John, am the one who heard and saw these things. And when I had heard and seen them, I fell down to worship at the feet of the angel who had been showing them to me. But he said to me, "Do not do it! I am a fellow servant with you and with your brothers the prophets and of all who keep the words of this book. Worship God!"

Then he told me, "Do not seal up the words of the prophecy of this book, because the time is near. Let him who does wrong continue to do wrong; let him who is vile continue to be vile; let him who does right continue to do right; and let him who is holy continue to be holy."

"Behold, I am coming soon! My reward is with me, and I will give to everyone according to what he has done. I am the Alpha and the Omega, the First and the Last, the Beginning and the End.

"Blessed are those who wash their robes, that they may have the right to the tree of life and may go through the gates into the city. Outside are the dogs, those who practice magic arts, the sexually immoral, the murderers, the idolaters and everyone who loves and practices falsehood.

"I, Jesus, have sent my angel to give you this testimony for the churches. I am the Root and the Offspring of David, and the bright Morning Star."

The Spirit and the bride say, "Come!" And let him who hears say, "Come!" Whoever is thirsty, let him come; and whoever wishes, let him take the free gift of the water of life.

I warn everyone who hears the words of the prophecy of this book: If anyone adds anything to them, God will add to him the plagues described in this book. And if anyone takes words away from this book of prophecy, God will take away from him his share in the tree of life and in the holy city, which are described in this book.

He who testifies to these things says, "Yes, I am coming soon."

Amen. Come, Lord Jesus.

The grace of the Lord Jesus be with God's people. Amen. (22:8-21)

. . . .

This is an epilogue at the end of John's book, balancing the prologue at the beginning. Between the two are the visions. The last half of chapter 22 is no longer part of the visions, but a direct and literal application of the visions to the seven churches and to us.

The Angel's Testimony

I, John, am the one who heard and saw these things.

John testifies that he did indeed see and hear these visions. We are assuming, in the absence of decisive evidence to the contrary, that it is the apostle John who is writing, not John the Baptist or John the Elder or some other unknown person by that name. He is describing the things he sees Jesus doing now from heaven on earth, the continuation of the things he had begun to do while on the earth himself. Jesus works now from heaven, in the church and by means of the gospel. John has seen a great many visions detailing how the gospel affects the course of human life and history.

And when I had heard and seen them, I fell down to worship at the feet of the angel who had been showing them to me. But he said to me, "Do not do

242

it! I am a fellow servant with you and with your brothers the prophets and of all who keep the words of this book. Worship God!"

John wanted to show his appreciation to his guide. He kneeled with his face to the ground in the traditional posture of servitude and respect. The Greek word here translated "worship" originally meant to show reverence by kissing the hand, then later by bowing down or prostrating oneself. The angel guide tells John not to do this, since only God deserves such reverence and worship.

Then he told me, "Do not seal up the words of the prophecy of this book, because the time is near."

The angel is telling John that when he finishes writing this book, he should not wrap it up and store it away on a shelf in a closet somewhere. "The time is near."

What John has seen in these visions is important, not only for himself but for his churches as well. They need to read what he has written and see through his eyes what he saw. They need the encouragement that these visions bring. So do we today.

The angel says the time is near. Everything in these visions is near. They are as near as now. What takes place in John's visions takes place in the present, not in the distant future. It continues indeed into the future, but its significance is always with us. It is always current. If we fail to see these visions with John, it is the equivalent of sealing them up and not reading them at all.

"Let him who does wrong continue to do wrong; let him who is vile continue to be vile; let him who does right continue to do right; and let him who is holy continue to be holy."

These first two clauses are surprising. They seem to negate the gospel, which proclaims forgiveness for all who repent. Are we then simply to allow the wicked to go on sinning without any effort on our part to change their commitment?

That is not what John's angel means. He is not implying that we should merely allow the wicked to wallow in their sins. He is telling us that we should recognize that however much the gospel is preached, however much it draws people to Christ, many people will still refuse to believe and reject the gospel. In any given cross section of time and in any given country, there will be people who continue to do wrong and "to be vile." The angel is simply reminding us of this fact and urging us to accept it.

At the same time, however, there will be many who do believe in the Lord Jesus Christ and who therefore will continue to do right and "continue to be holy," persevering in the faith. The good and the bad will continue to live together, side by side in the world. But these visions show how the inner dynamics of history work, how the good and the bad interact. They show how good exposes evil, draws it into conflict, and ultimately destroys it.

All of this is implied by the angel's words about continuation. The conflict between good and evil is there, and it will continue. Accept that and let the Spirit of Christ do his work.

Jesus' Testimony

"Behold, I am coming soon!"

The Greek phraseology used here is the same as in verse 7; the present tense is used, indicating continuing action in present time. This phrase is therefore a reaffirmation that these visions are not about some disputable set of occurrences far off in the future, but insights into what is going on all around us because of the gospel of Christ Jesus at work in and through the churches of this world. Ever since the great outpouring of his Spirit at Pentecost, Jesus has been coming among us and upon us. With his Spirit and with the gospel, he is establishing churches and calling sinners to repent and believe and be saved.

"My reward is with me, and I will give to everyone according to what he has done."

The preceding announcement refers to present time, and surely this one does also. When Jesus comes, that is, as he comes with the gospel, wherever he comes, in all the places and times and churches in which he comes, he carries his "reward" with him. The reward is not delayed until some indefinable future time; it is constantly with him wherever he goes.

This reward is precisely what happens to a person when he makes his choice either to believe the gospel or to reject it. When Adam and Eve chose to reject the command of God, they immediately felt its consequences: a guilty conscience, sexual aberration, discomfort in the presence of God, and an unwillingness to take responsibility for their actions. Their reward came with their sin, and it came in the form of punishment, of a curse.

Now, when Christ comes to us he too brings his reward with him. People who believe in him and follow him loyally experience a sense of forgiveness, they learn increasingly what it means to love and to be loved, they accept responsibility for the way they live, they develop inner peace and tranquillity, they become content, and they bring forth the fruits of the Spirit. These rewards and more are what Jesus brings with him when he comes into a person's life as Savior and Lord.

> *"I am the Alpha and the Omega, the First and the Last, the Beginning and the End."*

In chapter 1 these designations referred to God the Father. God is the original creator of heaven and earth; he is the Lord who controls all things and directs them to their appointed end.

Here the reference seems to be to Jesus rather than to God. Jesus is "the Alpha and the Omega . . . the Beginning and the End."

In the same sense in which John described Jesus as the Word become flesh (John 1:14), John now describes Jesus as "the First and the Last." The Word of God was there in the beginning when God created the world, for it was by means of the Word that he did so. The Word of God is also there throughout history until the end. Jesus incarnates the meaning and significance of that eternal Word of God, and he is in that sense "the First and the Last." It is through Jesus and the gospel that God is directing the course of human history from beginning to end.

> *"Blessed are those who wash their robes, that they may have the right to the tree of life and may go through the gates into the city. Outside are the dogs, those who practice magic arts, the sexually immoral, the murderers, the idolaters and everyone who loves and practices falsehood."*

This is another way of describing the rewards that Christ Jesus brings with him. Believe in Jesus, thus washing your robe, and you have the right to enter the holy city and partake of the Tree of Life. Refuse to believe in Jesus and you forfeit the right to enter this holy city, and must stay outside with your companions: dogs, magicians, sexual perverts, murderers, idolaters, and deceivers.

These alternatives describe life here and now whenever and wherever you live. If you follow Jesus Christ as Lord, every day you live you go through the gates into the holy city, and you eat from the Tree of Life.

"I, Jesus, have sent my angel to give you this testimony for the churches. I am the Root and the Offspring of David, and the bright Morning Star."

All this testimony, all these visions have their source in Jesus and their destination in the churches. The angel and John are the intermediaries, the messengers.

Put great emphasis on the phrase "testimony for the churches." Jesus is speaking to the Christians right there in the churches to which John sends these visions. He wants them to understand what is going on in their communities and to take courage to fight the good fight of faith. This is profound pastoral *testimony*. These visions are vital, current, contemporary, existential reports of what God is doing through Jesus from heaven. They demonstrate your current situation, whatever and wherever it might be.

The names Root and Offspring of David and Morning Star remind us that the work of Jesus Christ is the direct continuation and fulfillment of Old Testament Jewish history. Jesus is the Messiah long sought in Jewish tradition. Christianity is the direct descendant and heir of the Jewish legacy.

These names also assure us that the work of God in Christ is linear, that it functions in a horizontal, temporal, historical manner. The gospel works slowly, within time, much like yeast. It may take centuries or millennia for even the smallest gains to be made. Yet we should learn to see progress, gradual and minimal though it may seem to us, as the years pass and the gospel takes deeper root within the civilization of mankind.

Our lives are short. We would like to have immediate results from decisive action, but God does not work that way. With him "a day is like a thousand years, and a thousand years are like a day" (2 Pet. 3:8). God has all the time in the world — forever — to do his work. Our brief lives are but bit parts in the ongoing process by which God is creating a race fully imaging himself in its subjugation of the earth. Do not give up hope even when the tidal wave of sin and evil seems to engulf the world, for Christ is even now in the process of dethroning the devil.

John's Warning

The Spirit and the bride say, "Come!"

One of the most important operative terms in this chapter is the verb *come*, here used in the imperative voice. It is the same verb used earlier in the present tense to describe Jesus: "I am coming." Jesus is demonstrating in these visions how he is coming daily, regularly, and continually into the world. Now "the Spirit and the bride" echo his announcement.

"The Spirit and the bride" are two different entities, yet they should not be separated, for it is precisely within the church (the bride) that the Spirit of Christ is displayed. The one is the voice of God and the other is the voice of his people, yet they blend their voices into one as they echo the words of Jesus himself: "I am coming. Yes, 'Come! . . . Come!'"

And let him who hears say, "Come!" Whoever is thirsty, let him come; and whoever wishes, let him take the free gift of the water of life.

Anyone who hears this word from Christ should also echo the message. John is referring to anyone who hears the gospel, anyone who sees the true intent of these visions, anyone who hears in the sense of seeing what is going on in the world, seeing the process by which Christ is demolishing the stronghold of Babylon. Once a person sees this happening in his own life and world, the response should be a faithful and exuberant exclamation: Yes, yes, a thousand times yes! *Come, Lord Jesus!*

John assures every reader of these visions that they are eligible to change allegiance from Satan to Christ, to change residence from Babylon to Jerusalem, to escape the lake of fire and drink instead "the water of life." If the insights given in the book of Revelation whet your appetite and make you thirsty for truth and justice and goodness, then all you need do is *come*. The reward that Christ Jesus brings with him is entirely free. He is holding his reward out to you. Nothing is obscuring it, and there is nothing preventing you from coming to him. There is no obstacle to his reward whatsoever. It is there for all of us. Take the free gift, drink the living water, and come into the holy city, the new Jerusalem.

> *I warn everyone who hears the words of the prophecy of this book: If anyone adds anything to them, God will add to him the plagues described in this book. And if anyone takes words away from this book of prophecy, God will take away from him his share in the tree of life and in the holy city, which are described in this book.*

This is John's warning against tampering with his book. Similar warnings have been found in other ancient books: change anything I have written and may the curse of God descend upon you. Lacking copyright laws, this is the best these authors could do. Copyists, beware that you get everything right, just as I have written it.

But John's warning has much more significance. He is describing not what *might* happen but what *will* happen if people tamper with his reports. Change the reports in any significant way and you will miss their meaning. Tamper with them in any way which obscures the central thrust of Jesus' work, and you will obfuscate them. Interpret them in such a way as to misread them and you will nullify their impact. If anyone does this, John writes, "God will take away from him his share in the tree of life and in the holy city." Misinterpret this book of Revelation at your own peril — that is what John's warning is all about.

Final Summation and Benediction

> *He who testifies to these things says, "Yes, I am coming soon."*
> *Amen. Come, Lord Jesus.*
> *The grace of the Lord Jesus be with God's people. Amen.*

The whole massive affair of these intriguing visions is summed up in the words of Jesus from heaven, "Yes, I am coming soon." Jesus is in the process of coming. Ever since Pentecost he has been coming by his Spirit. He has been establishing churches composed of people who repent of sin and follow him in righteousness. He has been demonstrating within human culture how the lifestyle of righteousness contrasts with the lifestyle of sin. He has been challenging the forces of evil to do their worst, and has been defeating them. Yes indeed, he is *coming* promptly, swiftly, vigorously, and powerfully into the world. It is sure. *Amen.* This is the heart of the book of Revelation.

John's own response is to echo again, "Come, Lord Jesus." The reason John spent so much time and energy writing these visions was so he could do his part in the coming of the Lord to his churches, so the churches could see the Lord at work and could take courage and confidence from it.

And then the final benediction: "The grace of the Lord Jesus be with God's people. Amen." *Grace* is the Holy Spirit. The Holy Spirit creates in God's people the spirit of power, of holiness, of righteousness, of truth, of justice, and of all the other fruits of the Spirit. This is what the benediction affirms. It is so. Amen. And may it continue to be so with you!

Index of Subjects and Names

Index of Scripture References

(excluding Revelation)